In this book the author examines and ultimately rejects the conventional economic view that workers who have more dangerous jobs accept their risks voluntarily and are compensated through higher wages. In doing so, he attacks widely used techniques for assigning a monetary value to human life for cost–benefit analysis and other purposes. Arguments are drawn from the history of occupational safety and health, econometric analysis of wage and risk data, and formal models of the labor market. In place of the conventional view, Peter Dorman proposes a view based on new work in decision theory (thick rationality) and the theory of repeated games. These insights are combined with comparative policy analysis to support an approach to risk that promotes both regulatory effectiveness and democratic values. Despite its technical content, the book is written in highly accessible style, and is concerned with matters of general interest in the development of critical social science.

Markets and mortality

Markets and mortality

Economics, dangerous work,
and the value of human life

PETER DORMAN

CAMBRIDGE
UNIVERSITY PRESS

Published by the Press Syndicate of the University of Cambridge
The Pitt Building, Trumpington Street, Cambridge CB2 1RP
40 West 20th Street, New York, NY 10011–4211, USA
10 Stamford Road, Oakleigh, Melbourne 3166, Australia

First published 1996

Printed in Great Britain at the University Press, Cambridge

A catalogue record for this book is available from the British Library

Library of Congress cataloguing in publication data
Dorman, Peter.
Markets and mortality: economics, dangerous work, and the value of
human life / Peter Dorman.
    p.   cm.
ISBN 0 521 55306 7
1. Hazardous occupations – Economic aspects.
2. Industrial safety – Economic aspects.
3. Life – Valuation.   4. Risk.   I. Title.
HD7262.D58   1996
331.2–dc20   95–9287   CIP

ISBN 0 521 55306 7 hardback

CE

Contents

Preface

At some point, every careful reader of this book will begin to wonder just who it was intended for. Certainly I had in mind specialists and practitioners in the fields I have sought to cover: labor economists, personnel and safety officials, union activists, government regulators, and producers and consumers of benefit–cost analysis. This would explain the literature summaries and the analyses of statistical evidence and formal economic theory. But what accounts for the story-telling, the excursions into philosophy and psychology, and the other digressions that recur throughout this text? What is the point?

The simple answer would be to say that I had in mind the elusive educated lay reader. But why would this individual, the target of so many works, turn to a study of the economics of occupational safety and the valuation of life? Not for practical reasons, certainly, since this work is the product of an economist, not an industrial hygienist, and it contains no useful advice for avoiding the hazards of the workplace. My hope, rather, is that readers from a variety of backgrounds will find this topic interesting in ways that transcend its immediate concerns, as I have. Not that the human dimensions are not compelling: I have gone to greater lengths than most writers on this subject to make the consequences of dangerous work explicit and immediate. Yet it is the combination of intellectual complexity and life-or-death significance that makes this topic truly gripping – it presents a series of vexing theoretical and empirical puzzles that we *must* try to solve. Moreover, it is my view, which I attempt to communicate in this work, that the study of occupational safety provides a laboratory for the analysis of economics itself. The thread that begins with empirical anomalies in the "market for risk" leads ultimately to the foundations of economics as a social science, to its core behavioral and methodological assumptions. But, just as important, *the thread leads back again* to the world of practical policy decisions: we can propose fundamental changes in social theory and see

ix

how they might be reflected in new policies toward the allocation of risk. So this book is intended for a particular lay reader, one who cares about basic questions in social theory but appreciates the discipline imposed by the need to respond to the risks faced by real human beings in an economic environment that actually exists.

Even so, there remains the problem of mathematics. There is often pressure on writers of books such as this either to include mathematical material and target the work to specialists, or to leave out the math in hopes of attracting a more general readership. (In my case this pressure came from colleagues, not Cambridge University Press.) It is understandable that this should happen, since many readers who might otherwise be interested in technical subjects will be dissuaded if they find equations or matrices where they expected common English sentences. I am persuaded, however, that there is a political dimension to this problem that requires that the math be left in. Let me explain.

Mary Douglas (1985, p. 13) says, "The dialogue about risk and justice tends to be conducted in two languages: traditional English rhetoric on behalf of regulation and mathematical language on behalf of principles of free choice. This is reminiscent of a medieval law court in which the native plaintiffs made their vernacular requests and were answered in dog Latin." Indeed, there are two separate and highly distinct literatures on the economics of risk, one in narrative form that largely endorses the view that occupational risk is imposed on individuals by institutions and policies (and should perhaps be lessened), and another using mathematical optimization theory and econometrics that views this risk as freely chosen by individuals, and therefore more or less acceptable. Moreover, I believe that the balance of power is gradually shifting in the direction of mathematically informed analysis, and that this bodes ill for the view that risk, in a world of great inequalities in power, must be considered in relation to justice as well as efficiency. Of course, even were this not the case, the fact that two such strains can continue side-by-side for so long and influence each other so little is testimony to the extent of our society's two-cultures problem. One interpretation of the present book is that it is an attempt to overcome this stultifying divide. While I have gone to considerable lengths to translate the insights of the narrative literature into mathematical terms, and vice-versa, there are limits to this enterprise, and those who want to consider *all* the arguments must read both the sentences and the equations. I have tried to make this as painless as possible for the general reader, offering brief histories of the evolution of important economic concepts and techniques as well as providing intuitive accounts and examples. Nevertheless, portions of this book will require an extra dollop of effort from the non-technically inclined; if it is any consolation, these readers can pride themselves on contributing, in their own way, to dismantling the wall separating the two cultures.

This book developed over the course of a decade, and during that time I was given invaluable assistance from several sources. My greatest debt is to Herb Gintis, my dissertation advisor, who offered the patient support that too few graduate students receive; although he would find much to disagree with, this book reflects his influence from beginning to end. My thinking was also influenced by discussions with Sam Bowles and Bob Sass, but mention should also be made of the many members of the Progressive Economics Network internet list who offered their electronic advice on earlier drafts of some of these chapters. In its later stages the book was aided immeasurably by the wise criticism of two anonymous readers; they gave the work the sort of skeptical and comprehensive scrutiny that authors would like to impose on themselves, but usually cannot. Finally, it is significant that this book was written during a long sequence of temporary academic positions at colleges and universities across the United States. My connection with the economics profession became tenuous over those years, and without the help of faculty who found work for me at the last minute, year after year, this volume would never have come to be. I am pleased to have the opportunity to state publicly that I appreciate every one of those jobs and the friends and colleagues who made them possible.

PETER DORMAN

Prologue

Theoretical and statistical analysis alone cannot convey the full meaning of the daily exchange of risk for livelihood. Here are two narratives chosen for their historical prominence. For most of us who know them only dimly or at a distance they are like myths – dramatic, exemplary, and larger than life. But they are also real.

The Triangle fire of 1911

The Triangle Shirtwaist Company had offices and production facilities in the top three floors of the ten-story Asch Building, still standing half a block from Washington Square in New York City. Its business was the cutting and sewing of women's garments, a highly competitive field at the turn of the century, as it is today. Hundreds of workers, most of them young women, immigrants or the daughters of immigrants, put in long hours at low wages, suffering conditions that gave birth to the term "sweatshop."

From a business standpoint these women were not even employees of Triangle. The company hired a small number of master garment workers, and these in turn contracted for workers to fill out their teams. The contractors negotiated piece rates with the company, paid their helpers according to informal wage agreements, and pocketed the difference. In return for granting a job offering a few cents more per hour, the master contractor expected obedience and gratitude from those beneath him. The company, moreover, had no dealings with most of their work force; they kept no payroll records other than their piece rate payments for finished output nor did they even know how many workers were on the premises at any given time.

Shirtwaist-making was dangerous. With rags lying in wicker bins scattered about the factory and cotton dust in the air, the prime risk was fire. Triangle had a particularly bad safety record: between 1902 and

1

1910 there were no fewer than five fires for which insurance claims were filed. The industry as a whole was little better, however, and in the fall of 1910 a devastating fire at a garment factory in Newark, New Jersey killed 25 workers.

The women at Triangle were certainly aware of these risks. In 1909 they began a strike which rapidly spread to the rest of the shirtwaist industry in New York. Their demands included not only an end to the contracting system, but also drastic improvements in safety conditions. They wanted less crowding, open doors leading to the street, and adequate fire escapes. The strike succeeded elsewhere, but it was crushed at Triangle. Union organizers then filed a complaint with the State Labor Commission, claiming that the extreme crowding at Triangle constituted a safety hazard. The Commission ruled otherwise, noting that the company had provided the statutory minimum of 250 cubic feet of airspace per worker – although this was largely the result of high ceilings which in themselves exacerbated the risk of fire.

The catastrophic event occurred a few minutes before quitting time on March 25. A small fire broke out on the eighth floor and, feeding on the dry, combustible materials of the garment trade, spread quickly across the single large production room. Since it was the practice of the firm to have workers exit one at a time by a single door so that they could be inspected for possible pilferage, the other exit was locked. (This was in contravention of state labor law, which required that factory doors "not be locked, bolted or fastened during working hours" [Stein, 1962, p. 24].) Moreover, each door was so narrow that only a single worker could pass at once. A telephone connected the eighth floor with the tenth, where a connection could be manually set for the ninth, but it happened on that day that the regular operator was out; so when a distress call was made, it reached the executive offices on the tenth but not the crowded production room on the floor in between. The flames were not hindered, however: roaring through the open windows, they climbed from one floor to the next until all three were engulfed.

Many of the workers on the eighth floor were able to squeeze through the doorway and found refuge either on the street or, after that passageway had been cut off, on the roof. Others crowded into the two elevators which ferried dangerously heavy loads to safety. Those who climbed on to the fire escape, however, found that the narrow, flimsy structure was blocked by an open shutter locked into place. As more and more women piled on to it the structure buckled from the heat and collapsed, sending dozens of workers to their death eight stories below. Most of those on the tenth floor were able to escape either to the roof or by one of the elevators, which made its first stop for the executives. It was on the ninth floor, where workers had the least warning, that the fire was most deadly. Few were able to pass through the lone open door before the stairways were made impassable by flames. The fire escape was no longer an option, having already collapsed. The courageous operators of the elevator cars made repeated forays into the inferno, but one of the shafts twisted in the heat, while the other was stopped even more tragically: burning women broke down the doors to the shaft and threw themselves into it, so that the overburden of crushed bodies kept the second car stuck in the basement. For those remaining on the ninth floor there was no escape. Their bodies in flames, they leapt to the street below. They jumped by the dozens and crashed through the life nets assembled by the fire department. So many bodies were piled up on the sidewalk that one late jumper actually survived by landing on a heap of her coworkers. Other bodies were still burning even on the street and had to be hosed by the firefighters. In all, 146 workers died, all but a few in the first terrifying minutes of the fire.

The city responded with grief and outrage. On April 5, after all the other bodies had been claimed, the final seven unidentifiable corpses were carried through the garment district on their way to burial; police estimated that 400,000 turned out for the procession in pouring rain. The co-owners of Triangle, Isaac Harris and Max Blanck, were indicted on charges of manslaughter amid a general clamor for justice. The prosecution focused on the locked doors, which clearly violated state statutes; this, they claimed, was responsible for so many unnecessary deaths. The defense argued that, since the doors were not always locked, the owners had no way of knowing that they were locked at that particular time and could therefore not be held accountable. Moreover, they claimed, the real reason for the loss of life was the excitability and lack of intelligence characteristic of the immigrant working class. This argument, so unsavory to modern ears, resonated with several businessmen on the jury and was ultimately sufficient for acquittal.

Of somewhat less interest for contemporaries but critical for us were the bizarre revelations that surfaced concerning Triangle's insurance coverage. Triangle carried substantial fire insurance; why didn't the insurers demand safer business practices? The answer can be found in the role of intermediaries in insurance underwriting. First, brokers, organized in the New York Fire Insurance Exchange, were paid by commission; they actively *resisted* safety-improving practices, such as the provision by insurers of sprinklers in return for reduced claims, since they preferred to pass along higher costs in higher premiums. Second, coverage for firms like Triangle was pooled through a syndicate; 37 insurers, for instance, shared the Triangle account. A few influential brokerage houses assembled these syndicates, and insurance companies had to avoid the appearance of interfering if they wanted to be included in future projects. But the problem was not simply the lack of insurers' oversight. Triangle was starved for cash; at the time of the fire it was even in arrears in its insurance payments. Its access to credit was based on its insured value, but insurers participating in the syndicate never attempted to value its equipment or inventory. The result was that the coverage almost certainly exceeded the value of the firm, creating an economic incentive *for* a fire. After the smoke had cleared and the last bodies were tagged and carted away, Triangle submitted a claim for $199,750. Only one of the 37 insurance companies in the syndicate balked at immediate payment. They hired an accounting firm which, after inspecting Triangle's records, set an upper limit of $134,075 on the true value of the lost assets. In the end, however, all claims were paid, and the company, which had no liability whatever for the workers who died (most of whom were not even their employees), profited handsomely.

Many public meetings were held in the following months to draw meaning from the disaster. Some exhorted workers to be more careful; Fire Chief Edward F. Croker, for example, in a statement read to a memorial rally at Cooper's Union, said, "It would be my advice to the girls employed in lofts and factories to refuse to work when they find the doors locked" (p. 140). Others blamed the owners or the capitalist system in general. Perhaps the most eloquent statement was that of Rose Schneiderman, a leader of the Triangle strike two years earlier. Addressing a reform meeting uniting wealthy civic leaders and garment worker families, she concluded:

I would be a traitor to those poor burned bodies if I were to come here to talk good fellowship. We have tried you good people of the public – and we have found you wanting.

The old Inquisition had its rack and its thumbscrews and its instruments of torture with iron teeth. We know what these things are today: the iron teeth are our necessities, the thumbscrews are the high-powered and swift machinery close to which we must work, and the rack is here in the firetrap structures that will destroy us the minute they catch fire.

This is not the first time girls have been burned alive in this city. Every week I must learn of the untimely death of one of my sister workers. Every year thousands of us are maimed. The life of men and women is so cheap and property is so sacred! There are so many of us for one job, it matters little if 140-odd are burned to death.

We have tried you, citizens! We are trying you now and you have a couple of dollars for the sorrowing mothers and brothers and sisters by way of a charity gift. But every time the workers come out in the only way they know to protest against conditions which are unbearable, the strong hand of the law is allowed to press down heavily upon us.

Public officials have only words of warning for us – warning that we must be intensely orderly and must be intensely peaceable, and they have the workhouse just back of all their warnings. The strong hand of the law beats us back when we rise – back into the conditions that make life unbearable.

I can't talk fellowship to you who are gathered here. Too much blood has been spilled. I know from experience it is up to the working people to save themselves. And the only way is through a strong working-class movement. (Stein, 1962, pp. 144–5)

Eventually the labor movement, spearheaded by the Garment Workers Union, the ILGWU, organized the bulk of the New York garment industry, and disasters like the Triangle fire became less frequent. Yet with the decline of this movement in recent decades, reports of sweatshop conditions – and human carnage in production – have once again become common. Meanwhile, in the south, where unionism largely failed to take hold, safety and health standards remained abysmal, and a tragic echo of the great fire of 1911 occurred 80 years later, when 25 workers lost their lives in another fire at Imperial Foods, a poultry plant in Hamlet, North Carolina. Many of the details were identical, as if to defy our illusions of progress: the victims were nearly all women with families to feed and few alternatives, the employer a recent transplant with no ties or commitments to the community, looking to make a quick profit. Regulation was nonexistent; even the state's commissioner of labor admitted, "North Carolina has more people on the governor's personal security force than protecting the health and safety of 4 million workers at 180,000 workplaces" (James Brooks, quoted in Tye, 1991). Burning vats of oil, like Triangle's baskets of material, were an open fire hazard. And the doors: once again they were locked, to prevent workers receiving poverty-level wages from concealing a chicken in their purse at the shift's end. When a nozzle spraying hot fat burst open, their contents ignited by broiler flames to send streams of fire through the plant, the workers never had a chance.

The black lung movement

Underground coal miners breathe coal dust and develop chronic, debilitating lung symptoms, including tissue destruction, shortness of breath, and the inability to supply enough oxygen to the bloodstream. This has been known for more than 150 years, but it was not until the end of the 1960s that coal miners in the United States were able to win recognition of black lung as an occupational disease. To do this they had to wage a bitter, protracted struggle against the government, the medical profession, and even their own union.

Low-grade deterioration of the lungs was ubiquitous among miners during the nineteenth and early twentieth centuries. Referred to as "miners' asthma," it was viewed as an ordinary condition not requiring treatment, and, since the craft techniques used in mining had not changed in generations, the health effects were regarded as unavoidable. All of this changed with the introduction of the mechanical loader in 1930. This machine, which automated the process of removing the blasted coal from the mine, greatly increased the concentration of coal dust. Miners were alarmed. Said one delegate to a United Mine Workers of America (UMWA) convention in 1934: "Those conveyors are man killers and I believe this convention should do its utmost to find some way whereby those conveyors will be abolished ...The young men after they work in the mine six or eight hours daily become sick, either getting asthma or some other sickness due to the dust of the conveyors and they can no longer perform their duty" (Smith, 1987, p. 53). Soon additional aspects of the operation were mechanized, until the "continuous miner," a set of equipment that integrated the entire process from the initial cut to final removal of the coal, was installed after World War II. Productivity soared, but working conditions – noise, the pace of work, and, above all, the thick clouds of dust – were nearly unbearable. Year after year, rank-and-file miners introduced resolutions at UMWA conventions calling for a reduction in the dust and compensation for its victims.

Relief did not come. The mine owners had made a quiet, high-level agreement with the leadership of the UMWA: acceptance of the union and major wage and benefit increases in return for automation of the mines and reduction in employment. The union hierarchy, led by the autocratic John L. Lewis, feared that any discord over the health and safety consequences of this deal would undermine their entire strategy; so, while they gave lip service to the problem of coal dust, they carefully avoided taking any action.

Yet miners protesting lung disease had an even more formidable opponent than their own industry: the medical profession itself. From the beginning of the controversy during the 1930s and 1940s to the present day, most of the health community refused to recognize the existence of black lung as a general health impairment, nor did they agree that occupational health problems were epidemic among underground miners. There are two general reasons for this. First, most health professionals specializing in the condition of coal miners were company doctors until the system was reformed after World War II. Indeed, a federal survey taken in 1946 found that 97 percent of all coal miners in southern West Virginia, eastern Kentucky, Virginia, Alabama, and Tennessee were covered by "prepaid" company doctors. "Company doctors typically were called upon to testify in the operators' favor whenever miners filed workers' compensation claims ... Industrial accidents were attributed to individual 'carelessness,' and illness, to self-destructive personal habits like alcoholism" (Smith, 1987, p. 16).

Second, there was an enormous difference between the symptoms of black lung disease experienced by miners and the narrow technical evidence acceptable to the medical profession. Miners knew that prolonged experience underground breathing coal dust resulted in shortness of breath, general debility, and chronic lung disease. For the professionals, however, this "subjective" evidence had no standing. Their education had trained them to look for actual tissue damage in the lungs, and the most persuasive evidence of this was provided by X-ray photography. Thus was born "coal workers' pneumoconiosis" (CWP), a disease characterized by widespread lung damage as revealed by X-rays. After the watershed 1950 agreement between the Bituminous Coal Operators Association and the UMWA, the company doctor system was replaced by a union-operated network of clinics and hospitals. Doctors, adjusting to their new masters, began giving serious attention to the lung ailments of miners, but they did so according to their narrow interpretation of the problem. The result was a series of state and federal studies which revealed widespread, but by no means ubiquitous, health effects. Overall, between a fifth and a third of the mining population had either weak or strong evidence of pneumoconiosis, with higher percentages among retired miners and those with the most exposure to coal dust. But this did not lead to either compensation or prevention, because pneumoconiosis, defined as lung tissue damage revealed by X-rays, was only imperfectly correlated with actual disability. A worker could test positive and yet show no signs of an inability to perform the work, while workers who could hardly breathe or walk more than a few yards could come up negative. So medical evidence accumulated, but no action was taken.

What specialists did not know then, but what we know today, is that there is no single, uniform response of the human lung under the stress induced by coal dust. It appears that at least three major types of lung damage may be associated with black lung: the tissue destruction of pneumoconiosis, breathing difficulties related to bronchitis and similar diseases, and diminished oxygen supply to the bloodstream. A victim of black lung may have any combination of these. X-rays reveal only the first, but, except for the advanced stages of pneumoconiosis, the symptoms miners are most likely to *feel* are the result of the other two. On the other hand, it is not always possible to get physical evidence to corroborate bronchial or pulmonary vascular disabilities. It is not surprising, then, that one study published in 1964 found "a direct relationship between impairment of a miner's lung function and the number of years spent working underground, regardless of age, smoking habits, *or X-ray category of CWP*" (Smith, 1987, p. 28, emphasis added).

Workers' compensation boards in the coal-mining states refused to accept the claims of most black lung victims. (The British system accepted these claims beginning in 1943.) Administrators would accept only X-ray evidence, and even then required proof of exposure to silicon dust under the assumption, now known to be false, that only silicon is sufficiently abrasive to do lung damage. In this way, with only a fraction of a minority of black lung claims accepted, the system was virtually useless. Worse, in response to a financial crisis in the union's Welfare and Retirement Fund (the source of miners' medical funding, depleted by corruption and incompetence), its trustees ruled that permanently disabled miners would lose their medical coverage after four years – and receive that only if they were eligible under workers' compensation. Smith (1987) comments:

Until the late 1960s, most coal-producing states continued to award occupational lung disease compensation only for silicosis. Forty-year veterans of the mines who were so disabled that they could not walk up stairs or sleep in a prone position were denied compensation because their X-rays did not reveal the classic pathological changes associated with this specific disease. Even the disabled who showed evidence of silicosis rarely qualified for a lifetime award based on total and permanent disability. Many applied some time after they had retired from the mines, when their lung disease progressed to the point of causing severe debilitation; they were turned down because statutes of limitations typically restricted the time period between the last occupational dust exposure and the filing of a compensation claim. Most others received only a partial disability award – in West Virginia, $1,000 for first stage silicosis, $2,000 for second-stage. Unable to live on such a sum, they continued to work in the mines until some became so incapacitated by black lung that they had no choice but to quit. In many states, workers in this situation were prohibited from reopening their claims for compensation; a lump sum for partial disability was all they ever received. (p. 106)

Anger at the entire system – the coal operators, the union hierarchy, the coalfield doctors, and workers' compensation – erupted in 1968 with the founding and explosive spread of the Black Lung Association. A shoestring operation stitched together by antipoverty volunteers, dissident doctors, and rank-and-file union activists, the BLA fomented a wildcat strike movement first across West Virginia and then the entire eastern bituminous region. Their first target was West Virginia's workers' compensation board, which was pressured to make black lung disease, liberally defined, compensable. Their agitation further resulted in the incorporation of a black lung benefits program in the 1969 federal Coal Mine Safety and Health Act. Officials anticipated a small, relatively inexpensive program to defuse tension in the coalfields; the Surgeon General, for instance, estimated in 1969 that perhaps 100,000 coal miners had valid claims. Nevertheless, by 1971 almost 350,000 miners and widows had filed and program costs were mounting. In response, administrators retreated to a narrow definition of the disease, demanding X-ray evidence of pneumoconiosis. They justified this by arguing that only pneumoconiosis could be attributed with certainty to occupational causes, since bronchial and other disorders could be the result of a miner's "lifestyle"; moreover, the program required total disability, but this could not be granted if a worker was deemed capable of performing a desk job – not that there were many such jobs in Appalachia. A substantial majority of the claims were disallowed. "Miners who had spent thirty or forty years underground, whose breathing was a series of audible rasps, whose hacking coughs regularly produced inky black sputum, whose retirement did not include the hunting and fishing they had dreamed of, but, rather, short walks between the bedroom and the kitchen – all over the coalfields, such miners were denied compensation" (Smith, 1987, pp. 147–8).

The movement continued to agitate, using its proven ability to shut the mines down. In response, a Black Lung Benefits Act was passed in 1972 which liberalized the definition of the disease and permitted more forms of evidence. By the end of 1974 the total number of claims allowed exceeded 350,000, although more claims were still being rejected than accepted. Meanwhile, the budget for the program ballooned to a billion dollars per year, remaining at that level throughout the 1970s. A further round of liberalization was undertaken in 1977, along with a provision that would transfer financial responsibility from the taxpayer to the coal operator, provided the "responsible" operator could be found. With the dispersion of its leadership, the greater liberality of the benefit program, and emergence of other issues affecting the well-being of coal miners in the 1980s, the black lung movement lost its impetus.

The problems remain, albeit on a smaller scale. The benefit level was never more than modest, with average monthly payments under Part B of the program (pertaining to claims filed before the end of 1972) rising with inflation from $181.90 in 1970 to $376.40 in 1984. Simple expedients to reduce ambient dust in the mines, such as sprinkling the coal with water during extraction and loading, have improved conditions, although lung damage remains widespread. A National Institute for Occupational Safety and Health (NIOSH) survey taken at the end of the 1970s found that some form of bronchitis plagues 40.4 percent of all miners, 11.2 percent suffer from persistent breathlessness, and airway obstruction is "significant" in 24.2 percent. The effort to shift costs to coal operators has been generally unsuccessful; Barth (1987) estimates that only 4–6 percent of all compensation paid during the 1980s came from the operators or their insurers. And, most critically, the system of air quality monitoring within the mines, on which the compensation system, safety enforcement, and miners' medical assessment depend, is unreliable. Coal operators, who do the actual sampling, have an incentive to misinform federal regulators and their own employees, and the evidence suggests they do this routinely. As long ago as 1975 the US General Accounting Office found that "current procedures [make it] virtually impossible to determine how many mine sections are in compliance with statutorily established dust standards" (US GAO, 1975, p. 15). As recently as April, 1991 hundreds of mines owned by five major companies – USX, Bethlehem Steel, Du Pont, General Dynamics, and CLI – were fined a total of $7 million for tampering with air samples, joining Peabody Coal, which had been assessed $500,000 three months earlier for the same infraction (Kilborn, 1991). Perhaps the most dismal conclusion to be drawn concerning the health of coal miners is that no one really knows.

Note

The account of the Triangle fire follows Stein (1962). The section on black lung draws primarily on Smith (1987) and Barth (1987).

1 The economics of risk and the risk of economics

Each day millions of Americans go to work knowing that they run the risk of serious injury, illness, or death. Their fears are borne out by statistical evidence showing that work in America is dangerous and getting more so, and that public policies to reverse this trend have largely failed. This alone would be reason to write a book. But occupational safety and health is also a crucible for economic theory. Economists have developed an elaborate analysis of working conditions and their relationship to wages and employment decisions, and they have subjected it to dozens of empirical tests. They even claim to have developed the tools for assigning a dollar value to human lives saved or lost. As I will try to show, however, the theory they employ is fundamentally misguided, the tests are at best inconclusive and ignore massive amounts of counter-evidence, and, as a result, the economics profession has been unable to explain our predicament or help lead us out of it. The implications of this failure extend beyond the problem of workplace safety and extend to *all* of the issues addressed by contemporary market analysis, since the misguided assumptions that obscure the significance of dangerous working conditions are also in force whenever economists study the interaction between institutions and individual behavior in modern society.

Dangerous work: still a problem

Like the persistence of poverty, discrimination, and rampant inequality, the continuing threat of hazardous working conditions after centuries of economic development represents an indictment of our society. New products are engineered to accomplish astonishing feats of precision and economy, but the methods used to produce them often remain mired in an earlier age, as if the needs of workers, unlike consumers, are beneath consideration.

11

There are several questions we would like to be able to answer concerning occupational safety and health. (1) What is the level of danger today? Are jobs becoming safer, more dangerous, or staying the same? (2) How is occupational risk distributed across the population? Are some groups more at risk than others? Why? (3) How does the record in the US compare with that of other industrialized countries? Unfortunately, as we will see, there is no comprehensive, reliable source of information that can resolve these issues, and we must piece together what evidence we can find.

1   The level of risk

How dangerous are America's workplaces? Workers apparently feel they are unsafe. A poll of blue-collar workers taken in Indiana in 1990 found that nearly 30 percent considered their jobs "not safe," and those who felt their jobs less safe compared to three years earlier outnumbered those who felt their jobs more safe by 22.9 percent to 16.3 percent.[1] Almost three out of five reported that they had been *seriously* injured on-the-job; of these, a third reported multiple injuries. (The emphasis on "serious" was in the questionnaire.) When asked what priority his or her employer placed on safety, twice as many said "low" as "high" (The National Safe Workplace Institute, 1990a).

A more detailed survey was undertaken in 1985 by the National Center for Health Statistics of the US Department of Health and Human Services. They asked a sample of over 100,000 workers to assess the safety of their own jobs; a portion of the results appear in table 1.1. Note not only the large variation of perceived risk across occupations, but also the high level of overall risk, including lines of work usually regarded as "safe."[2]

It would be useful to check these impressions against the official statistics on occupational risk collected by the Bureau of Labor Statistics (BLS), but these are notoriously unreliable. Indeed, the National Research Council, an offshoot of the National Academy of Sciences that reports on public policy issues, found the BLS data inadequate for monitoring the effectiveness of safety programs (Saddler, 1987). There are several problems. First, the data are collected as part of the Occupational Safety and Health Act (OSHA) reporting system, which subjects them to distorting incentive effects. Firms are required to maintain logs of fatal and nonfatal accidents, but they have an incentive to underreport this information since it could be used as evidence to support workers compensation or tort claims by workers, and because

Table 1.1 *Percentage perceiving work-related hazards by occupation*

Occupation[a]	Hazardous substances	Hazardous conditions	Risks of injury
All	33.9	35.2	39.3
Cleaning and building service	47.1	18.7	36.4
Construction and extractive	63.9	50.1	71.9
Engineers	35.0	40.2	36.4
Fabricators, assemblers, etc.	60.1	47.6	50.8
Farm operators and managers	75.8	51.9	81.5
Farm, other agricultural workers	54.8	39.8	62.3
Financial records processing	13.6	17.8	7.1
Food service	19.2	28.8	50.7
Freight, stock, material handlers	45.7	41.0	56.5
Health assessment and treating	35.2	54.7	51.3
Health service	20.8	31.5	42.4
Health technicians	39.4	50.0	45.5
Machine operators, except precision	60.8	49.3	51.7
Management-related occupations	13.5	30.2	11.8
Managers and private administrators	23.5	32.6	30.8
Moving equipment operators	63.4	58.3	73.5
Mechanics and repairers	69.1	53.3	69.0
Motor vehicle operators	44.3	41.6	77.4
Officials and administrators, public	20.4[b]	32.6	16.8[b]
Other administrative support	19.1	28.2	19.6
Other professional specialties	11.3	38.7	21.9
Other protective services	28.5	38.9	63.8
Other sales	18.2	17.0	28.2
Personal service	33.4	18.8	20.6
Police and fire fighters	50.1	76.4	86.9
Precision production occupations	56.7	47.5	56.1
Sales representatives	15.8	25.1	32.9
Secretaries, stenographers, typists	10.9	18.1	7.8
Supervisors and proprietors	21.6	25.7	34.7
Teachers, librarians, counselors	22.4	32.3	20.5
Technicians, except health	39.2	40.3	32.1
Writers, artists, performers	27.4	28.2	27.3

Notes: a Occupation codes derived from 1980 Census Bureau codes.
b Estimated error greater than 30 percent.
Source: Shilling and Brackbill (1987).

OSHA administrators during the Reagan era focused inspections on those firms which *reported* the highest injury rates. Second, little effort is made to incorporate data on occupational disease, as against injury. The specific etiology of an illness is intrinsically more difficult to identify, since illnesses commonly have multiple causes, are only probabilistically determined by occupational conditions, and frequently appear only after considerable time has elapsed. As a result, BLS safety data do not reflect many of the most critical health concerns. These problems are compounded by the fact that there is no independent agency charged with compiling and verifying safety records.[3] This means that the criteria of public health professionals are not brought into the data-gathering process, and that conflicts between OSHA logs and medical records are not identified and resolved.[4]

Nevertheless, despite their shortcomings, these statistics and others collected by NIOSH are all that are available. Table 1.2 demonstrates the long-term historical trend in injuries for four major industries with significant safety problems.[5] In each case the record is U-shaped, with a historic high earlier in the century, steady reduction leading to a low generally in the 1960s or early 1970s, and then an upturn heading into the 1980s. (Note that data on the last two industries begin after the Second World War.) To interpret these numbers, we can convert them to injuries per full-time equivalent worker by letting 2,000 hours equal one working year.

A more focused look at the recent past is provided by figures 1.1 through 1.3, which track lost workday cases (occupational injuries or illnesses severe enough to result in at least one missed day of work), total number of lost workdays, and occupational fatalities. The first two are expressed as rates per 100 private-sector employees, the third as a rate per 100,000 employees. Before considering the trends they capture, a word of explanation is in order. Occupational safety statistics may rise or fall because of actual changes in the safety of work, but they may also fluctuate because of the changing composition of the economy. Some jobs, like retailing, are significantly safer than others, like mining. Over time, personal service and paper-pushing jobs have expanded, while blue-collar jobs (like mining) have contracted. Even without any change in the level of safety of each *type* of job, this will have the effect of making it seem that work has become safer. In order to control for this effect, I constructed "fixed-weight" indices of occupational safety and health by averaging industry statistics for each year as if employment in these industries were unchanged since 1980. That is, the 1980 data pictured in these figures are correct, but the 1981 numbers are slightly off: they represent the level of safety that would have been attained if the economy

Table 1.2 *The high-low-high pattern of nonfatal injuries in selected major industries. Incidence per one million hours (years in parentheses)*

Industry	High	Low	High
Manufacturing	24 (1926)	12 (1957)	23 (1979)
Mining	80 (1932)	25 (1971)	26 (1984)
Construction	41 (1949)	26 (1967)	34 (1984)
Trade	13 (1949)	10.5 (1975)	14 (1983)

Source: Robinson (1988).

had retained its 1980 structure (percentages of workers across industries), but with 1981 safety figures *within* each industry. With each succeeding year the fixed-weight average drifts further from the actual average, but the fixed-weight trend captures the true change in safety conditions on a job-by-job basis better than the actual averages would.[6]

With this out of the way, consider the evidence itself. Lost workday cases (figure 1.1) dipped during the severe recession of the early 1980s, then increased until the onset of the slowdown of the early 1990s. Two effects can be disentangled. First, there is clearly a "cyclical" component to safety: it rises during periods of economic hardship, and falls during periods of growth. This may be due either to the speed up in the pace of work when orders pile up (this is implicit in Okun's Law, according to which fluctuations in output exceed fluctuations in employment), or to the influx of new, inexperienced workers when hiring expands. In either case, long lines at the unemployment office seem to be good news for safety and health (as they are, incidentally, for the environment). Second, superimposed on these short-term fluctuations is a long-term increase in the frequency of serious injuries: compared to 1980, we left the decade with nearly an 8 percent greater chance that a worker in a given industry would experience a significant health or safety problem.

The situation appears more alarming when we consider figure 1.2. After the obligatory dip for the 1982 recession, the number of lost workdays per employee virtually explodes: the increase is more than 30 percent! Is this an accurate reflection of changing safety conditions during the 1980s? Some say that it is not, that the numbers reflect a milking of the workers' compensation system by dishonest workers angling to get a few extra days of paid vacation. I argue against this view in chapter 6, pointing out that it overlooks equally powerful pressures for workers to *under*report the extent of their illnesses and injuries. Moreover, as we will see shortly, case studies and journalistic accounts support the impression that, in many industries, the trend toward more dangerous work is incontrovertible.

Perhaps the sole ray of hope is found in figure 1.3, which shows the rate of occupational fatalities, as measured by the National Traumatic Occupational Fatality (NTOF) Surveillance Project. These numbers are constructed by the National Institute for Occupational Safety and Health (NIOSH) from a painstaking analysis of death certificates. Here the trend is unquestionably down, a drop of approximately one-third over the course of a decade. Several words of caution are in order, however. (1) Although it offers a more accurate accounting than does BLS, NTOF understates the number of fatal injuries by something like 20 percent (Stout and Bell, 1991). This is due to the failure of many death certificates to attribute job-related deaths to their true causes (if, for instance, a worker died in the hospital of complications following an occupational injury, or if the cause of death were a traffic accident while on company business), as well as to the difficulty of locating all of the qualifying deaths on a state-by-state basis. (2) NTOF restricts itself to deaths resulting only from injury, whereas BLS makes an (inadequate) effort to register illness as well. (3) The difference in trends between nonfatal and fatal accidents may reflect improvements in medical care rather than conditions on-the-job.

The previous discussion concerns fatal injuries, but in all likelihood this represents a small portion of the full human cost. Fatal occupational diseases, lightly covered by BLS and not counted at all by NIOSH, exact a far higher toll, but they are also, as indicated above, more difficult to recognize. An early attempt to provide a rough estimate of the number of mortalities attributable to industrial disease was undertaken by NIOSH in 1972. The procedure entailed calculating excess death rates of specific occupational groups relative to average mortality rates in the population as a whole (corrected for demographic variables), and then weighting by occupational density. One hundred thousand such fatalities per year were projected, a figure subsequently scaled down to 50,000–70,000 by the American Public Health Association (Landrigan, 1992). There have also been studies of particular causal factors in the workplace. Johnson and Heller (1984), for instance, report that between 8,500 and 10,000 individuals die each year from work-related asbestos exposure. A debate surrounds the evidence of industrial carcinogenesis; see, for example, the contrasting positions of Epstein (1979) and Doll and Peto (1982).

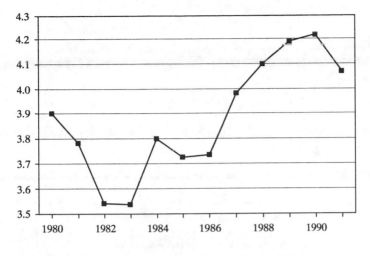

Figure 1.1   Lost workday cases per 100 employees (fixed weight)

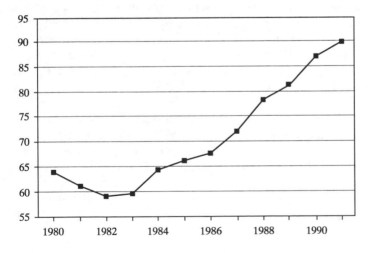

Figure 1.2   Lost workdays per 100 employees (fixed weight)

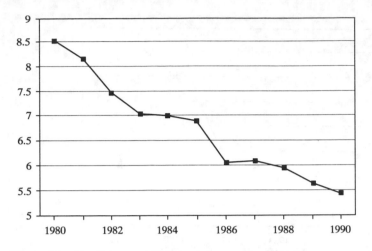

Figure 1.3   Fatalities per 100,000 employees (fixed weight)

Overall, it is likely that there are a great many more fatalities from illnesses than accidents on-the-job, but exact measurement will be difficult for some time to come.

On balance, the statistical evidence points toward worsening conditions in US workplaces. Overall, a worker has nearly one chance in twenty-five in a given year of experiencing an occupational injury severe enough to keep him or her out of work for at least a day, and can expect an average of approximately twenty-two lost workdays for each such episode. (These figures are based on the actual, not the fixed-weight, averages for 1991.) A similar view was offered by NIOSH during the mid 1980s; they estimated an annual rate of approximately 3 million "serious" injuries, in which the worker suffers some lasting impairment (Millar, 1985). Compared to employment levels, this figure represented an annual average of 8.0 injuries per 100 full-time employed workers. However measured, this upsurge in injuries, combined with the sky-rocketing cost of medical care, has created a workers compensation crisis in many states, with the result that state governments are being forced to hike their payroll tax (by 30 percent or more), slash benefits, or both (Freudenheim, 1991).

At the level of specific industries the gathering health and safety crisis of the 1990s is even more glaring. Intense pressure to speed up production and economize on personnel has led to bitter disputes over safety at USX, the nation's largest steel manufacturer, and General Motors; in one recent strike against GM in Baltimore, for example, workers protested a ten-fold increase in the injury rate following a management cost-cutting drive (Risen, 1987b; Tolchin, 1991). Even worse is the record at the Nucor Corporation, an aggressively nonunion operated specialty steel "mini-mills," where seventeen employees and contract workers have been killed on-the-job during the past decade – twice the industry rate. Critics point to corporate pressure to cut corners on training and safety conditions, as well as a productivity bonus system that holds workers' wages hostage to extreme risk-taking (Ansberry, 1991). Yet these conditions pale in comparison to those in the petrochemical industry, in which more than eighty workers have died and 1,000 have been injured in a series of catastrophic explosions during the last four years alone. A thread running through most of these episodes is the use of inexpensive – and inexperienced – contract labor, compounded by general understaffing and inattention to safety precautions (Schneider, 1991). In meatpacking the traditional risk of losing a hand to the cutting equipment has been augmented by repetitive motion disorders (RMDs, also referred to as cumulative trauma disorders), as production line speeds have been stepped up during the 1980s. RMDs cause loss of function in workers' wrists or elbows; they often require surgery to heal, and even then recovery is seldom complete. Nearly 8 percent of the workers in this industry report some form of this disorder, and in some workplaces the problem takes on near-epidemic dimensions. A NIOSH survey at South Dakota meatpacker John Morrell & Co., for instance, found that *half* the employees had RMD symptoms (Goldoftas, 1991). Morrell was subsequently fined more than $4 million dollars by OSHA for wilfully ignoring the effect of its relentless production pace on its workforce and for demanding that workers resume work within *hours* of surgery for RMDs. Inspectors found that workers were given an average of only 1.1 days to recuperate, and more than a third were permitted *no recuperation at all* (Ansberry, 1989). More generally, RMDs are taking their place as the occupational hazard of the new economic environment. In part this is due to the heightened pace of work dictated by unrestrained global competition, but it also stems from the introduction of computerized equipment to automate all but a few of the operations in the production process. The remaining human tasks, which may be knife cuts, welds, or keystrokes, are repeated thousands of times per day in a hectic effort to keep pace with the machines that perform the operations just before and after. Interestingly, white-collar and service occupations are as susceptible to this problem as traditional blue-collar work: RMDs have been found among telephone dispatchers, newspaper reporters, and supermarket checkout clerks. One study found that 20 percent of a sample of telephone operators had been diagnosed with either carpal tunnel syndrome, a painful condition which blocks functioning below the wrist, or tendinitis (Goldoftas, 1991). Finally, under conditions of extreme competition, even pizza delivery has become a high-risk activity. Intense pressure on employees to deliver their pizzas within 30 minutes of the initial order has apparently led to more than twenty fatalities at Domino's Pizza in the past few years (Kelly, 1989).

Of course, these anecdotes do not prove that working conditions in general are deteriorating. No doubt it would be possible to find other industries and employers where great strides were taken to promote safety during the same period. Yet there are two reasons to pay attention to these warning signs. First, safety improvements in some industries do not "balance off" declines in others. If new technologies or forms of workplace organization are making it possible to reduce the risks for some workers, this hardly provides a justification for lax conditions elsewhere: an unnecessary injury, illness, or death remains just that. Second, the anecdotal evidence corroborates the statistical evidence; both tell the same story. The long-term twentieth-century trend toward safer workplaces has come to at least a temporary stop, and changes in the economy during the past few years may even be making matters worse.

2   The distribution of occupational risk

It should come as no surprise that those who are most disadvantaged in the labor market generally – blacks, Hispanics, those with limited educational opportunities, and, above all, those confined by class to more limited social and economic options – suffer disproportionately from dangerous working conditions.[7] Robinson (1989) regressed occupational injury and illness rates for detailed occupations on worker characteristics for those occupations (California data). A relative risk measure (the risk for an ethnic group relative to that for whites) was computed from the coefficient on ethnicity. His results appear in table 1.3, where the numbers in parentheses represent 95 percent confidence intervals, and where the ratios are either adjusted to control for education and experience or displayed unadjusted. Several points stand out. First, whites clearly face less occupational risk; in only one instance was risk parity even on the boundary of the confidence interval. Second, Hispanic men are at greatest risk, although this may be specific to California. In the uncontrolled model they face more than twice the risk faced by white men. Third, despite the complications introduced by the relatively large difference in education between black and Hispanic women, the two groups are both at greater risk than white women. The disparity among women, however, is less than that among men, presumably since all are concentrated in "women's work." Finally, for all groups except black women, controlling for education and work experience substantially reduces the relative risk measure. This may be small consolation, however, since differences in educational attainment and job tenure are themselves primarily a consequence of discrimination. Overall, the impression is that differences in the risk of injury and illness on the job are consistent with, and therefore exacerbate, the other differences associated with race and ethnicity.

In another study Robinson (1988) merged several national labor market samples to construct mean characteristics for jobs that are safer than average and those that are less safe.[8] He found that, in general, dangerous jobs are bad jobs: they are less interesting, more authoritarian, impart fewer skills, provide fewer opportunities for promotion, offer less job security, and pay less. His results concerning average pay are important for the issues we will be considering throughout the book; they are reproduced in table 1.4.

To glimpse the human reality behind these abstract patterns, consider one group in particular, hired farmworkers. These workers, who number between one and a half and two and a half million, are more likely than the general population to come from minority and low-income backgrounds. Their work is difficult, sometimes backbreaking, but usually pays little more than the legal minimum. Farm work is often seasonal; many who do it must travel from one state to the next looking for work, undergoing long spells of no income at all. Unless they are among the lucky few to be unionized, farmworkers have no rights on-the-job whatsoever; in fact, many large corporate farms are run like boot camps. Add to all these hardships the extraordinary physical risks faced by farmworkers. Contrary to public stereotypes, many of these workers, some just children, operate heavy equipment. Until recent OSHA rulings, there was no requirement that employers provide any sanitary facilities at all, and even now the standard is not universally enforced. Above all, these workers are exposed to massive amounts of pesticides. According to the US Environmental Protection Agency, farmworkers receive as many as 300,000 acute injuries and illnesses from pesticide exposure; one 1990 study in western New York found that over 40 percent of the farmworker *children* interviewed said they had been directly sprayed by pesticides while working (US GAO, 1992).

The inescapable conclusion is that safe and healthy workplaces are rationed in the same manner as any other desirable, scarce good. Those who by virtue of class, caste, or simple good luck are able to acquire safety do so; they are also rewarded with jobs that are more interesting, skill-enhancing, and better paid. Danger and hardship are the lot of the poor and powerless. In this way, differences in the level of risk faced by workers correspond to the other differences in their life chances and thus compound them.

Table 1.3   *Occupational risk relative to white workers. (95% confidence intervals in parentheses)*

		Hispanics	Blacks
Men	*(Unadjusted)*	2.21 (2.04, 2.40)	1.41 (1.18, 1.69)
	(Adjusted)	1.33 (1.22, 1.45)	1.17 (1.00, 1.37)
Women	*(Unadjusted)*	1.49 (1.38, 1.62)	1.31 (1.14, 1.50)
	(Adjusted)	1.19 (1.09, 1.29)	1.31 (1.15, 1.50)

Note: Adjusted ratios control for education and work experience.
Source: Robinson (1989).

Table 1.4   *Hourly wages and annual earnings in hazardous and safe occupations*

	Hazardous occupations	Safe occupations	T
Hourly wage			
1978–1980 NLS	$6.11	$6.40	2.2
1974 PSID	$4.68	$5.86	9.9
1977 Manufacturing, CPS (all workers)	$5.32	$6.69	8.7
1977 Manufacturing, CPS (production workers)	$5.30	$5.97	6.4
Annual earnings			
1977 QES	$12,583	$14,669	2.0

Notes: T-statistics measure the confidence with which the null hypothesis – no difference in population means – can be rejected.
Source: Robinson (1988).

3   International comparisons

It would be useful to know how workplace safety in the United States compares to conditions in other countries. Unfortunately, the published data, such as those presented by the ILO in its *Yearbook of Labour Statistics*, reveal little, since they simply reproduce each country's internal statistics, which are compiled using radically different criteria and reporting standards. In most European nations, for instance, traffic accidents occurring during a worker's commute to and from work are counted as occupational; in the US they are not. A few countries, such as

Sweden, have an elaborate public health apparatus with a presence in most large workplaces, so that accident and illness data are generated as byproducts of monitoring and treatment. This is the most accurate and informative approach. In the US, on the other hand, data are derived from OSHA employer logs, creating, as we have seen, disincentives to honest record-keeping. Nevertheless, some rough comparisons are possible.

Table 1.5 summarizes a comparison between US and Australian fatality rates conducted by Stout *et al.* (1990); the differences are striking. With the exception of agriculture, forestry, and fishing and the two very low-fatality industries, trade and FIRE, Australian workers face far less risk of death than their US counterparts. Even so, the authors of this study, after taking a close look at the information-gathering mechanisms of the two countries, concluded that US fatalities are relatively more likely to be underreported, and so the true advantage of Australia is probably concealed. Assuming the numbers to be accurate, and further assuming that US deaths not classifiable by industry group are distributed in the same proportions as the classifiable deaths, by equaling Australian safety standards within each major industry the average US fatality rate reported by NTOF for 1980–5 could have been reduced from 6,757 to 5,006 – an annual saving of 1,751 lives. Expressed differently, a US worker has, on average, a 35 percent greater chance of dying on-the-job than an Australian, controlling for the industrial composition of the two countries. This computed difference, conservative in light of the bias in US statistics, is even more remarkable when it is realized that Australia is by no means a leader in occupational safety.

Even more interesting is a comparison between the United States and Japan. Japan enjoys a large trade surplus with the US; is it at the expense of the safety and health of its workforce? Unfortunately, differences in definitions and reporting procedures in Japan make a true safety comparison impossible, but Wokutch and McLaughlin (1992) reduced the discrepancy, in part by grouping injuries and illnesses into a single aggregate. (The Japanese draw the line between illness and injury differently than the US does, especially in regard to back problems.) Their results are summarized in table 1.6.

The order of magnitude difference between Japanese and US incidence rates is probably not reliable, since, as will be discussed in more detail in chapter 6, there is considerable pressure on both workers and managers to underreport minor incidents in Japan. The severity and fatality rates may be more accurate, however: these losses are more difficult to hide (particularly fatalities), and the relative performance of the two countries is comparable in both series. The conclusion would appear to be that US

Table 1.5 *Fatal injury rate per 100,000 workers: US and Australia*

Industry division	US	Australia
Agriculture/forestry/fishing	21.6	26.6
Mining	32.5	26.2
Construction	26.8	15.9
Manufacturing	4.8	4.0
Transportation/communication/utilities	26.5	14.5
Wholesale/retail trade	2.3	2.4
Finance/insurance/real estate	1.3	2.1
Services	3.9	1.9
Public administration	8.4	4.4

Source: Stout *et al.* (1990).

Table 1.6 *Injury and illness incidence rates: US/Japan*

Year and sector	Incidence rate	Severity rate	Fatality rate
Private sector (US/Japan):			
1983	3.6/0.61	90.2/60.0	4.1/4.0
1984	3.8/0.55	96.2/68.0	4.3/6.0
1985	3.7/0.50	97.9/58.0	4.4/4.0
1986	3.8/0.47	93.5/44.0	3.7/2.0
1987	3.9/0.44	99.6/40.0	3.8/2.0
Manufacturing sector (US/Japan):			
1983	3.5/0.39	87.0/44.0	3.5/2.0
1984	3.7/0.36	87.6/40.0	3.1/2.0
1985	3.6/0.33	91.6/38.0	3.4/2.0
1986	3.7/0.32	96.6/36.0	2.9/2.0
1987	4.0/0.30	101.6/30.0	3.5/2.0

Notes: Incidence rate: for the US lost workday cases per 100 full-time workers; for Japan lost time injuries and illnesses per 200,000 hours worked.
Severity rate: for the US days away from work per 100 full-time workers; for Japan days away from work per 200,000 hours worked.
Fatality rate: for both US and Japan fatalities per 200 million hours worked or, equivalently, per 100,000 full-time workers.
Source: Wokutch and McLaughlin (1992).

firms are more dangerous by a factor of nearly two. Some caution is in order, however. Even in fatalities, Japanese data may not fully reflect the performance of that country's smallest and most hazardous companies; on the other hand, US numbers were taken from the BLS which, as we have already seen, substantially underestimates our own injury, illness, and fatality rates. While the raw data are not decisive, then, they are suggestive, and Wokutch (1992), after detailed investigation of auto production in the US and Japan, concludes that, on balance, Japanese conditions are safer.

As a final observation on the state of occupational safety and health in the United States, note that the persistence of dangerous working conditions, their concentration in the most vulnerable sectors of the population, and their greater severity relative to other industrialized countries all remain pressing social problems despite the creation of a major new federal agency, OSHA, to address them. Why OSHA has been so ineffective is a topic that will have to wait for a more detailed treatment later; for now it is enough to say that workers in the United States are being grossly underserved, and that drastic changes in occupational health and safety policy are long overdue.

Through the looking-glass: how economics views occupational safety and health

If there is a widely held, "common sense" position on occupational safety and health, it probably goes something like this: High rates of injury and illness indicate that many jobs are still too dangerous. This is due to some combination of worker inattention and employer irresponsibility. The really hazardous jobs are, for the most part, performed by people who do not have the opportunity to avoid them; they are the most abused members of the labor force, and it is a public responsibility to improve their condition. Finally, if safety standards in general have improved over the last century, this is primarily due to the combination of government regulation and the struggles of the labor movement. The evidence presented in the first half of this chapter, along with the two case studies described in the prologue, clearly support this view, and it is, in my view, generally correct.

It is not, by and large, the view of the economics profession.[9] Indeed, there is probably no topic on which the chasm between public opinion and economic doctrine is wider; it is so wide that these two perspectives can barely recognize one another, much less debate their differences. The conflict between economic theory and popular perception is a central theme of this book; for now it is enough to sketch out the position taken by most economists, identify its central logic, and draw out its main implications.

Economists begin with the observation that workers *choose* dangerous jobs. It is rarely the case that a worker has no alternative at all to risky work; even the most disadvantaged have some scope for choice. A further postulate is that workers, indeed all of us, are rational: we seek out important information, process it efficiently, and make decisions calculated to best serve our interests. To propose otherwise, it is often said, would open the door to the paternalistic view that the liberties of the unenlightened must be restricted in their own interest. Eschewing this dangerous posture, economics counts itself on the side of the angels.

Yet why would a rational individual ever choose a dangerous job? Obviously, this could occur only if the total advantages of the job – its level of pleasantness, its future prospects, and above all its pay – were at least as great as, if not greater than, the next best alternative. This in turn implies that there must be other attributes of dangerous jobs that offset that particular disadvantage, so that they will still be rationally chosen by someone. This insight is generally traced to Adam Smith, who wrote that "the whole of the advantages and disadvantages of the different employments of labor and stock must, in the same neighborhood, be either perfectly equal or continually tending toward equality" (A. Smith, 1937, p. 100). Simplifying the matter to consider only the levels of risk and pay, we come to the theory of *compensating wage differentials*. Once we accept the postulates of free choice in the labor market and worker rationality in making that choice, it appears to be an inescapable conclusion that offsetting wage differentials must *fully* compensate workers for taking on greater risks.

This position has three profound ramifications for the way we understand occupational safety and health:

(1) In the economic view the presumption holds that, given existing technologies, consumer preferences, and worker attitudes toward risk, injury and illness rates are *not* too high, and occupational safety and health are not a problem. The logic is straightforward. The wage differentials required by workers to offset greater risk constitute a burden on employers. They can avoid these extra payments only by improving safety. More precisely, they have an incentive to make jobs safer so long as the marginal (added) cost of furnishing greater safety is less than the corresponding wage differential. Since this differential must fully offset the cost to workers of taking on dangerous work, the market is conducting an implicit benefit–cost analysis: improve safety if that is the least expensive way to satisfy workers, otherwise retain the risk and

pay compensation. Employer costs, meanwhile, are passed on to consumers, who must decide whether the value of the goods and services being placed on the market outweigh the expense. They too perform, in effect, a benefit–cost analysis, generating demand only for those goods whose contribution to social well-being offsets the costs – including the safety or risk compensation costs – of producing them. All in all, such a market produces the "right" amount of safety; government regulation, by tinkering with this result, can only make it worse.

In fairness to the economics profession, most of its practitioners recognise that, while the overall framework described above is correct, allowances must be made for market imperfections. The presence of friction in the labor market, for instance, which makes it costly for workers to locate and switch to alternative jobs, would mean that wage compensation would not have to be complete – just enough to dissuade workers from taking on the costs of mobility. Difficulties intrinsic to the insurance industry must also be considered. To avoid problems of litigation and insurers' "cream-skimming" (extending insurance only to the best risks), workers compensation was made mandatory and no-fault. But it still complicates the basic model, since it alters the calculations of workers and firms. (This will be discussed in chapter 4.) Above all, workers may not have enough information to make informed decisions, either because many safety issues are highly complicated and ill-understood, or because it is in the interests of employers to mislead workers into thinking that jobs are safer than they really are (so they will not have to pay wage premiums). This last argument has gained wide acceptance among economists and, while in their view it does not invalidate the model as a whole, it does provide a justification for public policies to disseminate safety information. But the ultimate goal of this and other interventions, for economists, is not to make workplaces safe *per se*, but to bring about greater convergence between real conditions and the free market ideal.

(2) The situation of workers in dangerous jobs cannot be improved by making their jobs safer. This follows directly from the free-market model for three reasons: First, forcing employers to make jobs safer than it would otherwise be in their interests to do has the result that workers must sacrifice a wage premium greater than the value of increased safety. (This will be shown more formally in the following chapter.) After all, if the employer could have restructured the total package – wages plus safety – to provide greater satisfaction to workers he or she would already have done so; this would make it possible to employ labor at the original total remuneration, but at less cost to the enterprise. If there is

no such opportunity for profitable reshuffling, government regulations cannot conjure them up. Second, it is an illusion to think that workers in dangerous jobs are worse off than those in safe jobs *because their jobs are dangerous*. True, on average, those who hold dangerous jobs will be the least advantaged workers, because employers can economize on wage premiums by hiring them. But they would be disadvantaged in any employment, and the theory of compensating wage differentials indicates that the condition of such workers cannot be improved by requiring them to take only safe jobs. Indeed, from this perspective the movement to regulate and improve working conditions looks suspiciously like middle-class paternalism. Richard Zeckhauser (1975, p. 457), perhaps the most influential public policy economist of his generation, put it this way:

The whole issue of denying the poor risks that they view as acceptable gets tied up with our perceptions of the income distribution. If we observe that poor people have to sell themselves into potential physical infirmities, we are forced to recognize that the income distribution is much more uneven or much more consequentially uneven than we have previously perceived. Prohibitions of this sort may be a way of salving the conscience of the middle class at the expense of the welfare of the poor. To the extent that it clouds perceptions about inequalities in the income distribution, it may do the poor a double disservice.

Finally, a free market in occupational risk permits workers and firms to seek out their most compatible partners. Some workers do not mind a little danger; they require less in the way of wage premiums, and so employers with unavoidably high safety costs will seek them out. Workers who place more value on life and limb will be unwilling to accept the wage bargains agreed to by their daredevil colleagues and will find their way into safer jobs. Overall, the market will perform a valuable matching service that has the effect of allocating risk to those most willing to take it. Once again, government tinkering, by changing the safety characteristics of jobs without attention to the preferences of those holding them, is inefficient. Risky jobs may be risky because those who are concentrated in them do not mind them that way. Taken together, these three arguments deny that the distribution of occupational hazards in society intensifies inequality.

(3) Occupational safety should be seen as just another commodity that is bought and sold in the marketplace; it has a price which reflects both its marginal contribution to worker well-being and its marginal cost of provision by employers. And just as prices for other goods are indicators of their relative worth, so also is the price of safety a measure of its value,

not to philosophers or political activists, but to those who actually produce or purchase it. From here it is but a short step to the proposition that information from the labor market can be used to construct a "value of life," a monetary equivalent of a single human life saved or lost. Two assumptions are required. First, assume that the price of safety improvements determined in the market reflects the preferences of workers "in general." Then assume that such workers are representative of the society as a whole, so that their choices are the ones we would all tend to make. Now the procedure becomes clear: calculate the wage differential required to offset a small decrease in safety, multiply by the number of such decreases that would add up to an expected loss of one life, and the result is the value of life. For example, suppose that it is discovered that workers are willing to accept an added 1/1,000 increase in the annual likelihood of death on-the-job in return for an extra $2,000 per year. Aggregated over 1,000 workers we would expect to lose one additional life, for which a total of $2,000,000 in compensation would be accepted.

Of course, matters are not quite so simple. It is difficult to estimate actual compensating wage differentials, since jobs have many attributes besides pay and safety, and because these differentials represent the spread between what workers get on their current job and what they *would* get in an alternative job with different safety conditions. This in turn requires detailed information about workers to evaluate their likely labor market options. Finally, it is evident that all workers do not share the same attitude toward safety, and that there will therefore be a range of values of life corresponding to differences in preferences, incomes, and other factors. Nevertheless, there have been scores of studies during the past two decades which have undertaken these measurements. Actual values have been proposed, and the results have been used in academia, government, and the courts to answer such questions as how much survivors should be compensated for the loss of loved ones and which environmental and safety regulations can be justified by their expected savings in lives.

These three implications of conventional economic theory have had far-reaching effects on public policy, despite their incompatibility with the views held by nearly all noneconomists. In the analysis which takes up the rest of this book I will refer to them respectively as the *efficiency*, *equity*, and *hedonic* properties of the competitive market model.[10] I will explore the underlying model on its own terms to determine more precisely the conditions that are required for each of these properties to hold. This will involve a detailed review of the theoretical structure of the model, as well as the econometric procedures required to compensate for the lack of fully satisfactory data.

Yet the popular view, that occupational safety is a problem requiring remedial measures by workers, employers, and the government, is based not on theoretical and statistical analysis, but on generations of experience with the thorny problems of labor relations, law, and regulation that have always surrounded the issue of dangerous working conditions. Economists, like fire chief Croker, may understand the Triangle fire entirely in terms of the free choice of the women who worked there, and who could have quit if they did not want to endure the risks, but most other observers would pay attention to the apparent negligence of the company, the powerlessness of the workers at their place of employment, and the ineffectiveness of the municipal and state agencies entrusted with upholding standards. These are conflicting ways of seeing the same events, and they lead to dramatically different conclusions. Much of the following analysis will therefore be taken up with the task of testing the market model against the evidence embodied in the social and institutional history of workplace safety in the United States and kindred industrialized countries. To the extent that the economic model is an appropriate lens, it should be able to explain this history; if the popular view is correct, however, the failure of economic doctrine to account for this mass of evidence should be traceable to defects in its underlying theory.

This preview suggests that two broad issues are at stake. Certainly the confrontation between the two perspectives sketched above has immediate implications for public policy. If the economists are mostly right, we do not need new statutes, standards, or inspectors to regulate working conditions; at most we need only provide the necessary information about the risks entailed in different jobs and clear away any barriers to competitive market conditions. Knowledge of the value(s) of life, moreover, can be used to provide an objective basis for policy decisions that have consequences for human health and longevity, such as how stringent our environmental standards ought to be and what medical procedures should be subsidized by the public. If the non-economists are predominantly right, however, the United States should begin looking to, or even beyond, other countries with better occupational health and safety records, while current estimates of the dollar value of life should be regarded with deep suspicion.

But there is a second, more general set of implications to consider, concerning the status of economic theory itself. The final years of the twentieth century have witnessed a great resurgence of the free market perspective. State-managed economies in eastern Europe are being dismantled in favor of systems built on privatization and the pursuit of profit. Neoliberal ideologies, not only in the United States and England where they present themselves under their own banner, but also under the "socialist" governments of Spain and France, advance deregulation and "competitiveness" as the basis for future economic growth. Expanding international trade and economic integration are reconstituting laissez-faire at the global level, while the impoverished nations of the south are informed that the price of continued credit is free market austerity. Behind this economic and political tidal wave is ostensibly the conviction that untrammeled markets can do the best job of producing and distributing the things people most want and need. Yet there can be no more valued good than continued life itself under conditions of health and comfort, and the theory of compensating wage differentials examined in this book plays the critical role of explaining and justifying the market allocation of this good. From a different perspective, the doctrine of wage compensation is just the application of market analysis to the particular good "occupational safety"; so it is reasonable to suspect that if there are serious shortcomings to this theory, as I will argue there are, then the current popularity of market-oriented institutions owes more to fashion and shifting balances of political power than to their actual virtues. The scrutiny of the compensating wage differentials hypothesis also promises greater precision in this critical enterprise: from the detailed discrepancies between theory and reality encountered in this study we can locate more exactly where, how, and why free market doctrine goes wrong.

2   The theory of compensating wage differentials

For Adam Smith, the theory of compensating wage differentials was little more than common sense, so he did not take much time to justify or support it. Modern economics, however, has no place for such casual attitudes and, like other theories inherited from the past, wage compensation has been transformed from a plausible insight into a necessary deduction from a tightly reasoned model. But the formalization of economic theory has not only had the effect of giving it greater credence (in the eyes of economists); it has made it easier to apply in empirical work, since the relationships that need to be measured, such as *ceteris paribus* wage compensation, can now be specified precisely. It is not enough, then, to scan the surface of this (or any other) branch of modern economics. Its mathematical expression is no longer simply a translation of its narrative meaning: it now forms the substance of the theory and determines its strengths and weaknesses. In this chapter I will begin with a brief overview of the historical debate over compensating differentials and then move directly into a streamlined version of the basic formal model. After considering the structure of this model and drawing out its key implications, I will explore some of the ways economists have tried to reintroduce a measure of realism into their analysis.

An old debate

Adam Smith's claim that workers in a competitive labor market would receive compensating wage differentials for all disagreeable aspects of their jobs, including the risk of injury or death, was an instant hit in England. The intellectual climate was already inclined toward social doctrines based on volition and contract, and the courts were discarding all barriers to the making and enforcing of market transactions. Smith in particular was held in high esteem, and his theory of equalizing differentials quickly found its way into jurisprudence and public policy.

(The mutual interplay of economic theory and common law is discussed at greater length in chapter 4.) Nor was there any serious dissent among the next generation of thinkers who viewed Smith as their mentor. Other Smithian propositions saw their stock rise and fall, but the presumption of equalizing differences seemed to follow so directly from the logic of free markets that it remained largely unchallenged into the middle of the nineteenth century.

Indeed, it was not until 1852 that the opposing view found its first prominent champion. John Stuart Mill, regarded then as today as a giant among social philosophers, was at first a proponent of the Smithian position; his *Principles of Political Economy*, a tremendously influential treatise, specifically endorsed (with a few qualifications) the doctrine of compensating differentials. It came as quite a surprise, then, when, in the third edition of this book, Mill turned against Smith and his many followers with a new argument:

If the labourers in the aggregate, instead of exceeding, fell short of the amount of employment, work which was generally disliked would not be undertaken, except for more than ordinary wages. But when the supply of labor so far exceeds the demand that to find employment at all is an uncertainty, and to be offered it on any terms a favor, the case is totally the reverse. Desirable laborers, those whom everyone is anxious to have, can still exercise a choice. The undesirable must take what they can get ... The hardships and earnings, instead of being directly proportional, as in any just arrangements of society they would be, are generally in an inverse ratio to one another. (Mill, 1852, p. 388)

Reading past the typical Victorian disparagement of the lower orders (did Mill assume that none of them would read his book?), we can recognize the modern institutionalist position that involuntary unemployment in conjunction with labor market segmentation defeats the hypothetical efficiency claims of the free market. This view eventually had a decisive impact on public opinion: by the end of the century few defenders of Smithian orthodoxy could be found. As I will argue later, however, this temporary reversal had more to do with the stubbornness of the evidence of inequality and abuse than with the logical force of Mill's argument.

A more perplexing case is that of Karl Marx. Marx, of course, had little impact on the thought, much less the policy, of his own time, but in retrospect his judgments are crucial. Marx was a close student of Smith; long passages in the three volumes of *Capital* and, particularly, his monumental *Theories of Surplus Value* attest to his conviction that Smith is such a commanding figure that each proposition in *The Wealth of Nations* must be held up to close critical scrutiny. It is also well known that Marx regarded the physical hardships of the proletariat as one of the most damning indictments of capitalism. Among the most memorable pages of *Capital* are those in which he documents the gruesome working conditions in the British mills, as his lifelong colleague Engels had done twenty years earlier. Surely Marx must have known that British judges and parliamentarians, in denying relief to workers, fell back on Smithian compensation theory: you knew the risks you were exposing yourself to; therefore you implicitly reveal your approval of these conditions in return for your earnings, and there is no basis for redress. *Yet nowhere does Marx ever take up Adam Smith's views on dangerous work.* In all of Marxology – indeed in all of Victorian intellectual history – there is no more startling omission. This is truly the dog that did not bark.

Why? In the absence of any hard evidence we can only speculate; here is one possibility. Marx in general does not take exception to classical economic theory at the level of the individual market. In a celebrated passage (Marx, 1976, p. 280) he writes:

The sphere of circulation or commodity exchange, within whose boundaries the sale and purchase of labour-power goes on, is in fact a very Eden of the innate rights of man. It is the exclusive realm of Freedom, Equality, Property and Bentham. Freedom, because both buyer and seller of a commodity, let us say of labour-power, are determined only by their own free will. They contract as free persons, who are equal before the law. Their contract is the final result in which their joint will finds a common legal expression. Equality, because each enters into relation with the other, as with a simple owner of commodities, and they exchange equivalent for equivalent. Property, because each disposes only of what is his own. And Bentham, because each looks only to his own advantage. The only force bringing them together, and putting them into relation with each other, is the selfishness, the gain and the private interest of each.

For Marx, market transactions occupy a middle layer in the hierarchy of capitalist social relations; the injustice of the system becomes apparent only below and above it, within the coercive production process by which labor-power, the ability to work, is transformed into actual labor, and at the level of the entire structure, where surplus value is transformed into profit. Although Marx disputed the invisible hand postulate on the grounds that day-to-day price fluctuations are not an adequate guide to production and distribution, he never claimed that market relations themselves are responsible for exploitation. The grisly record of injuries and diseases in British factories impressed Marx as characteristic of capitalist production – workers as raw material for the owners to "use up" – yet his bifurcated vision crippled Marx when he confronted Smith on this issue. The theory of compensating wage differentials pertains to the labor market, that realm of "Freedom, Equality, Property and

Bentham." Without any conception of the way the coercive nature of the labor process impinges on Smithian markets, Marx had painted himself into a corner. Accepting the assumptions of worker rationality and freedom of contract, he was left with no plausible rebuttal to the doctrine of wage compensation.

Nevertheless it *is* possible to do the job Marx left undone. In a later chapter I will offer a critique of compensating differentials that is consistent with Marx's more general position, and consider the extent to which it is actually effective.

A simple model of wage compensation

To bring the critical issues into the sharpest possible relief, the models developed in this book will abstract from a great many subsidiary questions. In this initial presentation of the mainstream model these simplifications include: all workers have identical skills and preferences, the unit cost of furnishing occupational safety is constant and exogenous, worker utility functions are well-behaved (exhibiting appropriate separability and diminishing marginal returns), all relevant information is costlessly available to all parties, and nothing is lost by considering a given firm in isolation from the rest of the economy (partial equilibrium). In this rarified world let workers' utility functions be

$$u = u(w, s)u_w, u_s > 0 \tag{1}$$

where w is the wage received and s is the amount of on-the-job safety. Labor market clearing requires that employers provide each worker with the going level of utility; hence $u = u_0$ for one and all. Firms must meanwhile attempt to set output and employment at their profit-maximizing levels, in the process selecting the least-cost way of providing u_0. However many workers they choose to hire, then, each employer must solve the constrained minimization

$$\min Z = w + ks + \lambda(u_0 - u[w, s]) \tag{2}$$

where k is the constant unit cost of s per worker.[1] Minimizing over w and s and rearranging the terms of the first-order conditions[2] yields the characteristic result

$$\frac{u_w}{u_s} = \frac{1}{k} \tag{3}$$

The left side of equation (3) represents the ratio of the marginal utility a worker would get from an increase in wages to the marginal utility of an increase in safety; the right side is the cost to the employer of a unit increase in wages (equal to 1 since the wage is paid in money) divided by the cost of providing a unit increase in safety. Thus the ratio of marginal costs equals the ratio of marginal utilities. The first of these, moreover, is equal to the slope of a line depicting the tradeoff between wages and safety for a given level of employer expenditure, while the latter is the slope of a worker's indifference (equal utility) curve – u_0 – at the market-clearing level. Thus the solution is a tangency: the slope of the market-clearing indifference curve where it just touches the lowest (closest to the origin) iso-cost (wage–safety tradeoff) curve. The implications of this for market-determined wages and safety are illustrated graphically in figure 2.1, where the equilibrium pairs (w_1, s_1) and (w_2, s_2) for two employers with different values of k are determined by the tangencies of market-clearing u_0 and iso-cost curves with absolute value of slopes k_1 and k_2.

This diagram tells us nearly everything we need to know about the logic of the theory. The steeper slope, k_1, corresponds to a solution with higher wages and less safety. This is reasonable, since it is more expensive for this firm to make its jobs safe. For accepting the higher risk $s_1 - s_2$ (recall that safety is "negative risk") these workers receive the compensating differential $w_1 - w_2$. Moreover, the three properties outlined in chapter 1 all follow, even in this highly simplified model.

1   Efficiency

Each firm is guided by market considerations to select the optimal level of job safety. In each case the worker satisfaction constraint is met in the most efficient way; any other pair of w and s would either violate this constraint or fail to minimize employer costs.[3] The efficiency of the market solution is also indicated by equation (3), which can be rewritten as

$$\frac{u_w}{1} = \frac{u_s}{k} \tag{3'}$$

This states that the added utility a worker receives from an extra dollar in wages is equal to the added utility she would get from an extra dollar (which buys $1/k$ units) spent on safety. It is not possible for the employer to reallocate expenses to make the worker better off, given whatever total amount of money is spent. Finally, note that the benefit–cost analyses implicitly performed by the market use the "right" prices. The wage differential $w_1 - w_2$ perfectly offsets the safety differential $s_1 - s_2$ *as determined by the workers themselves.* If the employer chooses to reduce safety, it can only be because it is more efficient to pay the extra wages; that is, the cost of safety to society (via the employer) is greater than its

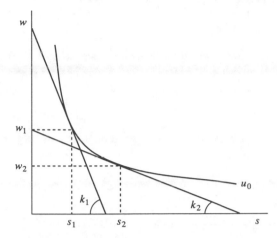

Figure 2.1   Equilibrium wages and safety under differing safety costs

benefit (to workers). And when consumers buy products made by workers in hazardous jobs, they have determined that the benefits of these goods outweigh the wage costs firms must pay to compensate workers for accepting the greater risks.

A corollary to the efficiency property is the observation that government regulation of working conditions not only cannot make anyone better off, but, in this simplified world, must make either workers, employers, or both *worse* off. To see this, consider figure 2.2, in which u_1 is an initial, presumably market-clearing, level of utility comparable to u_0 above, c_1 is an employer cost curve corresponding to k_1, and w_1 and s_1 are as before.[4] Now suppose the government intervenes and imposes a higher level of safety, s_2. Two extreme outcomes are now possible. First, if workers can costlessly move between this and other jobs, employers will have to continue to provide u_1. This means the best they can do is move to the higher cost curve c_2, cutting wages only to w_2 rather than w_3 as they would have preferred. On the other hand, suppose it is the workers who are captive, either because they cannot quit or threaten to quit, or because all the jobs they might switch to are being similarly regulated. Then they might absorb the full burden by dropping to the lower utility level u_2, while employer costs remain unchanged. In this case they will find themselves at (w_3, s_2). Of course, it is likely that the actual result will lie somewhere between, with each side doing somewhat worse. What is particularly interesting about this analysis is that, no matter how the burden is distributed, $w_3 - w_2$ (a negative amount) represents the net cost of government regulation. This can be interpreted either as the wage

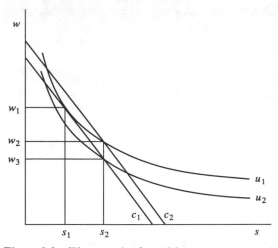

Figure 2.2   Wages and safety with government regulation

decrease that would return employers to their previous level of profitability (in the case when worker well-being is unchanged) or the wage increase that would return workers to their previous level of utility (in the case when company profits are unchanged), or some combination of the two. Thus government interference, as we would expect from the efficiency property of free markets, always flunks the social benefit–cost test; nobody benefits but someone, perhaps every one, must lose.

2   Equity

Workers getting (w_2, s_2) in figure 2.1 have safer jobs than those getting (w_1, s_1) but they are no better off: they are both at utility level u_0. This level of utility is set in the market for all such labor; recall that one of the assumptions is that workers have identical skills and are therefore, we can tentatively presume, of equal value to employers. If the labor market clears – if supply equals demand at a single, universal price – all labor must be rewarded equally. Figure 2.1 demonstrates that this is possible even though some jobs are more dangerous than others. We should therefore not shed any tears over workers in the k_1 firm; they chose to be where they are because it is no worse for them.

3   Hedonic

Workers, according to figure 2.1, are willing to accept a pay cut of as much as $w_1 - w_2$ to obtain an increase in safety equal to $s_2 - s_1$, a linear approximation to the slope of u_0 between these two points. In the language of economics this wage reduction represents their "willingness to pay" for the corresponding extra safety. We could adduce similar pay-for-safety exchanges for increments of s from one end of u_0 to the other; this would give us a willingness to pay schedule for the full range of safety improvements, as in figure 2.3. This curve must be downward sloping, since the shape of u_0 signifies that workers are willing to pay more for the first, critical improvements than for later refinements.[5] This diagram, with differences in income (willingness to pay) on the vertical axis, clearly depicts a demand curve for safety. This is true even though there is no market for workplace safety *per se*. Workers do not lay their money down and purchase a supply of safety, but they do (according to this model) accept lower incomes in return for less risk, which comes to the same thing.

Armed with this information, we can draw two major inferences. First, occupational safety can be regarded as a commodity like any other, with its supply (not pictured here), its demand, and its price. Moreover, the equivalence of the demand curve and workers' willingness to pay schedule indicates that the price is "right": it measures exactly the value that the last traded unit of safety has for the workers who "purchase" it. Thus, we do not have to ask what the value would be of a particular safety improvement under consideration; we have only to compute the compensating wage differential it commands in the labor market. Second, safety is a unique good; its importance derives from its effect on the probability of loss of life or health. It follows that the price of safety can be used to calculate the price of life itself. Suppose that the only risk workers face is that of sudden, accidental death. $w_1 - w_2$ therefore measures the value to them of a change in the likelihood of this particular event. If the change is some probability x (say 0.001), then it is reasonable to extrapolate and say that a statistical certainty of death should be valued at $(w_1 - w_2)(1/x)$ – in our case, $(w_1 - w_2) \times 1,000$.

But isn't there a problem with this procedure? Surely it is one thing to place a value on a small change in the probability of a drastic event like one's own death, and quite another to value the certainty of that event.[6] Economists have a convincing reply, however.[7] In most situations we are concerned with, such as deciding what regulatory standard to impose on the use of a hazardous chemical or how much to spend on a particular branch of medical research, we do not know in advance which individual lives will be saved or lost. The effect of the decision shows up in small changes in the survival chances of large numbers of individuals. To extrapolate from their willingness to pay for these small changes is therefore entirely appropriate, and what we arrive at is not the value of my life or yours, but the statistical expectation that the life of one of us is at stake.

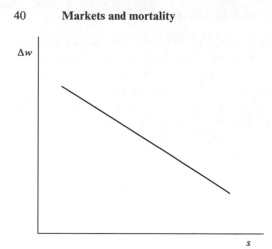

Δw

s

Figure 2.3   The willingness to pay for occupational safety

Finally, economists brush aside moral qualms about quantifying the value of human life by arguing that it is not they who make this calculation, but workers themselves when they weigh the costs and benefits of accepting dangerous jobs. The economist comes in after the fact, observes and records this tradeoff, and uses it in further analysis. You may like or dislike these numbers, but would you simply refuse to look at them, as the clerics were said to have refused to look through Galileo's telescope? And society *does* face inescapable tradeoffs between lives lost and dollars saved – would it be better to resolve these questions on the basis of gut reaction, the vagaries of popular sentiment, or (most likely) which interest group has the most clout? It is not enough to rail against the dehumanizing vision of the bean-counters; you must have an alternative.

For most economists who specialize in public policy issues, these arguments appear decisive. They have provided the basis for using value of life estimates in a wide variety of circumstances, while the views of those who oppose these procedures have been marginalized and discredited. Nonetheless there remain several unresolved ethical and practical problems with assigning a dollar value to life; I will address these in the following chapter.

To sum up, consider the meaning of these three economic propositions in light of the narratives offered in the Prologue. For economists, the key assumptions of the compensating differentials model are satisfied in both cases. Both the immigrant cutters and seamstresses at Triangle and the coal miners in Appalachia were intimately knowledgeable about the risks of their trade; indeed they protested these risks in the workplace and on the picket line. Both had available to them alternative sources of income, but took the jobs that eventually proved fatal to them, presumably because they paid more. There is no reason to suppose that either group of workers was irrational or otherwise unable to look after their own interests. Hence the properties of wage compensation apply in both cases: (1) the risk of fire at Triangle and the risk of lung damage in the coalfields were optimal, perfectly balancing the dangers perceived by workers against the costs faced by employers, and government regulation could not have improved matters; (2) these workers were just as well-off as millions of others in safer employments who faced little or no risk of injury or death; and (3) by sorting themselves into jobs of varying risk and monetary reward, coal miners and shirtwaist makers were simply reflecting the values of life characteristic of their era and class. If, in retrospect, large variations in risk and small differentials in pay indicate that life was cheap, then that must be accepted as a product of a poorer, harder past – or present.

These ideas will strike many readers of this book as bizarre, even grotesque. Their worst fears about the icy and impractical abstractions of economics will be confirmed. I would strongly urge them, however, to take the theory of wage compensation as a challenge, not an affront. Consider the formal model carefully. Its conclusions follow by iron necessity once its underlying assumptions are accepted. Thus, any disagreement must take place at this level, and it is the responsibility of critics of the model to specify exactly where and how they would differ. It will not take long before even the most hardened opponent of economic dogma finds that this is not easily done. Moreover, I will demonstrate repeatedly in the chapters to come that what appear to be "killer" arguments either dissolve into irrelevance or possess much less force than one might think. The critique of compensating differentials, so easy in the realm of historical and institutional experience, is a difficult under-taking at the level of theory. Those who accept this challenge stand to learn something.

Wrinkles and modifications

The model presented in the previous section was made as simple as possible to reveal the essential logic that drives it. Those who use it to study problems of occupational health and safety are quick to recognize, however, that many additional aspects must be included to arrive at a semblance of realism. Here I will briefly sketch some of the hesitations and adjustments made by mainstream economists; the more threatening doubts of others will be taken up in chapters 3 and 5.

1   *Friction in the labor market*

It is unlikely that workers can ever be *perfectly* free to switch jobs. A short list of possible frictions would include search costs for finding alternative positions, the acquisition of particular skills or experience which pertain to one job but not others (firm-specific human capital), and relocation costs. Thus a worker who discovers that her job is less safe than she thought may not be willing to leave, even if there is an alternative offer somewhere else that she would judge a little better.

It would seem at first glance that this is a potentially crippling observation, since it appears to strike at the heart of the wage compensation mechanism, the competition of jobs for workers. Yet this need not be the case. First, costs of job mobility matter only if workers are widely misinformed about safety conditions *before* accepting employment or if these conditions deteriorate *after* jobs are taken. Second, if comparable frictions impede workers in all the positions being compared to one another, and if employers generally take advantage of this by disguising their true safety conditions, then the frictions largely cancel out. To see this, consider figure 2.4. Workers accept work expecting to receive u_0, but employers deceive them to the extent of imposing u_1, the lowest utility level at which they will remain with the firm. The difference between them, $u_0 - u_1$, is the utility cost of the labor market friction. Workers in firm 1 must settle for (w_1, s_1'), workers in firm 2 for (w_2, s_2'). Now the first property holds, since we are still at a tangency between employer cost and worker indifference (although workers are worse off). Government regulation would be efficient, but only if it was designed to restore the type of outcome achieved by free markets without deception (figure 2.2 again). Meanwhile, the equity property remains intact, while hedonic measurements are distorted to the extent that we are now measuring tradeoffs at lower levels of safety, approximating movements along u_1 rather than u_0; given the increasing marginal value workers attach to safety as they get less of it, this will paradoxically tend to *increase* the value of life. Thus the introduction of mobility costs by themselves have relatively little impact; they matter only when they are distributed unevenly or when accompanied by other problems.

2   *Information*

This brief discussion of labor market friction indicates that the sufficient availability of health and safety information is essential to the compensation mechanism. There are several reasons why workers might be less than fully informed. First, some hazardous working conditions, particularly those associated with poorly understood, hard-to-identify occupational diseases, are simply not likely to be taken into consideration. Each

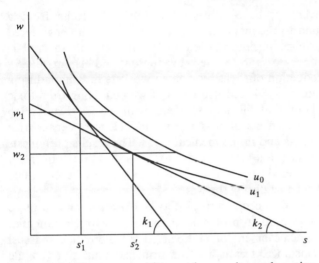

Figure 2.4 Wages and safety under employer deception and labor market friction

year, for example, thousands of new chemicals are introduced into the workplace; some of these will eventually prove to be dangerous, but how are workers to know today which ones they will be, or even to put forward a reasonable probability estimate of future harm? Second, for many on-the-job hazards the information is "there," but only if one is willing to invest considerable time and effort to dig it out. These costs may be beyond the resources of many workers, particularly those in the lower-paid occupations most at risk. Finally, information may not be available because firms have a powerful incentive to misinform workers, precisely to avoid the costs of wage compensation.[8]

Many of the most notorious cases of worker victimization have featured this type of behavior. A grim example, for which millions are still paying, is the suppression of information linking exposure to asbestos to the heightened risk of lung cancer. As early as 1918 insurance companies were quietly refusing to write policies to workers in asbestos-related occupations; medical researchers nailed down the direct causal link during the 1930s. Yet the firms producing and using asbestos managed to prevent any public disclosure of this knowledge, and it was not until the 1970s, after generations of workers had endured the crippling effects of asbestosis and lung cancer, that the public was finally informed (Selikoff and Lee, 1978). The sad sequel to this episode is played out not only in the critical care wards of the hospitals, but in the courtrooms where attorneys for Johns Manville, a major player in both exposure and cover up, have successfully siphoned profits from a settlement trust fund to the managers and shareholders who engineered this travesty.[9] Strategic misinformation may also arise in the public sector. A dramatic case is recounted by Ineson and Thom (1985), concerning the production of shells by women workers in Britain during World War I. There were 84 recorded cases of women dying from toxic jaundice in the plants that filled these shells with TNT. "From 1916 information about the effects of working with TNT were censored in both public newspapers and in the medical press. The results of inquests could only be published in a brief, standard form so that recruitment of labour was not hampered" (p. 91). Approximately one of every 1,000 women TNT workers died during the war.

Economists who study occupational safety and health tend to place more weight on information problems than on any other potential impediment to the achievement of compensating differentials. Viscusi (1983, p. 59), for instance, sees it as "the principal limitation," while Chelius (1974) considers information costs to be the only source of "friction" that would interfere with full wage compensation. To assess the ability of workers to overcome employer incentives, to discover and act upon the risks of employment, Viscusi (1979) and Viscusi and O'Connor (1984) have studied whether workers who are likely to have stumbled into a job more dangerous than they had supposed are also more likely to quit – in the words of one of the studies, whether workers are "Bayesian Decision Makers."[10] Since workers in such situations are more likely to escape them, this is taken as evidence that employer deception wears off and is therefore not a large problem for economic analysis. Nevertheless, economists generally support government agencies like NIOSH that disseminate information on occupational injuries and illnesses, and they also tend to endorse hazard disclosure requirements, even over the stiff opposition of employers.

3   Safety as a public good

When an employer decides to what extent investments will be made in making jobs safer and healthier, it is usually the case that hundreds or thousands of workers are affected at once. Most workplace hazards, such as the use of toxic chemicals or the pace and physical demands of production, are shopwide; if some workers are to be exposed, then so must the others. This would not present a problem if all workers really did have the same preferences, since the solution embodied in equation (3) would apply to each worker equally. But workers are not all the same; they have different attitudes toward risk in general, and even different attitudes toward particular types of risks. The optimum wage-plus-safety package for one worker may be completely inappropriate for another. This difficulty, it should be noted, would exist under any system: so long as there are irreducible job hazards toward which workers have different attitudes, while working conditions and, to an extent, pay are largely equalized, some workers will be better served than others. The question then is, how is this problem resolved under a market system, and to what extent does this solution undermine the three properties of market allocation?

There are two rules employers might follow in trying to determine how to set the terms of the compensation package. They could get a sense of the "average" preferences of the workforce as a whole, so as to minimize the shortfall of total workforce utility compared to the (unavailable) alternative of a unique (w, s) for each worker. Or they could provide the package best suited to those workers who are the most mobile – generally those with the least seniority. This latter group consists of "marginal" workers, in the sense that they are those likely to be added to or subtracted from the larger work group. Economic theory suggests that employers are, in fact, likely to go with this second approach, since only the most mobile workers will act on small changes in wages and safety. The immobile majority, on the other hand, will continue to settle for what they get, provided it is not too far out of line. Unfortunately, the tradeoff between wages and safety most amenable to the marginal workers is unlikely to be the one which best approximates the average preferences of the entire group, particularly since mobile workers are likely to be younger, less experienced, and less concerned with family responsibilities than the average. If this in turn implies that they are likely to be less averse to occupational risks, then all three properties are altered: less safety and more wages are provided than would be efficient, the average worker is worse off in industries with a more footloose marginal component, and estimates of the value of life will overrepresent the preferences of the risk-takers.

The consequences may not be so stark, however. Employers may be able to structure the work process in such a way that the newest workers, who are least troubled by it, are exposed to the greatest risk. It may also be that the preferences of marginal and average workers are not far apart. For instance, while young workers may be more willing to take a given risk, any accident or illness is also a greater risk for them, since they have more future years of life at stake. An extreme case is presented by the exposure to substances that can cause disease decades in the future: why should older workers worry? If the psychological traits and real personal interests of different age groups are offsetting, marginal and average preferences may well converge. Finally, there is an alternative bargaining mechanism available to millions of workers who have a collective interest in their workplace: unions.

4 *Collective bargaining*

While the percentage of the labor force organized in unions has declined from one-third to one-sixth in the past thirty-five years, unionism remains an important influence. Not only are many of the more hazardous jobs in unionized firms, but nonunion employers are often compelled to offer comparable wages and working conditions to keep unions out. The influence of unions matters for our purposes if it alters the incentives to employers to provide safety or otherwise changes the properties of market allocation. The answer depends on how union bargaining objectives are determined.

Several theories of union decision making have been proposed. One is derived from a principle of vote maximization, the median voter rule. Suppose union leaders must face election and need to win a majority of the votes. They will have committed supporters who strongly agree with them; their opponents will have equally committed supporters on the other side. The contest then takes place over the crucial votes in the middle, the median voters. If the burning issue before the union, for example, is wages versus safety, the successful candidates for union office will be those who did the best job of catering to the swing voters whose preferences do not fall strongly either way. Once elected, these officials would presumably continue to cater to this interest and adopt an "intermediate" bargaining position. From the standpoint of economic analysis, this is all to the good, because it generates precisely the kind of "average preference" rule that served as a benchmark for efficiency in the discussion of safety as a public good.

A second theory simply proposes that unions act instrumentally as "utility maximizers" for the entire bargaining unit; their goal is to maximize either utility per worker or the total utility of the workforce, depending on how they approach it. In either case the result would be nearly identical to the median voter rule, at least as far as the tradeoff between safety and wages is concerned, since it approximates what most workers want. Again collective bargaining "works."

A third theory is more problematic. It claims that unions are political hierarchies, pyramidal power structures with power concentrated at the top. Most rank-and-file workers, like most ordinary citizens in modern democracies, have little say in the decisions made by the institutions they nominally control. In this model effective decision making power is vested in the groups near the top of the pyramid, presumably the most senior workers who have ascended to the best jobs, have the most security, and are best connected to the networks of information and influence. If this view is correct, it is not the youngest, but the oldest workers whose preferences will be best represented in unionized workplaces. Now the bias would be a mirror-opposite of that in the marginal-worker system: too much safety would be provided at the expense of wages, and measurements of the willingness to pay for safety would overrepresent its average value across all workers.

Which is right? We will look at the evidence for wage compensation in unionized firms in the following chapter, but for now consider an ingenious study by Kahn (1990) which uses safety and other information to test different theories of collective bargaining. She begins by asking, how could we relate the actual provision of workplace safety to the relative influence of different seniority groups? Suppose workers with different numbers of years on the job have unequal influence. This could be measured if we conducted a regression in the form of the following equation

$$A_i = \alpha + \pi_s b_i z_{si} + \varepsilon \tag{4}$$

where A_i is the accident rate for industry i, α is a constant, z_{si} are the demographic characteristics (related to safety preferences) for seniority group s in industry i, b_i are the weights (regression coefficients) attached to each type of characteristic, and π_s are the weights attached to each seniority group.[11] (ε is a random error term.) The idea is that information on workers such as their gender and marital status would enter into the determination of industry-wide safety through their preferences as estimated by the bs, while these preferences in turn would be weighted according to how much clout their seniority group (new hires, long-timers, etc.) had in the overall explanation of A. Thus if the b coefficient on marriage were negative, we would conclude that, all other things being equal, industries with a higher proportion of married workers among the groups they pay attention to will have fewer accidents. If, on the other hand, a π coefficient for a particular tenure group is close to zero, or even negative, it means that the characteristics of this group, whatever their preferences, are disregarded in the determination of safety. To put it differently, for above-average marriage rates in an industry to have a negative impact on the accident rate two things must be true: marriage must be negatively associated with accidents (negative b) *and* the above-average incidence of marriage must occur within seniority groups who count (positive π). As in all regressions, the estimates of all the πs and bs are those calculated to produce the least error in predicting each industry's accident rate.

Unfortunately, the problem is a little more complicated than this. An industry's accident rate is not only the result of the decisions made by employers but also the behavior of the workers themselves. Accident rates may be lower for married workers not only because these workers demand a safer workplace, but also because they take more precautions when they work. How can these two effects be separated? Here Kahn finds a nice solution: she adds an additional explanatory term to the right side of the equation to measure the direct effect of a worker's traits on an industry's accident record, and then changes the original model so that the πs and bs weigh the effect of *coworkers'* characteristics. The idea is that each worker's characteristics may affect safety by affecting her behavior, but the characteristics of those she works with will affect her safety by influencing company-wide factors. For example, suppose an industry has a high accident rate. This will be due to the effect, call it m, of each worker's own traits z, such as marital status, and the familiar product of π, b, and the traits of each seniority group in the industry, but these can now be represented as z', since they represent the traits of the other workers. The full model Kahn estimates, then, is

$$A_i = \alpha_i z_i + \pi_s b_i z_{si}' + \varepsilon \tag{5}$$

Her results were weak in some respects but very strong in others. The estimates of the αs and bs, the coefficients that translate worker characteristics into "preferences" or "accident prone-ness," are mostly signed as one would expect, but in most cases are not significant. The real news, however, is in the πs, the coefficients that determine which seniority groups have influence. In repeated variations on the model, with slight differences in specifications, she found the same results: workers with the most influence in unionized industries are those who have been on the job either relatively little (zero to three years) or relatively much (over ten years); and *only* the least experienced workers have equivalent clout in nonunionized industries. In both types of industries workers with three to ten years of experience seem to have little say.[12] What this suggests is that employers, when unimpeded by unions, tend to gear their safety decisions to interests of marginal, newer workers; unions make their demands based on the preferences of the most senior workers; and the result in unionized industries is that both new and old workers are represented, while workers in between are not. What does this mean in light of the theory of compensating differentials? Neither employers nor unions, it seems, are very democratic about taking into account the attitudes of all workers equally, but the combination of the two is probably a better approximation than either alone.

5   Compensation before and after the fact

The simple theory of compensating wage differentials outlined above assumes that the only compensation workers will receive for enduring hazardous working conditions is a wage premium, paid from the moment they start working. This is *ex ante* compensation, paid in anticipation of a potential future harm. But workers may also be paid *ex post*, after an injury or illness, and the knowledge that this future compensation awaits them may reduce the need for extra payments before. For many years, in fact, the main recourse for workers was to try their luck in the courts by suing their employers for negligence. This was generally unsuccessful, as I will show in chapter 4, and it was superseded by the introduction of workers (née workmen's) compensation in the early decades of this century. Workers compensation makes payments to workers who suffer injuries and, in a few cases, illnesses as a result of their jobs, without requiring a legal showing of fault. In addition, there has been an increasing trend toward filing civil and criminal suits in particularly egregious cases on top of workers compensation liability. These include not only negligence suits against employers, but claims against the original suppliers of dangerous equipment and materials. Indeed, the expectation of *ex post* compensation has become so widespread that its denial, as in the case of black lung, is usually seen as an outrage. What implications does this alternative channel of compensation have for economic theory?

In principle, it is not difficult to incorporate *ex post* compensation into the model. Workers now decide whether to accept or keep a job based on three factors – the wage, the level of safety, and the expected value of workers compensation and other awards. This in turn suggests that employers can simply deduct the present value of *ex post* compensation, figured at the chosen level of safety, from the wage, and the worker will receive the same total amount of compensation as before. In other words, compensation after the fact does not really matter; it is simply income transferred from the present to the future. Once again, all of the properties of perfect wage compensation hold, provided, of course, that estimates of the value of life are adjusted to factor in *ex post* compensation. Perhaps the most interesting conclusion, however, is that workers will have no interest either in a workers compensation system or in a system of negligence litigation: an expected dollar from either is a dollar out of the paycheck. Note that this result, like the others, follows directly from the formal model presented earlier in this chapter; to escape it one must drop at least one of the assumptions, such as rational worker foresight. Did coal miners wage the black lung movement out of ignorance, failing to recognize that they had nothing to gain from it?

The five modifications to the theory presented in this section are seen by most economists as providing the necessary dose of realism to render the basic model operational. As we have seen, some of them are quite easily incorporated, while others require a bit of backing and filling. Taken as a group, however, they do not fundamentally challenge the logic of wage compensation, nor its practical implications. Later in this book, after a detour through the historical evidence, we will return to consider more serious challenges to economic doctrine.

3   Putting a value on human life

The bad old days of valuing lives

When I was in grade school, I was impressed by the "scientific" judgment that a human being is worth only $3.76 – the value (in 1950s prices) of our bodily chemicals if sold on the open market. It never occurred to me that it would cost much more than this to *extract* these chemicals, so that the true "scrap" value is zero. (This must be why people are generally buried or cremated.) Looking back, however, what makes the strongest impression is my willingness to affix a number, *any* number, on the value of a life.

In fact, from the time of Hammurabi attempts have been made to establish the "value" of the lives of different classes of people, primarily for the purposes of punishment and restitution. A prince would be worth so many peasants in the harsh calculation of early justice, and no justification would be provided other than that of power and tradition. With the spread of markets, however, people came to think in terms of the calculus of wealth, and the idea dawned that prices could set the value not only of the things people own and use, but of life itself.

The main occasion for this development was the problem of establishing awards in wrongful death judgments. Clearly it is not enough to demand reimbursement for the direct economic costs of dying, such as burial and funeral rites, since this does not cover the opportunity cost: the income a deceased person would have earned had he or she lived on. Thus the courts gravitated to a procedure that came to be called the "human capital" approach: calculating the present value of the income stream foregone due to premature death.[1] According to this method the value of a person's life increases with her earning ability and expected longevity, and decreases with her age and the interest rate chosen for discounting.[2] Leonard (1969) cites cases dating back to 1916 in which expected future earnings were used to compensate wrongful deaths, but even in recent times this has been the most widely used approach. The scope of this industry can be seen in Leonard's account of his own experience as an "econometric appraiser": he claims to have prepared more than 110 future-earnings appraisals during 1963–9, and adds that his colleagues in the American Society of Econometric Appraisers have participated in hundreds more. Viscusi (1986) provides a survey of recent court awards in wrongful death cases, noting that the values determined by the human capital method are generally far lower than those that would have resulted from the hedonic studies we will be looking at. The average compensation for fatal bodily injury in product liability cases, for example, was $212,000 in 1982 dollars (p. 202).

Human capital measurements also attracted the interest of policy analysts charged with evaluating public programs that might have the effect of saving lives. They drew from economic theory the notion that, in general competitive equilibrium, a worker's wage is equal to his marginal product. The present value of lost future wages, then, could be used to measure the value of economic output lost due to premature death – as plausible a measure of the social cost of such deaths as any other. Thus, of the 22 benefit–cost analyses surveyed by Graham and Vaupel (1983) 15 employed the foregone earnings approach. This method was employed in regulatory and program analysis as late as 1972; examples, for instance, include the US Office of Science and Technology, *Cumulative Regulatory Effects on the Costs of Automotive Transportation* (1972) or the US Department of Transportation, National Highway Safety Administration, "Societal Costs of Motor Vehicle Accidents" (1972).

Unfortunately, the human capital approach is deeply flawed. From a social standpoint it is perverse to value citizens only in their capacity to produce; it is as if people were no more than means of production with body hair. This is particularly apparent when such studies reveal that individuals who are victims of discrimination and therefore earn less than their coworkers are "worth" less, while those who are retired or unemployable are worth nothing at all. Calculation of expected future income requires heroic assumptions concerning a wage-earner's chances for promotion and occupational mobility, not to mention changes in the wider economic environment that could also affect future earnings. And there are many reasons for doubting that an individual's income necessarily corresponds to her economic contribution to the community. Above all, reliance on foregone earnings is objectionable since it makes no effort to incorporate the value that individuals place on their own lives.

Feeding the numbers racket: the rise of benefit–cost analysis

While lawyers and consultants were poring over earnings projections and actuarial tables in wrongful death cases, a new development within the political system was taking place which would ultimately transform the life-valuing trade – benefit–cost analysis. Although the pressures emerging in Washington and the states for more and better numbers by which to measure life, health, and other intangibles are tangential to the technical story to follow, they are central to the prominence of what would otherwise be an arcane and little-noticed corner of economic research.

Benefit–cost analysis (BCA) rode into Washington, DC on a white horse after World War II. The Bureau of Reclamation, the Army Corps of Engineers, and other federal agencies had engaged in an orgy of dam-building, river diversion and other projects far past the point of economic (not to mention environmental) rationality. By what standard could reformers select the most ill-advised programs, and how could they create a consensus to shut them down? They found the answer to both questions in what had once been a stagnant backwater of applied economics, BCA.

In principle, BCA is simplicity itself: add up the benefits of a project, add up its costs, and make approval dependent on whether the difference, total net benefits, is written in black ink or red. Of course, close up this simplicity disappears; there are great technical hurdles to be overcome in such areas as valuing intangible or difficult-to-measure costs and benefits, deciding on the rate of discount to apply to outcomes that will occur in the future, and, if the analyst is conscientious, adjusting for the effect that income inequality has on the dollar value of outcomes to different social classes. This keeps economists busy. Despite these complications, however, they can appeal to the overall common sense of the benefit–cost framework to gain support in the political process. In the early applications to water policy the technical problems were not important – the most wasteful projects were easily identified – but as the use of BCA widened the problems increased, and different studies of the same proposal would often come up with wildly divergent numbers.

BCA took a great leap forward in importance under the Carter administration. An internal war broke out within the executive branch over the fate of the regulatory explosion of the 1970s. On one side were the activists, drawn from the ranks of consumer, public interest, and other advocacy groups, demanding a fulfilment of the promises of such agencies as the Environmental Protection Agency, the Food and Drug Administration, and the Occupational Safety and Health Administration.

On the other were economic advisers worried about inflation, as well as the possibility of sending unfriendly signals to the business leaders who, regulation or no, still had their hands on the throttle of the national economy. It was in this context that the economists chose benefit–cost analysis as their weapon of choice. Each new regulation or administrative change had to be subjected to this sort of analysis – conducted by a special task force dominated by economic policy officials, of course – and before long most of them were judged "inefficient." Armed with this verdict, opponents of regulation were able to win most of their battles, especially after 1979 when the White House veered sharply to the right.

The next logical step was taken by the Reagan administration upon assuming office in 1981: by executive order *all* substantive regulations had to pass a benefit–cost test. Skeptics pointed out that this was a thin disguise for a general hostility to all measures that attempted to protect the public interest at the cost of business profits, but even so the apparently neutral format of BCA rendered the process palatable to the public. BCA had arrived: no longer merely one piece of the decision making process, it had become the process itself.

But this ever-widening scope, in which BCA was, as Hubert Humphrey once described the political invocation of God, "poured over everything like catsup," stretched the methodology to its limits. This is because it is not enough for BCA simply to identify all the benefits and costs; each must be given a value in dollars so that their totals can be compared. The procedure had won its spurs with the reasonable task of assigning dollar values to the power and recreational benefits of dams, but it now had to do this for the costs of lung damage due to air pollution or excess deaths due to a less stringent standard for radiation in the workplace.

Under these circumstances economists were under pressure to devise a new, technically sophisticated, and philosophically plausible method for attaching a dollar value to human life. In the following pages we will trace a course of development that leads from pure speculation to hard numerical calculations. Although research in these areas occurred simultaneously, we will consider them in a logical order that begins with the least convincing and ends with the most influential.

The theorist's corner, or Bentham and nothingness

As we have seen, the human capital approach to valuing life is clearly inadequate, but just *how* inadequate? Economic theorists took up this question during the 1970s and 1980s, devising theoretical models based on the premises of expected utility theory.[3] Their hope was that, by making a few plausible assumptions concerning the way individuals might view the prospect of death, it could be possible to characterize the economic valuation of life in qualitative terms. In particular, these researchers were interested in the relationship between an individual's willingness to pay for a reduction of the risk of early death and the extra earnings that reduction would make possible, in order to demonstrate (in their own vernacular) the insufficiency of human capital calculations. In addition, they were also interested in the likely effects of differences in wealth, the magnitude of risk reduction envisaged, and the baseline level risk from which reduction would hypothetically occur.

But how to model the impact of impending death on utility? A first generation of studies, including Linnerooth (1979), Bergstrom (1982), and Shepard and Zeckhauser (1982), emphasized the fact that an early death reduces the opportunity for future consumption. In the simplest possible terms, their typical formulation looks like this

$$EU(w,p) = u(w)(1 - p) \tag{1}$$

This is a one-period model in which the expected utility derived from a quantity of wealth w and a risk of death p is equivalent to the likelihood of surviving $(1 - p)$ times the utility of surviving with that amount of wealth.[4] By adding additional assumptions concerning the shape of utility functions and the possibilities for shifting income between different time periods through life insurance, these theorists have established several expectations: that individuals will indeed be willing to pay more to reduce the risk of death than simply the income they might otherwise lose, that greater wealth or earning ability will lead to higher willingness to pay for risk reduction, that this willingness to pay will likely rise early in life to a peak in early middle age and decline after this, that progressively greater increments of risk reduction are subject to diminishing returns (declining willingness to pay), and that, at least in some models, higher baseline risk leads to higher willingness to pay for its reduction. While most of these results are strictly qualitative – asserting general relationships between factors rather than calculable amounts – the hope of their sponsors is that they can be used to assess the reliability of empirical estimates and explain their discrepancies.

How credible are these efforts? While their ingenuity cannot be challenged, their basic assumptions are deeply implausible. It is astonishing (but, unfortunately, not unexpected) that economists speculating on our relationship to death would blithely lay down propositions without any reference to the record of thousands of years of human engagement with this problem. To be more precise, there are two senses in which we can understand these theoretical exercises, either as stylized descriptions of how most people really react to the risk of death, or as formulae that people should follow if they are to be truly rational. In neither case do these expected utility models make sense.[5]

Begin with the notion that economists are modelling probable responses of the wider public. In fact, much has been written on the history and current state of popular attitudes toward death. It has been argued, for instance, that until relatively recent times death was commonly viewed as the capstone of life rather than primarily, much less solely, a limitation to it (Ariès, 1981). That is, it was believed that one should live one's life in such a way that a "good" death would result. In literature, echoes of this view can be found from Sophocles' *Antigone* to Tolstoy's *Death of Ivan Ilych*. Of course, in all ages human beings have also been subject to the primordial drive to survive at all costs. No doubt, over the eons many an individual has wrestled with the conflict between a refined, culturally sanctioned view of death and raw, irrepressible dread. To make matters even more complex, a large percentage of moderns, even a majority in some countries, profess to believe in the existence of an afterlife. From this perspective, death is little more than a transitional moment between the middling business of this world and the transcendent glory (or damnation) of the next. Finally, a new view of death has emerged in recent years that sees it as simply one more, and last, stage of the life process (Kübler-Ross, 1969). This outlook, which has become popular in the therapeutic and self-help literatures, sees death as a generally benign event, provided it occurs after the individual has had a chance to go through a process of acceptance. What does all of this mean for utility theory? It would be difficult to say. At the very least, it calls into question the simple assumption that death is viewed by most people primarily as a loss of consumption opportunities. Most of the views sketched above also place great emphasis on exactly *how* death occurs – whether it follows naturally on a biological process of decline (and can therefore be entered knowingly), whether it is at least partially under our control (so we can make it *our* death), whether or not it is brought on by "honorable" life choices. Needless to say, in many cases the very act of transacting for risk of death, taking extra chances in return for cash payments, could impinge on the type of death that results.

Matters hardly improve when we turn to the second interpretation of utility theory, as a prescription for the rational life. Philosophy, as the famous aphorism of Camus advises, has long considered whether death should be welcomed or shunned, and its speculations have been joined with those of fiction, poetry, theater, film, and the other arts. It would be impossible to recount here all of the approaches that have been taken, even if we were to limit ourselves only to the last few decades. One particular insight, however, seems especially apposite. Modern thinkers have been struck by death as a state of nonbeing: the "experience" of being dead probably resembles that of not yet having been conceived and born. It is, in other words, a radical, endless void. From this possible fact various conclusions can be drawn, ranging from a posture of morbid absurdity, as in the works of Samuel Becket, to a heightened appreciation for each moment of life, as recommended, for instance, by Heidegger and Sartre. However one wishes to respond to it, the view of death as the inescapable end of human existence *and meaning* is deeply at odds with the presuppositions of expected utility analysis. In particular, the fact that an early death eliminates potential future consumption (or other worldly satisfactions) is quite immaterial, since foregone consumption will not matter after the moment of death, *and the rational individual knows this in advance and therefore attaches no significance to it in anticipation.* One might say, "I hope I live long enough to see my grandchildren graduate from college," and this certainly means that, from today's vantage point, longer life is preferred to shorter, but it does not mean that I can in any way compare the utility of *actually* living that extra year to the "utility" of dying instead, just as I cannot say that I am better off today than I would be if I were dead instead. Death is a state in which questions of utility, and all other questions, cease to apply.

A more recent theoretical approach, however, has avoided these pitfalls – only to stumble into others. Jones-Lee (1989), improving on Dehez and Drèze (1982) and Jones-Lee and Poncelet (1982), bases his model entirely on the effect that changes in expected longevity have on the quality (not quantity) of potential life and therefore sidesteps the confusion between accumulating years and accumulating utility. His formula for utility is

$$EU(w, \tau) = U(w_1, 1), p_1 + U(w_2, 2)(1 - p_1)p_2 + \dots \qquad (2)$$

where τ is the current life expectancy and w_i and p_i are the level of wealth and the probability of death for each period i. The series is summed up to T periods, where T is the longest conceivable lifespan. In the light of the previous discussion two points deserve particular notice. First, by placing the expectation of remaining periods of life inside each period's utility function, Jones-Lee captures perfectly the common sense interpretation of the desire to live on into the future. This represents the contemporaneous effect of such an expectation, as in "I hope I live to see x or accomplish y." Second, by summing the probabilities p_i he is not accumulating utility-years in the manner criticized above, but merely providing a weighted average of quality-of-life expectations. Increasing life expectancy, according to this approach, does not automatically increase expected utility (as it would in models beginning with equation (1)), but increases τ by 1 in each period (which is normally utility increasing) while slightly decreasing the near-term ps and increasing the long-term ps (whose utility effect depends on whether life is expected to be better or worse as one grows older).

The utility formulation used by Jones-Lee is more defensible than the others we have surveyed, but, by itself, it is less capable of generating the sort of results theorists have generally pursued.[6] But Jones-Lee's main interest lies elsewhere: he wants to develop a determinate relationship between the willingness to pay or be paid to avert a marginal increase in risk, a measure of the individual's risk aversion, and the maximum acceptable total risk increase. Jones-Lee asks us to imagine a risk increase Δp above the initial risk $\bar{p}$ so large that $\bar{p} + \Delta\bar{p} = 1$. Surely, he suggests, no one would ever permit such a large change; the compensation required to induce one to accept it, v, would approach infinity. By the same reasoning we could imagine slightly small Δps that would elicit the same response. Eventually, by slightly varying Δp we would arrive at the lowest value consistent with infinite v, which he labels Δp^*. Any proposed risk increase below this amount will correspond to a finite monetary settlement. Once Δp^* is calculated, Jones-Lee demonstrates, we can use information concerning an individual's general willingness to embark on certain forms of risky behavior to work backward to the valuation of Δps of real-world dimensions.

The relationship between Δp^*, $\bar{p}$, and v is depicted in figure 3.1 below. (Note that $\Delta p^* = p_{max} - \bar{p}$.) Two risk valuation curves are drawn, each representing a different degree of risk aversion. Where such a curve intersects the vertical line at $p = \bar{p}$, its height represents the willingness to pay for a small decrease, or to avoid a small increase, in risk at its initial level. v is assumed to approach zero as the level of risk becomes zero. The more risk-averse individual would have a higher v at $\bar{p}$; shifting p_{max} to the left (reducing Δp^*) would also have the effect of raising v at $\bar{p}$. What makes this analysis potentially powerful is its implications for measurement: in principle, we should be able to measure both Δp^* and the degree of risk aversion; this would make it possible to construct a quantitative estimate of v for marginal risks – a far more ambitious goal than simply describing its qualitative relations to other variables, as before.

Unfortunately, the assertion that such a Δp^* generally exists, which is central to Jones-Lee's project, is not grounded in his analysis, it is simply

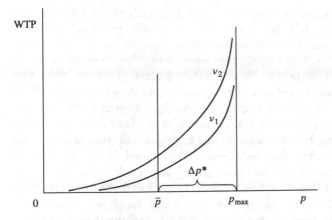

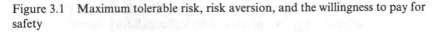

Figure 3.1 Maximum tolerable risk, risk aversion, and the willingness to pay for safety

an assertion. As a general proposition it is unlikely to be true. Many individuals (especially as they grow older!) would be willing to accept certain or near-certain death in return for very large rewards. Indeed, if wealth is interpreted broadly, such rewards can be reputational, ideological, or otherwise "psychic." Once we take this more expansive view it becomes obvious that people voluntarily assume substantial probabilities of death every day. If we see less of this spirit of self-annihilation in the world of monetary transactions, it is perhaps due either to the relative smallness of offered compensation or the tendency toward nonutilitarian responses to imposed risk – about which more in chapter 5. Even in conventional economic arenas, however, individuals, particularly those with drastically limited life opportunities, often take extraordinary risks, certainly larger than Jones-Lee's supposed lower bound of 1/1,000. (Recall the women of Triangle Shirtwaist Company, who knew from other garment industry fires and their own dangerous environment that their risk of death in the year 1911 was probably much higher than 0.0001. They continued working for minimal compensation after their strike was defeated.) On the other hand, some people, as we will see in chapter 5, refuse to accept even the most minimal increases in certain risks, whatever the offered compensation. Cairns (undated), for instance, surveyed 27 individuals described as "emergency planners and their scientific advisers" – presumably a sophisticated sample. Of these, four refused to identify *any* increase in risk for which they were prepared to receive compensation. (Cairns assigned them a zero value of life.)

In fairness to Jones-Lee, it should be pointed out that many others have assumed the existence of Δp^*. One approach to the life-valuation problem, which I will not detail in this work, proceeds from the assumption that existing regulations setting forth maximum permissible exposures to risk reflect social judgments of this sort. Examples would include Starr (1969) and Health and Safety Executive (1988). The latter, for example, makes this claim: "Broadly, a risk of death of 1 in 1,000 per annum is about the most that is ordinarily accepted under modern conditions for workers in the UK ... and it seems reasonable to adopt it as the dividing line between what is just tolerable and what is intolerable ... the maximum level that we should be prepared to tolerate for any individual member of the public from any large-scale industrial hazard should be not less than ten times lower, i.e., 1 in 10,000" (p. 23). Risks below the intolerability cutoff, on the other hand, are said to be permissible if their benefits exceed their costs. In making these judgments, the Health and Safety Executive is adhering to Hegel's dictum that "what is real is rational" by interpreting existing regulatory stringency as a revealed social preference. If, on the other hand, regulations arise out of social conflict and reflect the balance of power between risk-creators (business and government) and risk-bearers (workers, consumers, and local inhabitants), no such interpretation is possible. From this second, *realpolitik* perspective, for example, the disparity between "worker" and "public" risk standards can be traced to such factors as class-based differences in political resources and the greater resistance of business to restrictions on authority in the workplace. Thus the existence of regulatory standards should not be invoked to demonstrate the existence of a Δp^*, much less fix a particular value on it.

Even were we to accept the view that, for most people, there exists a maximum compensable risk, however, it would not follow that this would be the same for all manner of risks. As we will see in chapter 5, there is considerable evidence that indicates that most people regard risks quite differently, depending on such factors as the type of risk and the degree of personal autonomy in bearing it. It is probably true that a majority of individuals will refuse to accept any compensation for risks that appear to be imposed by others solely for their personal gain; they adhere to a standard of "thou shalt not harm or accept harm" that does not make room for monetary adjustments. If this is the case, even if we were to identify a Δp^* in one context, we could not assume that it applies in others, or even that the existence of this value in one context implies its existence in others. The same argument, incidentally, applies to Jones-Lee's measure of risk aversion: willingness to gamble, to trade a small chance of great loss for a large chance of small gain, is unlikely to be constant over *types* of risk.

Finally, Jones-Lee's approach is vulnerable to the same criticisms that apply to other applications of conventional expected utility theory: it assumes too much willingness and ability to calculate, and it assumes that individual decisions are made in a bubble, unaffected by the choices of others. These themes are developed at greater length in chapter 5, and so will not be reproduced here, but, by way of preview, the basic points are these: (1) individuals cannot foresee all potential consequences of a given risk, much less assign utility values to each of them and construct a probability function of their likely occurrence; (2) individuals cannot examine all potential sources of risk to which they are exposed, which is to say they will "overconsider" some and "underconsider" others; and (3) individuals will rely on simplifying rules or benchmarks to guide their response to risk, influenced primarily by risk norms established in their community. Thus there is no reason to expect that stable relationships will emerge between the parameters, like risk aversion and subjective probability, that govern expected utility analysis and real-world attitudes toward specific risks. (Interestingly, Cairns surveyed his sample to determine their values of v, Δp^*, and risk aversion. His results did not support a set of hypotheses derived from Jones-Lee's theoretical model.)

Ultimately, Jones-Lee's exercise attempts to estimate one difficult-to-measure value, v, from putatively easier-to-measure data, risk aversion and Δp^*. But risk aversion and, above all, Δp^* remain elusive; his Rosetta stone, it turns out, is yet another hieroglyph. The attempt to characterize individuals' hypothetical willingness to pay for changes in risk confronts a quandary: either it makes assumptions concerning life and death that stretch expected utility theory beyond the bounds of reason, or it simply cannot generate meaningful results. And so the trail leads once again to direct quantification.

Just ask: the survey research approach to valuing life

The most straightforward approach to the problem of valuing changes in fatal (and nonfatal) risk would appear to be that of simply asking a cross-section of the population to state their own values. Indeed, if life is to be treated as a commodity, why not emulate the proven methods of market research? In fact, the survey approach is as reasonable as any other, although it is beset by its own characteristic problems. Some of these are endemic to any form of survey research, such as accounting for response bias, the framing effect of different ways of eliciting information, and differences in the way respondents understand the questions being put to them. In addition, questionnaires asking individuals to put a price tag on risks to life and health encounter unique difficulties: in what narrative context can such a demand make sense, and how will responses change from one such context (say, traffic safety) to another (nuclear power)? How should we understand the refusal of many respondents to make such tradeoffs – to offer zero bids for risk reduction or to say that no level of compensation will induce them to accept an increase in risk? And how much credence should be placed in responses to purely hypothetical questions, when respondents can simply throw out numbers with no apparent consequences for themselves and others?[7] As we will see, creative survey design can address these issues but not dispose of them altogether. Here is a representative selection:

1 Acton asked three groups of 36 people to state their willingness to pay (or to advise having others pay) to reduce the risk of death by heart attack. The primary hypothetical life-saving measure was an increase in local ambulance services, although in one question he brought up the possibility of improved screening. Acton received answers which, taken at their average and extrapolated to the saving of one predicted life, occupied a range from $7,400 to $47,000 in 1970 prices. These results, far lower than most others have found, can probably be traced to the nature of the hypothetical exercise: individuals rightly fear the experience of having a heart attack itself and question whether their post-attack quality of life will suffer. On the other hand, we must all die someday and a fatal heart attack may not be such a terrible exit if it is swift and is accompanied by loss of consciousness. Moreover, death by heart attack is considered "natural" and is therefore more likely to be accepted than other, artificially created hazards. Finally, it is possible that most of Acton's respondents had already contemplated the prospect of a heart attack at some point in the past and had taken the path of putting such thoughts aside. If so, the questions put before them would incite a measure of "cognitive dissonance," and it is plausible that the response would be to trivialize Acton's risk-reducing schemes.[8] All of these factors conspire to limit his results.

2 Mulligan (1977) had the prescience to ask a random sample of 82 residents of Lewiston, Pennsylvania, near-neighbors of the Three Mile Island power plant, to value small changes in nuclear safety – before the famous near melt-down.[9] She varied her questions in two ways. First, she asked about descending (or, in half the surveys, ascending) magnitudes of risk change: from 1 in 1,000 to 1 in 10,000, from 1 in 10,000 to 1 in 100,000, and so on up to 1 in 100,000,000. Second, she asked each respondent how much he or she would be willing to pay to reduce risks by these amounts, and how much compensation would have to be offered

to gain acceptance for a similar increase in risks. Unfortunately, she did not specify just what the risks themselves consist of – whether death, serious illness, birth defects, or otherwise – and this makes interpretation of the results more difficult. The responses are summarized in table 3.1.

The value of life (measured in thousands of 1977 dollars) in column 5 is drawn from the means reported in column 2 and calculated on the assumptions that all risks are fatal risks and that they are assumed to apply in the current year.

These are clearly fascinating results, although it is somewhat less clear how much credence should be placed in them. Since the values in columns 2 and 3 pertain to the increments in column 1, it is clear that the economic valuation per unit change in risk rises rather than falls as the baseline risk is lowered. This is reflected in column 5, which reveals a three-to-four order of magnitude difference! It is difficult to believe, however, that this is reflective of the respondents' "true" values. Since the bids remain relatively constant as the tens in the denominator of the risk variations mount, it is plausible to suppose that what is actually being represented is confusion surrounding numbers that are much smaller than most people are familiar with. (This observation is confined to the WTP answers, which, as we will see, are much more reliable.) Another possibility is that, for many or most respondents, values are being given not for specific quantities of risk reduction but for the "idea" of risk reduction itself; that is, they reflect ethical judgments in which quantities matter little if at all, rather than instrumental judgments in which quantities are everything. Since additional questions that could have probed the respondents' understanding of numerical probabilities were never asked, we can only speculate on the actual mechanism at work.[10]

Equally dramatic is the cascade of refusals to accept compensation in the WTA portion of the questionnaire; refusniks number between 66 and 75 out of a sample of only 82. (Since the other WTA results are based on so few cooperating respondents, they are of little value.) Even in the WTP segment, however, significant numbers of individuals simply refuse to pay anything. Does this signify a zero value of life for such people? This is what the methodology of value-of-life surveys implies, and their proponents take refuge in the hypothesis that the denizens of column 4 just do not understand the rules. Violette and Chestnut (1983), for instance, suggest that zero bids and nonbids can be reduced by adding an introductory portion of the questionnaire that explains its logic more clearly. This, they say, would "[get] people to think about such tradeoffs in a more pragmatic way" (p. 4–29). The alternative position would be to take these respondents at their word: they *do not* think safety (at least in this case) can be traded off against income, and

Table 3.1 *Willingness to pay and willingness to accept for changes in nuclear safety*

Change in risk	Mean bid	WTP Questions Median bid	Number of zero/nonbids[*]	Value of life (thousands)
9×10^{-4}	3.41	1.50	6	45
9×10^{-5}	2.36	1.40	12	315
9×10^{-6}	1.97	1.20	16	2,627
9×10^{-7}	1.65	0.97	25	22,000
9×10^{-8}	1.53	0.86	30	204,000
		WTA Questions		
9×10^{-4}	2.00	0.80	75	
9×10^{-5}	15.71	4.00	75	
9×10^{-6}	8.75	2.50	74	
9×10^{-7}	8.18	4.38	71	
9×10^{-8}	17.94	10.00	66	
$N = 82$				

Note: *This column reports the number of zero bids for the WTP questions and the number of refusals to entertain bids in the WTA questions.
Source: Mulligan (1977).

they refuse to do so. In particular, while they may have become accustomed to the level of risk that now exists, the notion that measures taken by government or business might increase it further violates their sense that such actions *should not occur*. We will explore the cognitive bases for such judgments in chapter 5. For now, it should be enough to point out that the assumption underlying utility theory that all outcomes are commensurable is simply an assumption, and that individuals are no less rational for behaving differently.

3 Frankel (1979) asked 169 academics and business executives about their willingness to pay for reductions in the risk of fatal aeroplane accidents.[11] Five questions were posed: how much would you pay to reduce this risk by 1.5×10^{-6} on a single flight? By 1×10^{-3}? How much would you be willing to pay for a one-year increase in life expectancy? How much would you be willing to pay for the *certainty* of an extra year of life? How much compensation would you require to accept a one-year loss in life expectancy? Extrapolating from the answers to the first question, the mean statistical value of life was $12,000,000; the

median $3,000,000. Interestingly, 23 percent of the sample replied that they were unwilling to pay *anything* to increase safety. The second question increases the potential risk change by over two orders of magnitude, and, consistent with the previous study, the mean value of life fell by more than two orders of magnitude to approximately $50,000. (But this hypothetical risk change greatly exceeds the total risk from air travel, so the question may be spurious.) In response to the third question (willingness to pay for a one-year increase in life expectancy), the mean value exceeded $1,000, but the median was only $5.33. This remarkable difference is explained by the fact that 44 percent of the respondents were unwilling to pay anything at all! The mean willingness to pay for a certainty of one extra year of life, however, was substantially more, over $1,800, and the median of $500 implies far fewer zero bids. Finally, when the question was changed to how much compensation would be required to accept a one-year loss in life expectancy, only 3 percent said nothing; the mean was $45,000 and the median $30,000.

How can these confusing responses be interpreted? The mean and median values offered in reply to question 1 are plausible, but it is striking that nearly a quarter of all respondents entered a zero bid. Either this reflects extreme fatalism, or a belief that aeroplanes *should* be safe, and it is not up to travellers to pay extra for this. The fatalistic interpretation gains strength from the refusal of nearly half the sample to pay for greater expected longevity – although their stoicism withers in the face of a guaranteed extra year. Finally, the tendency to value gains and losses relative to the status quo differently is dramatized by the surge in WTP in question 5. What emerges from the study as a whole is a jumble: radically different valuations are produced depending on the narrative, the perception of probability versus certainty, and whether risks are contemplated to rise or fall. Moreover, a substantial number of respondents answer in a way that results in their being given a zero value of life. It is difficult to see these results as anything but bad news for those who would use surveys to establish a single number, or even a range of numbers, for the value of life in benefit–cost analysis.[12]

4 Smith and Desvousges (1987) asked a stratified random sample[13] their willingness to pay for reductions in the risk posed by hazardous waste facilities. To explore the relationship between these values and the dimensions of risk involved, they repeated this question varying the amount of risk reduction and the baseline risk from which the reduction would occur. Their results were consistent with conventional expectations in some respects but not in others. There was a widespread willingness to pay for risk reduction, but, rather than increasing as

baseline risk increased, it generally fell. (This implies increasing returns to safety, since the safer one is to start with, according to this study, the greater will be the demand for further safety.) Those with greater income expressed a willingness to pay more – an expected result – but there was a much greater WTP to reduce risk from a higher level to a lower one than to avoid increasing it from the (same) lower level to the (same) higher one. This asymmetry, irrational by the standards of expected utility theory, is becoming familiar to us.

This study is also interesting for its examination of zero bids. These were designated as "protest bids" if "the respondents' answers to follow-up questions indicate that zero was given for reasons *other than* as a reflection of the value of the risk reduction to them or as an indication of their budget limitations" (p. 99, emphasis in the original). Approximately 15 percent of all responses (both to lower and avoid raising risk) were placed in this category. We have already considered some of the reasons individuals might refuse to place a price tag on their life or health; what do Smith and Desvousges think? They proceed from "the hypothesis that a nonzero bid was more likely to be associated with greater under-standing of the valuation question ..." (p. 101). To test this hypothesis, they examined the relationship between the probability of offering a positive willingness to pay (not protesting) and two variables intended to reflect understanding, the respondent's level of education, and the number of newspaper articles he or she had read about the problem of hazardous wastes in the past three months. (Other control variables, not discussed here, were also employed.) They found that, as they expected, greater education leads to a greater willingness to pay for safety, but, unexpectedly, greater familiarity with the issue led to less. Smith and Desvousges placed a favorable spin on this result, claiming that it gives overall support for their view and downplayed the relevance of news-paper reading. Their reason is that those who follow the papers may expect the government to intervene to clean up the mess no matter what choice they make – hence, no willingness to pay for a cleanup on their own. Of course, it might be otherwise. Education is highly correlated with income (which was not used as a control), and this, naturally, leads to fewer nonzero bids. (Greater education, especially in college, can also lead to more exposure to textbook economics, which encourages students to regard all goods as simple commodities.) On the other hand, it is difficult to believe that anyone who followed the news coverage of hazardous waste disputes closely could put much faith in the ability of the government to cope; particularly during the Reagan era (the time period of this study) there were frequent stories about corruption and incompetence in the Superfund program. All in all, it seems reasonable to interpret their results as an endorsement of a very different position, that even highly sophisticated respondents may violate the dictates of expected utility theory.

5 Finally, Philips, Russell, and Jones-Lee (1989) surveyed a stratified random sample of British adults to determine their willingness to pay for the reduction of traffic accidents and related phenomena. After asking a number of questions concerning risk perception and checking for an understanding of probability theory, they posed such problems as, how much extra would you pay to take a bus in a foreign country to lower your risk of a fatal accident from x to y, or how much would you pay for a new car safety feature that would lower your risk from x to y? After removing outliers (probably due to coding errors), their results indicate a value of statistical life in the range of £1,210,000 to £2,210,000 (£1982).[14] Once again there were the refusniks: between 14 percent and 30 percent gave zero answers to the most pertinent valuation questions. Despite a somewhat more elaborate attempt to explain these refusals than that of Smith and Desvousges, however, they were unable to locate any aspects of an individual's background or circumstance that could predict whether they would be hold-outs.[15]

This concludes our brief review of value-of-life surveys.[16] In part, they uphold the commonsense notion that if you want to obtain information from people you should ask them. Most respondents to these surveys do offer responses that can be aggregated to produce a monetary value of life. Of course, the fact that people reply in this way when they are asked does not guarantee that this is their view when they are not asked, or that they would not answer differently if they were asked differently.[17] Moreover, a sizeable minority does *not* offer a monetary value of life even when directly asked to produce one. Add to this the uncertainties stemming from the subtle impact of different narrative contexts, difficulties in processing minuscule changes in probability, and asymmetries between reducing risk and avoiding its increase, and it becomes clear that, even taken together, these studies do not produce a practical answer to the question, how much is it worth to save or take a life?

The origins of hedonic analysis

Knowledge often grows by what, to outsiders, looks like free association. Obscure technical threads, invisible to the untrained eye, connect advances in one field to apparently unrelated discoveries in others. Only to the specialists in these fields, for whom the foreground and background of intellectual life are reversed, does the process seem to make sense.

In a way, our story in this chapter begins with the pioneering work of such luminaries as Nobelist Simon Kuznets in constructing and measuring the national income and product accounts, the mundane categories that have transformed the original Keynesian vision of the *General Theory* into practical, workaday macroeconomics. National income accounting has enough grey areas and unresolved issues to maintain a small army of professional statisticians, and one of the most troublesome is the problem of representing changes in the quality of goods and services. Measurements of output in different sectors of the economy, aggregated into such totals as the GNP, are calculated according to precise, consistent rules from one period to the next, and are then compared to determine rates of growth. The accuracy of these comparisons is crucial for a wide range of economic purposes, such as the measurement and prediction of business cycles, estimation of the rate of inflation, and the analysis of productivity growth. However, while the rules for measurement may remain the same, the actual goods and services do not; they generally improve in quality over time, as new techniques of design and production are developed and commercialized. An important recent example is the computer industry. Each year both personal and mainframe computers become more powerful, not only doing the old tasks more quickly but extending themselves to new applications. Until recently, though, these machines were simply tallied as "computers," unchanging as tons of coal or bushels of cucumbers. If prices of computers rose this was attributed purely to inflation, while computer input into other manufacturing and service industries was deducted to compute the appropriate value added. By not adjusting their measurement of real computing output for quality changes, statisticians were overestimating both inflation and the net product of industries which use computers – not at all an insignificant error in the age of the microprocessor.[18]

The principle of adjusting for quality is clear enough, but how to go about it? How, for instance, would one measure the change in useful computing power from last year's model to this year's? Simply comparing technical features like processing speed or data storage is misleading (not to mention hopelessly labor-intensive in an economy with millions of different products), since what counts is not the difference in hardware but the difference in the value attached to it by those who purchase and use it. A group of econometricians, working without any guidance from economic theory, came up with a possible solution during the 1950s: why not regress a product's price on its qualities to get each attribute's contribution to the market value, and then measure quality change by the calculated "value" of each change in attributes? In a celebrated example, Harvard's Zvi Griliches assigned the final value of a car to such factors as horsepower and wheelbase (remember, this was the 1950s), so that, if a new model introduced a more powerful engine, all he had to do was multiply the change in horsepower by its regression coefficient (its imputed value) to measure the value of the model change.[19] Of course, it was not long before the companies producing these goods got wind of the new measurement techniques, recognizing that these same methods could be highly valuable in their own development and marketing campaigns.

It took another decade for economic theorists to catch up, which they did in Kelvin Lancaster's "New Approach to Consumer Theory" (1966). He specified more precisely the assumptions in utility analysis required to apportion the willingness to pay for a product to its component attributes. In his own words: "Consumers whose choices represent points on different facets of the efficiency frontier are equating their marginal rates of substitution between characteristics to different implicit price ratios between characteristics" (p. 152). Since the object of this approach is to assign utility values to the characteristics of goods, it became known as "hedonic" analysis. Its fundamental vision is that anything people buy can be thought of as a package of characteristics, and that the price they pay is nothing more than the sum of what they would be willing to pay for these characteristics separately. People want roominess, power, maneuverability, etc. in a car; add up the value they attach to each of these and one arrives at the price they are willing to put down on the whole machine.

Unfortunately, the Lancaster model is incomplete, since it looks only at the behavior of consumers, whereas the market price is determined jointly by demand and supply. If the price changes, a part of that may be attributed to the response of consumers to the changing mix of product characteristics, and part to possible changes in the cost of production passed on by producers. Disentangling these two is not easy. The solution was reached by Rosen (1974). He imagined a world in which there are many buyers and many sellers, each with her unique tradeoff between characteristics, whether in terms of utility or of costs. Instead of working with a changing quality mix over time, it is possible to work through the more tractable problem of comparing different mixes at the same time, as different buyers and sellers are "matched" in the marketplace. Thus, some firms might find it cheaper to produce small, fuel-efficient cars and position themselves in that market niche; there will also be consumers who want that particular package and will buy from them. The same would also be true of other types of cars, so that hedonic analysis can now be performed on a cross section rather than a time series. Under this set of assumptions there emerges a single curve in a diagram relating prices to product qualities, and its slope, measured by the coefficient on quality in a price regression, is tangent to both the indifference curve of the consumer represented at each point and the corresponding cost curve of the producer she buys from.[20]

Figure 3.2 illustrates this relationship for a good whose variable attribute is its safety: some versions of it are safer than others. For simplicity, three pairs of buyers and sellers are singled out, although the curve assumes an infinite number of intermediate cases. Producer 1 faces cost curve c_1 and sells to a buyer whose indifference curve is u_1; the same for producers 2 and 3. Assume further that all firms are in long run equilibrium and therefore earn zero rates of economic profit (equivalent to the economy-wide average rate of nominal, or accounting, profit); this means that they will be setting prices such that these particular cost and indifference curves, rather than others closer to or further out from the origin, are settled on. We can connect these and kindred market-transacting points to form the hedonic curve H. The slope of H at any point is both the seller's and the buyer's optimal tradeoff, in this case meaning that it measures not only the marginal cost of providing this particular unit of safety, but also its marginal value to the consumer who buys it.[21]

In principle we could look to any market in which some choices are safer than others to get a measurement of the value of safety, and therefore the value of life. Since any such market will do, we will begin with various consumer studies before taking on the main concern of this book, the "market" for occupational safety and health.

Buyer beware: risk and choice in consumer studies

As with the questionnaire method, we will look at a few examples that represent a much larger literature.[22]

1 Blomquist (1979) studied the decision to wear seatbelts, which he interpreted as a tradeoff between risk and time. Riders can "purchase" greater safety at the expense of the time it takes to fasten the belt. Blomquist measured this delay, assigned it a monetary value based on earnings, and multiplied it by the inverse of the change in probability of death to arrive at a final number. But, as most other observers have noted, it is unlikely that time, rather than effort, is the chief cost of seatbelt use. Moreover, it is not apparent why the value of time at work

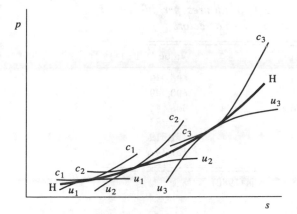

Figure 3.2

should be used to value time during nonworking hours. (Even assuming that work hours are perfectly flexible – which they clearly are not – so that the wage earned in the last minute worked equals its marginal value as "leisure," each additional minute of nonwork will presumably have a lower marginal return, and exactly which of these minutes represents the appropriate value for this study?) Finally, this analysis, like many others of its ilk, suffers from "selection bias": its sample is not a randomly distributed subset of the population, but a specific, self-selected group which differs from the rest in a relevant way. Those who do not buckle up, we can assume, have a greater than average tolerance for risk, and it would be misleading to generalize their preferences to the entire population.

2 Dardis (1980) examines the costs and benefits of purchasing smoke detectors in the hope of deriving a monetary value of life. The method is straightforward: compute the marginal contribution of smoke detectors to reducing injury and death, compute the present value of purchasing a smoke detector, divide the second amount by the first, and the result is the average number of dollars per lives and injuries saved. Assuming for the sake of simplicity that consumers care only about fatal rather than nonfatal injuries, this amount can serve as the lower bound to the value of life for those who buy smoke detectors and the upper bound for those who do not.[23] As it happened, however, changes in the production process for smoke detectors had the effect of lowering their cost to consumers continuously throughout the period she looked at, and this necessitated a different calculation for each year. Dardis' main results are reproduced in table 3.2.

Table 3.2 *Expenditures per life saved purchasing smoke detectors*

Year	Value of life ($)
1974	606,013
1975	600,949
1976	308,544
1977	222,785
1978	171,519
1979	137,342

Source: Dardis (1980).

The dramatic decline in her valuation of life is not due, of course, to any real change on the part of consumers; it is strictly a result of declining production costs. Which number is the right one? Dardis' solution is simply to *average* them, and she produces the figure $256,652 as the appropriate value for benefit–cost analysis. This procedure is arbitrary, however; there is no a priori reason, given her methodology, for selecting this over the 1974 amount or the 1979 amount. In fact, there is no reason to suppose that *any* number in column 2 corresponds to a central tendency in the social valuation of life and health, since the marginal buyer is unrelated to either the average or median buyer. Finally, as with the previous study, it is doubtful that the real cost of safety is being recognized. While some people may choose not to buy smoke detectors because they feel they cannot afford them, in most cases we would suspect that the main impediment is the sheer bother of locating, purchasing, and installing a device that will have only a minute impact on one's chances for survival.

3 In a more conventional hedonic analysis, Portney (1981) examined housing prices as a function of a variety of characteristics, among them life-threatening air pollution. In a regression of these prices, the coefficient on pollution was interpreted as the value (negative) assigned to the altered risk of death, and the actual health effect of dirty air was then used to extrapolate to the value of a statistical life. As in the Blomquist study, however, selection bias is a problem: the people who choose to live in polluted areas have different preferences, on average, from those who do not. A more complex problem for Portney, however, is raised by the possibility of omitted variables. If any relevant characteristics have been left out of this study, estimates of the effects of

those that remain will be unreliable. To dramatize this point, consider a pair of locations not in the Portney study, Costa Mesa and Corona. Both are cities in Southern California, but Costa Mesa is on the ocean south of Los Angeles while Corona has sprung up in a desert environment 60 miles inland. Winds off the ocean keep Costa Mesa's air clear and unpolluted year round; Corona is in the middle of a smog bowl, and its air is virtually unbreathable for months at a time. While housing is much more expensive in Costa Mesa than it is in Corona, it would be a mistake to attribute this difference solely to the health effects of differences in pollution. To begin with, pollution is objectionable in many ways other than its physical damage; it is ugly and offensive. But there are other factors that must be considered as well. Costa Mesa has beaches (and the Southern California beach culture to go with them); Corona has dust and chapparal. Costa Mesa has better schools and less crime. It has bigger malls (an important consideration for the locals) and better cultural amenities in general. Finally, and perhaps crucially, the temperature in Costa Mesa fluctuates around 75° all year long, while Corona bakes in triple-digit misery through much of the summer. So if one were to try to explain why housing is more expensive in Costa Mesa than it is in Corona, but fail to include a few of these salient differences – differences that are correlated with air quality – the result would be an overestimation of the effect of differences in air pollution alone. Since most locational characteristics are difficult to quantify, however, such a result is almost inevitable. For this reason in particular, Portney's estimations are likely to be off the mark.

4 Finally, Pauline and Richard Ippolito (1984) analyzed the decision of most smokers to continue smoking cigarettes even after new information was released on the health risks of smoking. If we can assume that smokers passed from a state of ignorance to one of wisdom upon the inauguration of the Surgeon General's warning, such an individual would continue to smoke only if the satisfaction from doing so would outweigh the health risks. To an economist, moreover, the satisfaction from smoking is captured in its price, so once again we have a method for assigning a dollar value to life. Divide money spent on cigarettes by projected lives lost, and the result should be a willingness to accept a single expected death for at least this subset of the population. It is odd, however, that the Ippolitos, whose methodology is quite sophisticated in many respects, failed to consider the most obvious problem with their enterprise: the fact that nearly all regular smokers are addicted to nicotine. Quite the contrary: they analyzed smoking as if it were as amenable to models of rational choice as, say, buying a vacuum cleaner.

But if smoking is a *compulsive* activity that is undertaken irrespective of its impact on real well-being, addictive smoking behavior is a poor guide for rational decision-making in the presence of risk.[24]

The fragility of these and similar attempts to value life through studies of consumer behavior is well recognized by economists; nevertheless, there has been a general consensus that these problems apply with much less force to studies of the labor market. Here, it is said, markets are competitive and well-developed, information is widely disseminated, motivations are uncomplicated, and the theory of how wages and working conditions are determined can solve any remaining problems. We have already seen the doctrinal arguments in the previous chapter for this point of view, but how has it turned out in practice?

The risk of death and the value of life: hedonic analysis of dangerous work

If there were a single labor market, in which workers could compete equally for all available jobs, and if all jobs were identical except for the risk involved, all we would need to know in order to estimate compensating wage differentials would be the riskiness of each job and how much it pays. Of course, these assumptions are not valid; so we need to know a great deal more. To correct for the fact that there are many labor markets we need to know more about worker characteristics; from these we can determine which jobs make up each worker's reference set (alternatives for comparison). Since jobs differ in many ways other than safety, and since these differences are correlated with safety (as we saw in chapter 1), we should also incorporate more job attributes in our analysis.[25]

In practice, only the first of these two adjustments is commonly made, and researchers usually estimate a model of the following form

$$\ln w_i = \alpha + \beta_M M_i + \beta_i K_i + \beta_R R_i + \epsilon_i \tag{3}$$

Here, for convenience, I have divided the regression coefficients into three groups: β_M, β_K, and β_R, representing labor market variables (such as region of the country), human capital (age, experience, etc.), and measurements of on-the-job risk.[26] There will be as many of each of these variables as the researcher wants to include – or is able to locate. (In other words, each β is a vector.) The subscript i identifies the value of these attributes for the ith worker; as usual, α is a constant and ϵ is the residual. A logarithmic form is used for wages since logarithms measure rates of change, and it makes sense that a percentage change in income (say 10 percent) is a better measure of utility gain or loss than a simple dollar amount (say $2,000).[27] In theory, the combination of the M and K variables should adjust for differences in labor market opportunities: if, by chance, two workers were perfectly identical in these variables, the entire difference in their wages would be attributable to differences in safety conditions. In real life, however, those who do these studies generally throw in other variables which are expected to influence a worker's wages, whether theoretically motivated or not. Thus, it is common to include the worker's race and gender, lest wage differences attributable to discrimination be wrongly assigned to working conditions, and sometimes the size of the worker's company, which is also correlated with wages, even though we can only speculate why. In all, as many as 30 or 40 such variables may be thrown in, with the maximization of adjusted R^2 (a measure of predictive power) usually taking precedence over theoretical justification, despite the misgivings of the econometric priesthood.[28]

Information on the labor market and human capital (and atheoretical but empirically useful) attributes of workers in the United States is available in a number of government data sets, including the monthly Current Population Survey (CPS) conducted by the Census Bureau and special studies which follow a sample of workers over the course of several years (longitudinal studies). Unfortunately, neither the BLS nor most of the other sources provide information about the job hazards faced by individual workers. Under these circumstances, the second-best solution is to *assign* a particular level of risk to each worker, based on one or more attributes for which there *is* adequate information. This, in fact, was the approach taken by the "breakthrough" study in this field, Thaler and Rosen (1976). They constructed R_i by matching each worker with the "excess death" measurement for his or her occupation, according to a survey by the US Society of Actuaries. Thus, while this variable does not measure an individual worker's true level of risk, it does measure the average risk for that worker's occupation. The coefficient on this variable, then, should represent the compensating differential received by virtue of being in that occupation. This result was indeed positive and significant for Thaler and Rosen, marking the first "hard" estimate of the value of a life: depending on particular assumptions, within the range $130,000 to $260,000 (1967 dollars). So striking and, for them, plausible was this result that they took it as evidence for the existence of fully compensating wage differentials and the overall effectiveness of the market in allocating safety.[29]

Others were not so impressed. The obvious flaw in the Thaler and

Rosen approach is that the life expectancy of those holding an occupation is not the same as the risk of the occupation itself. This was first pointed out by Lipsey (1976), who noted that many occupations rated as risky by the Society of Actuaries are disproportionately filled by people whose overall life circumstances put them at greater risk.[30] Thus, cooks and waiters have a much higher risk factor than fire fighters, while bartenders are even with mine workers. In fact, Thaler and Rosen's own analysis supports this objection. Their simple correlation between average wage and average life expectancy (in the absence of the other variables incorporated in M and K) across occupations was also negative, which would appear to suggest that, viewed across labor force strata, occupational safety is an inferior good: at higher incomes people purchase *less* of it. This is hardly believable, and so we are left with the conclusion that the actuarial data are not an accurate measure of true occupational risk.[31]

In response to this problem, economists turned to a more promising source of information, the Bureau of Labor Statistics series on fatal injuries by two-digit SIC.[32] Despite the known shortcomings of these data described in chapter 1 – the unreliability of employer record-keeping and the exclusion of most fatal illnesses, as opposed to injuries – the BLS series at least has the virtue of counting only those deaths that are attributable to working conditions. Since the data are broken down by industry rather than occupation, a worker is assumed to face the average risk of fatal injury which applies to her industry, whatever her occupational role. It is easy to object to this procedure, but in a large enough sample, and the census (and other similar data sets) permits thousands of observations, it should still be possible to measure this industry risk effect.[33]

During the past 15 years many such studies have been conducted, and nearly all of them have produced results that supporters deem plausible; the most prominent of these are displayed in table 3.3.[34] Smith (1976) and Olson (1981) drew their samples from the CPS, while Viscusi used the Michigan Survey of Working Conditions in his 1979 study, and then switched to the Panel Study of Income Dynamics (PSID), a longitudinal set, in Moore and Viscusi (1990). Taken as a group, they estimate a value of life between $2.4 and $6.2 million (1990 dollars). After the National Institute for Occupational Safety and Health made its NTOF data base available (see chapter 1), Viscusi returned to the PSID sample. He found that, both because NTOF reports increased risk across the board and because it changes the rankings of industries with respect to risk, using this source instead of BLS effectively doubled his monetary equivalent of life to nearly $7 million.

Table 3.3 *Labour market studies of the value of life*

Authors	Sample	Risk data	Value of life[a]
Thaler and Rosen (1976)	SEO	Soc. of Actuaries	0.8
Smith (1976)	CPS	BLS	4.4
Viscusi (1979)	SWC	BLS	3.9
Brown (1980)	NLSYM	Soc. of Actuaries	1.5
Olson (1981)	CPS	BLS	4.9
Viscusi (1981)	PSID	BLS	6.2
Moore and Viscusi (1988)	PSID	NTOF	6.9
Moore and Viscusi (1988)	PSID	BLS	2.4

Note: a In millions of 1990 dollars.

From one perspective, the similarities between the results summarized in table 3.3 suggest that there really is something we might call "the value of life" out there to be measured, and that the various studies approximate it to a greater or lesser extent. But one might just as well ask why the *differences* between these studies are so great; after all, the high end of the range is nearly ten times the low end. Of course, using different samples of workers and different measures of personal risk will lead to disparate results, but there may be something more fundamental at work. Recall from figure 3.2 that the slope at any point of the market wage/risk curve represents some worker's value of life. As we move up or down this curve, we are, in effect, switching from worker to worker, and the value of life changes. Some of this is captured by making the dependent (left-hand) regression variable the natural logarithm of wages, rather than their absolute level, as discussed above. Yet there is no reason to suppose that the curvature provided by taking the log of wages is the same as that of the "true" market tradeoff curve. Large samples may therefore generate an "average" value of life in percent-of-income terms which differs from the true *range* of these values.

One approach would be to focus an entire study on a specific occupation, so that only one slope along the wage/risk curve is actually being estimated. In general, the problem is that few if any professions have such detailed risk data that a researcher could make comparisons within the group. Nevertheless, a brave attempt was made by Low and McPheters (1983), who regressed police wages by city against risk of death, community income, crime rate, and regional dummies (to pick up other, unspecified factors affecting wages that may differ from region to region). The point was to determine if police officers receive more money for taking on a greater risk of death on the job, and, if so, how much this amounts to when extrapolated to a statistical life. Interestingly, despite the relatively high level of police wages compared to the largely blue-collar workers surveyed by CPS and PSID, the resulting value of life was just under $1 million (1990 dollars). This is well below the bottom of the pack represented in table 3.1.

In part, the explanation may be, as Leigh (1986) pointed out, that the risk measurement used in this study is highly suspect. Low and McPheters assigned to each officer a risk equal to the total number of police deaths in that city, not the deaths per capita or per officer. To the extent that this variable is arbitrarily randomized, there is a downward bias on the risk coefficient, β_R. Yet there is an even more problematic aspect to this study. The Low and McPheters model assumes that police wages are market-clearing in each city, but in actuality there is nearly always a long waiting list for these jobs. As a result, the actual wage offered must, in general, exceed the "reservation" (lowest acceptable) wage of many, if not most, individuals in the applicant pool, and it is no longer clear what, if anything, is being measured. A portion of a police officer's wage is "extra" – not required to meet a labor supply constraint. It would be more accurate to say that police wages are determined politically, by the degree of moral and political power police officers and their allies are able to bring to bear on mayors and city councilors. We shall see later that this is a particular instance of a general, and probably insurmountable, problem with hedonic analysis: wages are not set to equilibrate supply and demand.

The alternative approach to this problem is exemplified by Leigh and Folsom (1984). They assumed a nonlinear wage/risk tradeoff and conducted their study on two different data sets to arrive at a range of values, rather than a single one. Using the PSID they arrived at $5.0–$11.7 million (1990 dollars); using the QES it was $6.3–$11.0 million. They concluded from this that individuals at the top of the range (highest income) place approximately twice as much value on their lives as those on the bottom. In a sense, we have come full circle: we began by rejecting the so-called "human capital" (discounted future earnings) approach in part because it simply translated greater worldly success into a higher personal "worth," but now the same results appear in the hedonic approach. Yet this should not be surprising, since any attempt to derive values from consumer demand in the marketplace will attach greater weight to the most affluent consumers. Highly paid workers have a higher value of life, just as they express a higher value for horsepower if they buy Porsches and BMWs. How could it be otherwise?[35]

To put the matter this way, however, is to identify an analytical difficulty. Dangerous work is held to contribute to higher wages, but higher wages can also result in less danger if better-paid workers demand higher wage premia. In other words, rather than one-way causation running from risk to wages, we see mutual causation between them. Moreover, it is possible that other factors, such as special abilities or inabilities to do hazardous work, can simultaneously influence both variables. The remedy for such a situation is the technique of estimating simultaneous equations: in separate stages estimating each partial causation separately and then their simultaneous effect. One study that employed this approach was Garen (1988). First he conducted a conventional wage/risk estimation, regressing wages on risk and other variables in the usual manner. Then, using the simultaneous equations approach, he re-estimated the same risk premia, with the result that the coefficient on fatal risk increased by 50 percent. Finally, he repeated the process, this time using an estimator he developed to control for outside interactions (joint cause) as well simultaneities. This had the effect of increasing the risk coefficient by yet another 50 percent – a combined increase of 125 percent over the conventional single-equation estimation. This increase represents the fact that better-off workers, who are calculated to place a higher value on their life, are underrepresented in dangerous jobs and therefore undercontribute to aggregate estimates of willingness to pay unless measures are taken to offset this effect.

Wage compensation and the market for safety

The studies described above are custom-designed to generate coefficients on the risk of death, but an attempt to model the wage compensation mechanism in all its subtleties requires a broader specification of job attributes. After all, if workers are remunerated for accepting risk, this must include the loss of a hand or a bout with carpel tunnel syndrome as well as the risk of imminent death. Thus, the more sophisticated studies of compensating differentials may produce a value-of-life statistic as a byproduct, but they have other purposes and must be evaluated according to different standards. The question is not, how much is a life worth, but, are workers actually compensated for dangerous working conditions?

This more general body of research is vast and difficult to classify. Samples are partitioned in various ways to focus on particular groups of workers, the mix of working conditions incorporated as "risks" changes from one study to another, and the list of other explanatory variables expands and shrinks. Without getting into enormous detail, we can only view the surface of this literature and note its high points. My plan is to begin with a few general surveys and then move to a brief look at some of the key issues which have emerged. Serious criticism will be postponed until the following section.

The basic design of broad-spectrum compensating wage differential studies is the same as that for the value of life: regress wages (generally its natural log) on market conditions, human capital and other wage-related variables, and various measures of dangerous or otherwise undesirable job characteristics. In principle, the latter could include *anything* that a worker might wish to avoid, such as the risk of a layoff, the lack of promotion opportunities, or low social status. Moreover, a "correct" study would include all of them, since leaving any out biases the coefficients on those that remain. Of course, analysts must make do with insufficient information and simply hope that the variables they are forced to omit will not greatly devalue the results.

This tension between the demand for and the supply of data has led to an interesting dynamic, as the fruitless results of each generation of studies inspires greater creativity and sophistication in the next. The saga begins with the early work of Thurow and Lucas (1972), who found that coefficients on working conditions variables were generally insignificant, with some (including hazardous conditions) wrongly signed – suggesting, in the context of wage differential theory, that workers are so eager to be exposed to occupational risks that they would also be willing to take a pay cut. Lucas (1977) continued this line of inquiry and found that positive compensation is associated with repetitive work and obnoxious working conditions. The results were not significant for strenuous effort, however, and were perverse (negative compensation) for supervision. Another attempt to measure differentials was Hammermesh (1978), which utilized self-reported data on working conditions in a study of "job satisfaction" – a single index of workers' valuation of the complete job package. Hammermesh found that coefficients on working conditions variables in his wage equation were all insignificant. He discounted this result by observing that these variables were measured subjectively (responses by workers to interviewers), and that higher-paid workers may be less likely to identify poor working conditions. His study offered additional evidence of weak or no compensation, however: workers whose wages were above the level predicted in their respective wage equations were more likely "all in all" to be "very satisfied" or "somewhat satisfied" with their jobs. Hammermesh interpreted this as evidence that such workers are simply lucky in a labor market with uneven and largely uncontrollable rewards, but it may also indicate that "compensating working condition differentials" (which make up for unequal wages) are weak.

Brown (1980) presented a comprehensive survey of the evidence up to that point, finding the results mixed. He suggested that measured differentials may be biased downward by omitted variables in M or K. If factors such as education, age, and job tenure, for instance, fail to capture differences in worker "quality," and if there is a raw correlation between true quality and good working conditions, a portion of returns to quality will show up as reduced or even negative compensating differentials. To correct for this potential source of bias Brown used the National Longitudinal Survey (NLS) Young Men's sample for years 1966–73, in which job and wage changes occur for the same individuals. The Dictionary of Occupational Titles (DOT), which presents "standard" responsibilities, qualifications, and working conditions for thousands of occupational categories, was used to generate working conditions, along with our now-familiar Society of Actuaries study of excess mortality by occupation. Nonetheless, the results did not confirm the hypothesis of compensating differentials: once again most of the relevant coefficients were wrongly signed or insignificant.

Additional controls were introduced by Duncan and Holmlund (1983). They reasoned that previous studies may have failed to properly attribute working conditions to individuals, since they relied upon merging different files. Thus, Brown had assigned working conditions by merging DOT data with individually reported occupations.[36] Duncan and Holmlund, however, used longitudinal data on Swedish workers between 1968 and 1974 which not only tracked wage and occupation changes for the same individuals, but included self-reported data on working conditions as well. To further control for individual-specific variables that might influence wage outcomes, they regressed the log of overall wage growth – ln(1974 wage) − ln(1968 wage) – on changes in working conditions, measured in such a way that higher values represent poorer working conditions, and on worker characteristics, but their results were inconclusive. Two attributes had positive coecients significant at 1 percent, two positive and significant at 5 percent, four positive but not significant, and four negative but not significant.[37] Finally, Biddle and Zarkin (1988) find that using simultaneous equation techniques (broadly comparable to Garen, 1988, discussed above) on data from the 1977 QES, the coecient on risk of injury more than doubles.

Thus far, the studies have assumed that wages and working conditions are determined in a competitive labor market, but what about the effect of unions? Unions, as we saw in the previous chapter, could bargain for greater wage compensation for their members, but they might also bargain for standardized wages that do not reflect differences in working conditions – a negative byproduct of "taking labor out of competition." Researchers have attempted to account for the influence of unions either by partitioning their samples (studying union and nonunion workers separately) or by "interacting" union membership and working conditions variables (creating a new variable by multiplying a job characteristic rating by the unionization rate). Typical was a study by Duncan and Stafford (1980). They began with an entirely different problem: economists have been interested to measure the "union wage premium," the extra pay attributable to union membership alone. It is not enough to just compare the wages of unionized and nonunionized workers, however, since many other factors also affect wages. Once again, the correct method is to perform a regression of the form

$$w_i = \alpha + \beta_X X_i + \beta_U U_i + \epsilon_I \tag{4}$$

where U is either a worker's union membership status (taking the form of a 0 or 1) or the unionization rate of the worker's industry and X is everything else specific to a worker which might influence wages. Within this catch-all category, as it happens, are undesirable working conditions, and so Duncan and Stafford tested for their effects incidental to their real purpose, estimating a union wage premium β_U. They found that inclusion of working conditions variables reduces estimated union wage premiums by at least one-third, indicating that much of it is attributable to compensating differentials. This implies, of course, that unionized workers have, on average, worse working conditions, and they speculated that this in turn may reflect the employer response to higher wages caused by unionization in the first place: cut where you can. If this is true it would reverse the flow of causation, turning Adam Smith on his head. An additional possibility, however, which Duncan and Stafford did not consider, is that working conditions may "explain" a portion of the union wage effect through a different channel if poor conditions on the job are more likely to convince workers that they need unions.[38]

In a later review of this topic, Dickens (1984) found an interesting pattern: in a majority of the studies unionized workers receive *negative* compensation for nonfatal risk, while nonunionized workers receive negative compensation for fatal risk! Following Olson (1981), he hypothesized that unions protect workers who take extra time off following an injury, and this "compensation" eliminates the need for the monetary variety. He found the anomalous result for nonunion workers more difficult to explain, however, so he retested it in a variety of specifications which controlled for unmeasured differences between industries. Reproducing this result – wage *reductions* due to the presence of deadly risk – Dickens could conclude only that wage compensation simply does not work for the bulk of the labor force unprotected by unions. It is important to point out in connection with Dickens' work, that most recent studies that interact a union dummy with risk – that allow for the possibility that the risk variable can have one coefficient for unionized workers and another for the nonunionized – find that nearly all the wage compensation for risk goes to the union section. Unorganized workers in these models receive little if anything for their troubles. (We will have more to say about this later.)

Thus far, the studies I have described are all predicated on the assumption that monetary compensation for both fatal and nonfatal accidents take place only through the medium of wages. This is contradicted, however, by one of the central pillars of the US occupational safety and health system, workers compensation (WC). Since workers anticipate receiving, or having their heirs receive, WC benefits, the standard theory holds they will rationally deduct them from the wage compensation required of employers. For this reason, regressions that do not include measures of expected WC benefits (preferably interacted with risk, since the greater the likelihood of an accident, the greater the expected value of WC) are incomplete. The literature on the mutual interactions between wages, safety conditions, time away from work, and the liberality of WC provisions is immense, since the workers compensation system is one of the country's largest and most important public programs – with predictable effects on the grant spigot.

Incorporating the effects of WC is generally accomplished by assigning to each worker his or her specific state workers compensation benefits, since the system's rules and benefit levels vary from state to state. The result is a wage regression with additional terms, and therefore additional coefficients to interpret. Perhaps the most startling example of this type of study is that of Moore and Viscusi (1990). They used coefficients for both the risk of a lost workday(s) due to injury and workers compensation benefits to calculate what the compensating differential would be if workers compensation provided complete income replacement; depending on the specification used it was either $20,700 or $31,400 (1990 dollars). This they identified as the nonmonetary ("pain and suffering") value of an injury. (The average injury in the BLS series required missing 13 days of work.) In addition, they found that the compensating wage differential for workers compensation eligibility – the reduction in pay due to the benefits offered by the program – was such that there was more than a dollar-for-dollar replacement for employers: for every dollar they pay into the program employers save even more by being able to reduce wage compensation for risk. In other words, workers compensation is a net benefit for the firms that finance it! They also find, on the other hand, that *marginal* increases in benefits are a net cost to firms, so that their opposition to the expansion of the program is not irrational. Nevertheless, their overall results would come as a shock to most corporate executives, and, for that matter, to most workers, who think that the system, while inadequate, is better than nothing.

A few of the studies we have looked at are summarized in table 3.4. A positive coefficient on the job characteristic variable signifies that workers exposed to this condition receive higher wages; since these conditions are undesirable, the theory of compensating wage differentials requires that this be the case. A negative coefficient, on the other hand, contradicts the theory, as, for that matter, does a coefficient indistinguishable from zero. Note that many of the job variables studied are similar to those which figured prominently in the Triangle and black lung histories – hazardous materials and equipment, restrictions on movement, etc. If the evidence shows that workers generally receive adequate wage compensation for these conditions, and if we believe we can infer that this was also true for the Appalachian coalfields and the sweatshops of New York City, we would have to conclude that worker protests, such as those recounted in the Prologue, are uninformed. Surely workers would not object if they knew that they were being fully reimbursed for their troubles, and that improving working conditions would lead inexorably to a corresponding reduction in their wages. Once more, then, we face the conflict between the views of economists and those of nearly everyone else – and, in particular, the convictions of the workers directly involved. Overall, which view is supported? Table 3.4 demonstrates (and the broader literature not depicted in this table confirms) that the evidence for wage compensation is weak at best: few of the coefficients are significant, and they are nearly as likely to be negative as positive. For economists this is a puzzling anomaly – where, they ask, have our studies gone wrong?

The dubious foundations of the compensating differentials literature

Bismarck is reputed to have said that there are two things into whose manufacture one should not inquire too deeply, sausages and legislation; the moderns have added a third, statistics. Those with only a passing familiarity with the tools of modern statistical analysis – linear and nonlinear regression, multistage analysis, sophisticated data transformations, and customized estimation algorithms – may be convinced that the final output is the immaculate product of Science, but those who do this work for a living know only too well the problematic assumptions made along the way. This is unavoidable in the social sciences, since the perfect

Table 3.4 *Selected tests of compensating wage differentials*

Study	Data sources	Job characteristics	Coeff.
Lucas (1977)	Survey of Economic Opportunity, Dictionary of Occupational Titles	Physical conditions[a]	
		white males	0.068*
		white females	−0.077
		black males	0.033
		black females	0.195*
Hammermesh (1977)	ISR Survey of Working Conditions	Noise	
		white males	0.151
		white females	0.139
		Dirt	
		white males	−0.007
		white females	−0.006
		Hazardous materials	
		white males	0.037
		white females	0.033
		Hazardous equipment	
		white males	0.033
		white females	−0.156
		Miscellaneous hazards	
		white males	0.029
		white females	0.050
Brown (1980)	NLS Young Men's Sample, DOT, Society of Actuaries	Repetitive work	−0.056*
		Work under stress	−0.019
		Physical strength requirement	−0.009
		Bad working conditions	−0.037
Duncan and Stafford (1980)	SRC Time Use Survey, PSID, QES[b]	Not free to leave work	0.031
		ln (work effort)	0.066*
Duncan and Holmlund (1983)	Swedish Level of Living Surveys[b]	Inflexible hours	−0.001
		Difficult to run errands	−0.032
		Heavy lifting	0.010
		Physically demanding	−0.006
		Daily sweating	−0.007
		Noise	0.044*
		Smoke	0.038*
		Strong vibrations	0.020
		Toxic chemicals	0.012

Notes: a Exposure to either extreme temperature, wet or humid conditions, substantial noise, risk of bodily injury, or noxious working environment.
b Data limited to white males.
* significant at 5% level or better.

data set never appears and controlled experiments are either impossible or immoral. Of course, there is no need to reject all empirical work in the social sciences out of hand, since the assumptions might be close enough to the truth to get by, and results obtained using one method can be corroborated by similar results using another. Nevertheless, skepticism is always in order, and no discussion of empirical research is complete without close scrutiny of the underlying assumptions.

Earlier in this chapter I mentioned two of the characteristic problems with compensating differentials studies: the poor quality of the data on working conditions and the risk that important determinants of wages might be left out of the regression models. The first of these, what economists call the "error in variables" problem, is the result of the inadequate system of occupational safety and health record-keeping in the US. Studies that rely on the BLS injury data employ numbers that are self-reported by businesses and, as we have seen, often self-serving as well. They partially reflect the risk workers face due to on-the-job accidents, but they are entirely inadequate guides to the much more important risk of occupational illness. Even the superior NTOF series on occupational fatalities covers only injuries and, according to NIOSH, may represent no more than one-half the true number of fatal accidents.[39] The second problem, the possible omission of key variables, undermines the integrity of the coefficients on all variables estimated. It is likely, however, that there are many such omitted variables, since we still know relatively little about the factors that enter into wage determination in the real world.

What are the likely effects of these problems? Both will tend to produce risk coefficients lower than the true wage–risk tradeoff. The error-in-variables effect can be derived from econometric theory (although it is possible under some circumstances for random mis-measurement to bias the corresponding coefficient upward); the second results from patterns we have already observed in the labor market. This is because, as we saw in chapter 1, overall, workers in the highest-risk jobs also get the lowest pay, and the purpose of including variables representing market conditions and human capital is to isolate the effect of hazardous working conditions *within the worker's reference group*. Only if that effort is successful could occupational risk be associated with higher wages. Omitting some of these other explanatory variables would jeopardize this effect, reinstating the original connection between high risk and low wages. Together, then, these two problems would tend to produce too few significant coefficients and too many with the wrong sign – exactly the result we found in the previous section.

This theoretical possibility was elaborated in Hwang, Reed, and

Hubbard (1992), who asked, how large an effect would a "small" misspecification of workers' human capital have on the regression's risk coefficient? They demonstrate that the answer also depends on two other variables, the percentage of the total compensation package received in the form of wages and the marginal utility of money. As with human capital, both of these are subject to potential, even likely, measurement error. By working backward from the formula for the ordinary least squares (OLS) estimator, the most common algorithm for hedonic regression models, the authors were able to calculate the difference between the computed and the true coefficients on risk as a function of the three mis- or unmeasured variables. They made the assumption that the wage share of total compensation is in the range of 65–75 percent, since that appears consistent with economy-wide estimates drawn from BLS data. The variance in the marginal utility of money (not captured by the use of $\ln w$) was variously estimated at 0.10, 0.20, and 0.30 (not "large"), and disturbance effects on β_R were calculated across a broad range of possible human capital measurement errors. The results were striking: overall, as expected, the effect of these discrepancies is to reduce the measured coefficient on risk, but even modest assumptions were sufficient to reduce this coefficient by half or more, or even reverse its sign.[40] Their conclusion is that, in view of the paucity of data available to researchers (reflected in typical R^2s of less than 50 percent in wage regressions), estimated risk coefficients – and therefore extrapolations to willingness to pay for life – bear little relation to their true values.

Preston (1986) conducted an empirical test for this type of effect using an ingenious technique to simulate the method of "reverse regressions." To understand her approach, consider the very simple regression model

$$y = \alpha + \beta x + \epsilon \tag{5}$$

Once a β is estimated, the regression generates a "trend" line in an x,y diagram, due to the presence of a residual, ϵ; of course, the actual values of y given x may lie above or below this trend. Suppose, however, that you suspect a problem, such as omitted variables, in the absence of which the "correct" trend line would be above or below the one you obtained: how could you check for this possibility? You could run a reverse regression, estimating

$$x = \alpha' + \beta'y + \epsilon' \tag{6}$$

where α', β', and ϵ' are the coefficients and the residual corresponding

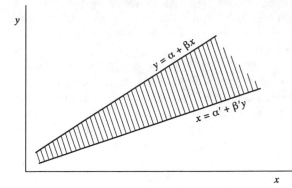

Figure 3.3

to this backwards version of the model. Now, suppose further that the graphs of these two regression lines appear as in figure 3.3. Our suspicion is that both of these are wrong, but we now know the range within which the true regression line must fall, the shaded area in this diagram. This is a useful bit of information, because it tells us that our original estimate, with its α and β is biased *downward*. If the positions of the two "false" lines were reversed, our bias would have been in the opposite direction.

So far, so good. But the method cannot be applied with more than one x on the right-hand side, since in that case the reverse "regression" would have more than one dependent variable, and that's not a regression. It is interesting to see how Preston solved this problem. First, she used two data sets, the 1977 Quality of Employment Survey and the 1980 Survey of Job Characteristics developed by the Harvard Sociology Department, providing information on wages, working conditions, and other variables X (our M and K) for workers in each. Then she performed standard wage regressions on these data, which we can represent by

$$w_i = \alpha + \beta_X X_i + \beta_C C_i + \epsilon_i \tag{7}$$

where C are the working conditions variables. She got results which appeared to contradict the theory of compensating wage differentials: for four working conditions variables, and for each sample, the coefficients were wrongly signed. But Preston then subjected the same data to a canonical correlation, a different kind of test which permits multiple dependent variables, of the form

$$\beta_X X_i = \alpha + \beta_w w_i + \beta_C C_i + \epsilon_i \tag{8}$$

where the β coefficients, while attached to the same variables, have different values because of the difference in techniques. (Recall that these βs are *vectors*.) She demonstrated, however, that these coefficients are identical to those in a hypothetical regression

$$x_i = \beta_w w_i + \beta_C C_i + \epsilon_i \tag{9}$$

where x_i is an "x-score" for each individual, constructed from the sum of the individual's "other" variables weighted by the coefficients β_x derived in the canonical correlation. This rearranged model is shown to have the properties of a reverse regression, making it possible to infer the bias in the coefficients on C. As in the simple $x - y$ example, compare the coefficient on X from the original regression with its counterpart in the reverse model, β_C/β_w.[41] Once more, the "true" coefficients on C, the compensating differentials, would lie between the two. What Preston found confirmed her suspicion that wage compensation has been underestimated: β_C/β_w was strongly positive for all but one of the undesirable working conditions. While there are no appropriate significance tests for these coefficients considered singly, the overall correlation is strongly significant and the coefficients represent "large" – in some cases unreasonably large – wage increments. Preston correctly points out that her results do not "prove" the existence of compensation any more than previous, weaker results "disproved" it, but they do indicate strongly that the conventional wage regression underestimates true compensation. She interpreted this as demonstrating that omitted variables are a chronic problem in such studies, although *any* problem which tends to produce a downward bias on measured wage compensation would achieve the same result; in chapter 5 I will speculate further on what some of these might be.

Even if economists had access to perfectly accurate, perfectly complete data concerning all the variables, including working conditions, that are related to wages, estimates of the value workers place on safety would be skewed by the presence of unemployment. This was considered in the case of the police officers studied by Low and McPheters, but it is implicit in any work that identifies the coefficient on risk in a wage regression with the value workers place on their own well-being. If leaving a job entails the risk of unemployment, a worker might continue to accept inferior working conditions even without a completely offsetting wage differential.

A useful way to think about this problem is in terms of the so-called Coase Theorem (or more accurately, the Coase Conjecture), which contends that in a wide variety of situations, where an individual does not initially own a good and must pay to acquire it or where he or she does and must be paid to be willing to part with it, the *price* paid and the *quantities* held after market transactions are complete will be unaffected. For example, consider one of the cases discussed in Coase's original article (Coase, 1960). A railroad passes through a farmer's corn field. Sparks from the train occasionally ignite fires which are costly to the farmer. By running fewer trains the railroad company can reduce the risk of a fire, but it also incurs its own costs associated with rerouting, reduction in service, etc. A court might rule that the farmer has the right to forbid *any* activity which potentially damages her crops, and in that case the railroad would have to pay enough money to convince her to permit some of the trains to run anyway. On the other hand, a court could rule for the railroad. Now it is the farmer who must pay to persuade the railroad to run fewer cars. Coase claimed that, either way, when all negotiations are complete there will be the same number of trains running per week, and the price per train, whoever pays it, will be the same as well. From the standpoint of the farmer, we can call the amount she would pay for an incremental reduction in traffic her "willingness to pay" for reducing the risk of a fire, and the amount she would demand (if she had the right) her "willingness to be paid" for increasing it.[42] Each is, in a sense, a measure of the value she places on a marginal change in this risk, and Coase's conjecture is that, if there are no problems of information or transaction costs, they will be identical. In practical terms, if he were right we could use price information from markets to infer the value people place on tangible and intangible goods, irrespective of whether they were buying or selling them. For our purposes, it would not matter whether workers have a right to safe working conditions and have to be bribed by employers to give them up, or whether they have no such rights and must effectively purchase safety by giving up wages.

Coase's claim challenged the thinking of lawyers and economists alike. Many of the arguments for environmental regulation, contract enforcement, and other areas of jurisprudence and public policy were suddenly at risk. In response, economists examined the proposition carefully and found that, strictly speaking, it was false: in general, one would *not* expect willingness to pay and willingness to be paid to be equal. The most universal reason is this: the value people tend to place on goods depends, in individually diverse ways, on their income, and, since incomes depend on who has the initial rights (and will therefore be a money-taker rather than a money-giver), prices must also be different. Somewhat less general but much more potent is another observation: if borrowing is difficult or costly, the amount people can pay is limited by their incomes, but there is no corresponding limit to the amount they can demand to be paid. An example will make this clear: consider the difference between your willingness to pay and your willingness to be paid to protect the Grand Canyon. If the public has no right to this natural wonder, a company can choose to flood it to build a hydro-electric dam. Your only recourse will be to contribute money to what amounts to a protection racket: pay off the dam builders so that they will not build. On the other hand, suppose that companies do not have the right to flood the canyon, but they can purchase it by bribing you and other citizens to gain your permission. Whatever your attachment to the Grand Canyon, it is certain that the first amount will be less than the second. In fact, some people will not sell off the canyon at any price; this is effectively the same as setting an infinitely high price, but clearly this is possible only because it is money they would receive and not pay.[43]

Oddly enough, the fact that the Coase Theorem is false has not impeded its usefulness in many applications. Exhibit A could well be the effort to divine a value of life: if a worker's willingness to pay for reducing the risk of death is either unknowable or understated because of the effect of unemployment, we could just as well try to determine the willingness to be paid for accepting this risk, by considering situations in which the shoe is on the other foot and it is the *employer* who must pay to gain the worker's consent. What might such a situation be? A clear case would be that of an already employed worker who is offered a voluntary relocation to a dangerous field office, such as in a country in the midst of civil war, where, in lieu of acceptable compensation, the worker could choose to stay just where he is. In the terms of the Coase Theorem, this worker has a right to remain at the initial level of safety and must be paid to accept any reduction. Unfortunately, there are relatively few such cut-and-dried cases, and it would be difficult to track them down and get full disclosure of terms offered and accepted. Yet it is plausible that there is an entire class of workers who, in a sense, exercise the freedom to say no to their employers and who therefore must be courted with extra inducements: voluntary job leavers. Of course, simply running a wage regression on this subset does not work, since it is precisely the inadequacy of the offered wage compensation (or some other aspect of the job) that inspired them to quit in the first place. Nonetheless, there is a solution; it involves weighing the relative effect that wages and risk have on the decision to quit.

Just such a study was conducted by Herzog and Schlottmann (1990). They began by performing a conventional wage regression of the form represented by equation (1) on a sample (the Public Use Sample of the 1970 census) for which there is a record of which workers switched industries, and therefore jobs. This permitted them to estimate standard coefficients for the M and K variables, as well as the risk of death. From these estimates they derived w^*, the predicted wage, which differs from the actual wage by ϵ_i for the ith worker. Now they expressed the likelihood of switching jobs S as a function of X (combining M and K), R, and w^*

$$S = S(X, R, w^*) \tag{10}$$

(They used the predicted, and not the actual, level of wages to control for the effect that randomly "good" and "bad" wages have on the quitting decision.) Assuming that (8) is linear, the coefficient on each variable is the derivative of S with respect to that variable; thus the coefficients on R and w^* can be used to determine the offsetting movements of R and w^* that would leave S exactly unchanged. For example, if β_R is larger, it means that a smaller change in R is required to offset a change in w^*. This, of course, is a measurement of wage compensation for risk of death, but, instead of inferring it from wages directly, Herzog and Schlottmann have derived it from a study of the factors that make workers prone to quit. It would be reasonable to conclude that this represents a willingness to be paid for incurring risk, since, whereas the employer exercises the right to set pay levels, the worker exercises the right to quit. The worker, in effect, "purchases" higher wages by acceding to the employer's reduced safety, but he or she must be "paid" in some fashion to forego the quit option.

Two samples were considered, all workers and full-time workers only, and two specifications of wages were used, its actual value and its logarithm. Together with the two methods of imputing worker preferences, equation (1) (willingness to pay) and equation (8) (willingness to be paid), this generated eight different measurements of the value of life.

In each case the job-switching approach yielded a substantially higher value than the conventional wage approach – in the full sample approximately twice as high. As Herzog and Schlottmann point out, this is due not only to the general tendency for willingness to be paid measures to exceed willingness to pay (the lesson from the Coase Theorem), but also to the presence of unemployment which at least partially disables wage compensation in the market, but not the relative weights workers place on wages and safety when deciding whether to quit. The second column of results in table 3.5, then, can be considered "unemployment-proof" measures of the value of life.[44]

Even if the results of the foregoing studies can be taken at face value, however, there is strong evidence against the view that the measured

Table 3.5 *Value of life: willingness to pay versus willingness to be paid (millions of dollars, 1990)*

		Earnings equations	Industry switching equations
All workers	Weekly earnings	5.785	10.342
	Ln (weekly earnings)	7.361	16.599
Full-time workers	Weekly earnings	6.248	8.207
	Ln (weekly earnings)	7.596	11.663

Source: Herzog and Schlottmann (1990).

coefficient on risk represents a true "willingness to pay" for anything. Every study that has estimated separate risk coefficients for union and nonunion workers finds them significantly different, and in most cases (all cases involving risk of death) the union worker receives relatively large wage premia while the nonunion worker receives little or nothing. (We will see further evidence of this phenomenon shortly.) What does this mean? Either workers who happen to belong to unions put vastly greater prices on their life and health, which is difficult to believe, or one or both of the coefficients is "wrong." But which one? According to Violette and Chestnut it is the coefficient on union risk that should be discounted: "union bargaining power may also push risk premiums higher than they would be under competitive equilibrium conditions" (pp. 2–6). Why should this occur, however? As we demonstrated in the previous chapter, under competitive equilibrium conditions unionized workers would have no incentive to demand excessive wage compensation; this would be equivalent to demanding too much money and too little safety, thereby ending up on a lower indifference curve. In fact, on the basis of conventional economic analysis, there is no satisfactory explanation for the magnitude of the union–nonunion risk compensation differential that preserves the interpretation of measured wage compensation as a willingness to pay.

Finally, over the course of this chapter we have seen increasingly sophisticated attempts to overcome the problems which bedevil hedonic wage analysis. From simple, unadorned wage regressions we moved to partitioned samples, inclusion of workers' compensation benefits, canonical correlation to test for implicit bias, and an estimation of the likelihood of job-switching to circumvent the difficulties connected with unemployment. It is true that these more refined methods yield results that are stronger and more significant than those of the first generation, and this fact has convinced most economists that they are on the right track: the proposition that markets generate wage compensation is believable, and the efficiency, equity, and hedonic properties follow in good order. Economic science, having stumbled about at first, has now found the proper path. What I will now show, however, is that *all wage/ risk studies, including the most sophisticated, are based on assumptions that have already been refuted by labor market research*. This means that their results, until proven otherwise, must be rejected as spurious.

Recall the initial problem we encountered in the pioneering Thaler and Rosen study. They attempted to isolate the effect that risk of death has on wage rates for various occupations, taking their risk data from a Society of Actuaries study of life expectancy by occupation. This approach was seen as flawed, since the longevity of those who hold an occupation may be only slightly related to the actual risks imposed by the occupation. The alternative, which nearly all subsequent studies have employed, was to use the average risk level for an industry as reported by the BLS (or NIOSH) as a proxy for the risk faced by each individual worker in that industry. The logic could be expressed this way: many factors affect a worker's wage, including the risk of injury or death on the job. We do not know the specific risk each worker faces, but we do know the average risk for his or her industry. Workers in high-risk industries will, on average, have higher risks, and we anticipate that they will be paid more for bearing them. Of course, since we do not know the true risk at the individual level, what we are measuring is the wage premium for belonging to a high-risk industry. To say that this is the same as a true compensating wage differential is to say that high-risk industries pay higher wages, once we control for the other variables that define or impinge on their members.

Rather than simply *assuming* that this relationship between risk and industry wage levels exists, we can *test* it directly by looking at the research that has been accumulating on the interindustry structure of wages in the US and other capitalist countries. Numerous authors have found that some industries pay more than others, that the list of high-paying industries is fairly constant over time and across countries, and even that there is a tendency for *all* workers to share in their industry's fate, irrespective of their own occupation within it. According to a review of this research by Dickens and Katz (1987), for instance, between 7 and 30 percent of the total variation in individual wages can be explained by these broad industry differentials. In a recent influential study by Krueger and Summers (1986), the standard deviation of industry wage ratios (the percentage difference between an industry's average wage and the weighted average of all industries) was 15–24 percent, depending on measurement assumptions. These results would hardly surprise most job-seekers, who learn early on that there are choice jobs in each local area, with "good" employers or industries. Let us take a closer look at the characteristics of these differentials and the ways they have been measured.

Industry differential studies look much like wage/risk studies, only larger. They include all, or nearly all, of the variables included in conventional wage regressions, plus dummy variables for each industry and additional characteristics of jobs and market conditions which might also explain wage patterns. One basic form is

$$w_i = \alpha + \beta_x{}'X_i' + \beta_I I_i + \epsilon_i \tag{11}$$

where X' is an expanded list of wage-related variables, and I_i is a set of variables, one per industry, which take the value "1" if the worker is in that industry and "0" if he or she is not. The coefficients on I, then, represent the reward or penalty simply for being in that particular industry – the industry wage differential. As a second step, one might want to explain these variables by running another regression such as this

$$D_j = \alpha + \beta_Y Y_j + \epsilon_j \tag{12}$$

where D_j takes the value of β for the jth industry from equation (11), the Y_j are characteristics of each industry, and ϵ represents the unexplainable portion of the variation in D. What are the typical suspects for inclusion in Y? In their review of ten previous studies, Krueger and Summers (1987) located several promising candidates: overall industry profitability (and to a lesser extent the level of concentration within the industry), the labor share of costs, the capital–labor ratio, and the percentage of the industry's workforce which is unionized (union density). Each of these seems to have some effect, although most studies continue to show a substantial portion, as much as 50 percent, of industry differences which are unrelated to them.

One possible explanatory factor which has *not* made much of an impression is compensating wage differentials for hazardous or otherwise undesirable work. Dickens and Katz (1987), for instance, worked on a large scale: they pooled twelve consecutive monthly surveys from the CPS and incorporated, in addition to the standard fare, a long list of variables most other studies have ignored: the percentage of an industry which is black or female (to pick up the effects of discrimination that might spill over to all workers in that industry), the layoff rate and the number of hours of work available in each industry (to pick up other compensating differentials), the industry unemployment rate and its union density (to capture aspects of the industry's labor market), firm size, the extent of oligopoly, the capital–labor ratio and the ratio of R&D spending to sales, fraction of production workers in each industry's workforce, and industry-wide profitability (to capture the effects of technology and the market conditions facing firms). To this they added a dummy (0 − 1) variable for each three-digit SIC. Then they divided their sample into union and nonunion workers, under the assumption that the wage determination process would be different for each. Juggling their various explanatory variables, they tried out 216 specifications on each sample. The result was a tidal wave of coefficients, but little comfort for supporters of wage compensation doctrine. The coefficient on the industry's injury rate was insignificant in nearly all specifications; it was generally positive for the nonunion sample, but was often negative for unionized workers. As Dickens and Katz point out, this makes sense in light of their finding that high-wage industries pay higher wages to all their workers: production workers, clericals, engineers – *everyone*. Even if an industry's injury rate were high, why would this affect workers in all occupations and departments?

Krueger and Summers' (1986) results are even more damaging. In one part of their study they performed an expanded wage regression similar to (11) using data from the University of Michigan's Quality of Employment Survey. This enabled them to incorporate ten different quality-of-work variables to represent characteristics such as the presence and seriousness of health hazards, as well as the availability of full-time and overtime work, the burden of commuting, and the general pleasantness of the demands made by the job.[45] What they found was that including these working conditions variables increased the adjusted R^2 of their regression from 0.496 to 0.519 but also *increased* the standard deviation of the industry wage premia (adjusted for industry weight) from 11.3 percent to 11.8 percent. This has serious implications for the validity of the studies we have been considering throughout this chapter. To see this, return to the logic of conventional hedonic wage regressions, whose underlying assumption is that industries which are more dangerous than average will pay higher than average wages, after accounting for the other effects, such as the demographic characteristics of the workforce, which are already incorporated in the study. The Krueger and Summers result throws a monkey-wrench into this hypothesis. What their work shows is this: to the extent that there are positive compensating wage differentials for undesirable working conditions, then high-wage industries have, net of all other effects, *better* working conditions, so that attributing (negative) compensating differentials to them increases the true *industry* wage differential. But this in turn indicates that the guiding assumption of the studies we have looked at in this chapter is false: workers in high-risk industries generally earn less, not more, and by not including a variable to incorporate this effect, researchers will get misleading results.

A fascinating echo of these results appears, almost in passing, in a study by Dillingham (1985). In the course of testing five different approaches to attributing risk to individuals (by major or detailed industry, occupation, or some combination thereof) he ran each specification with, and then without, dummy variables for a subset of occupations and/or industries. (He used as many as 157 industries and 83 occupations, but only six industrial and five occupational dummies to avoid problems of collinearity.) This gave him ten sets of results, five for each specification with dummies and five without. In his dummy-less models he obtained positive coefficients on risk significant at the 5 percent level (two-tailed) four out of the five times. When dummies were inserted, however, only one of the coefficients remains significant at 5 percent, one is significant at 10 percent, and the others are insignificant. Moreover, in each instance, adding a set of dummies reduced the size of the coefficient. Occupational dummies cut it in half, industry dummies (in the detailed industry models) by more than 75 percent. This is fully consistent with the interindustry wage differential literature, since it shows that even partial incorporation of industry effects wreaks havoc with conventionally measured risk coefficients.[46]

A similar result was obtained by Leigh in a recent study (Leigh, 1994). Leigh estimated a conventional equation – the log of wages as the independent variable, fatal risk and the standard set of controls as independent variables – using the 1981–2 PSID and both the BLS and NIOSH risk measures. He found positive, significant coefficients on risk, replicating the usual results. Then, however, he re-estimated his equations, this time with the addition of dummy variables for major industry categories, hoping to pick up interindustry wage differentials. As he had expected, controlling in this broad way for industry effects virtually wipes out measured risk premia. His evidence is summarized in table 3.6.[47]

To perform an even more direct test of the interindustry hypothesis, Paul Hagstrom and I have estimated compensating wage differentials for the 1982 panel of the PSID using conventional controls, industry dummies, and a broader set of industry-level variables (Dorman and Hagstrom, 1993). In keeping with current practice we chose a seven-year average of the NTOF major industry-by-state observations as our fatal

Table 3.6 *Risk coefficients without and with industry dummies*

Risk variable	Without dummies	With dummies
BLS	0.00275*	−0.00033
	(4.726)	(−0.456)
NIOSH	0.00036*	0.00051
	(5.331)	(0.378)

Note: * Indicates significance at 5% (one-tailed).
Numbers in parentheses are t-statistics.
Source: Leigh (1994).

risk variable and the BLS series on lost workday injuries at the three-digit industry level as our nonfatal risk variable. We also incorporated the usual set of demographic and human capital control variables. OLS estimation of log wages was then conducted under a variety of specifications, incorporating the permutations of the two risk variables, in each case separating out the effects for union and nonunion workers, and incorporating explanatory variables representing a "traditional" wage regression (primarily individual-level data), "traditional plus major industry dummies," and "full interindustry" (using a range of industry-level data). The full interindustry model included such variables as the industry-average capital–labor ratio, the average establishment size, the four-firm concentration ratio, and the percentage of the industry's workforce covered by a collective bargaining agreement. In all, we tested nine models. Table 3.7 summarizes our regression data for the two risk variables and two union statuses under the three alternative specifications. Each risk category has three rows and two sets of columns. Columns marked "I" reflect models in which only that form of risk (fatal or injury) was incorporated, while those marked "II" reflect models with both forms of risk entered simultaneously. For each risk/union status group the first row displays regression results using the basic model, the second the model with industry dummies, and the third the full interindustry model.[48]

Other than the results for fatal risk for unionized workers, the overall pattern strongly supports the hypothesis that the measurement of wage compensation depends strongly on whether industry-level data are incorporated in the study. In all specifications, fatal risk for nonunion-ized workers and nonfatal risk for unionized workers decline in significance as more industry-level variables are added, with measured compensation falling by 22–37 percent. Compensation to nonunion

Table 3.7 *Selected regression results: risk coefficients*

Dependent Variable: LOGWAGE
$N = 931$

Variable	coeff.		t-stat		cwd	
	I	II	I	II	I	II
nu-fatal (I)	0.0026536**	0.0028962***	2.16	2.34	340.7	371.8
	0.0024999*	0.0025694*	1.43	1.47	320.9	329.9
	0.0020528	0.002242	1.17	1.28	263.5	287.8
u-fatal (I)	0.0046981***	0.0041158**	2.65	2.31	370.4	324.5
	0.0047759**	0.0039558**	2.12	1.74	376.5	311.9
	0.0052189**	0.0045905**	2.30	2.02	411.5	361.9
nu-inj. (I)	−0.0003471	−0.0004573	−0.91	−1.19	−308.2	−406.1
	−0.0007668**	−0.0007241**	−1.92	−1.81	−680.9	−643.0
	−0.0011691**	−0.0011177**	−2.21	−2.10	−1038.1	−992.5
u-inj. (I)	0.0010627***	0.0009453**	2.53	2.24	786.6	699.7
	0.0008995**	0.0008491**	2.15	2.01	665.8	628.5
	0.0006636*	0.0006087*	1.44	1.32	491.2	450.6

Notes: * indicates significance at 10%.
** indicates significance at 5%.
*** indicates significance at 1%.
u = union.
nu = nonunion.

workers for nonfatal risk was actually *negative*, and became quantitatively larger and more significant as more explanatory variables were added. In other words, the more we control for other influences on the wages of nonunion workers – the vast majority of the workforce – the more we find hazardous working conditions associated with *lower* pay. The only exception to this pattern is compensation for fatal risk to unionized workers, which grows slightly in size (although not significance) in the full interindustry specification. Combined with the result for nonfatal union risk, whose significance survives the inclusion of industry-level variables, the clear implication is that only those workers most insulated from market forces are able to extract higher wages in return for accepting greater risk. Presumably this is *not* because they place a higher value on their life and health!

These and other interindustry wage studies seriously disable all previous (and, alas, continuing) efforts to identify compensating wage differentials for industry-related job risks. Until it is shown that significant coefficients on risk can be obtained for all (or even most) workers in regressions that incorporate *all* of the factors which affect wages, we cannot endorse either the purported evidence for wage compensation or the related estimates of the value of life.[49]

Hedonic estimates of the value of life: squeezing a stone from blood

Not every car an engineer might design should be built, not every new strain of corn a geneticist might breed should be planted, and not every coefficient an economist might estimate should be promulgated as a valid and useful statistic. There are two questions that must be answered: does this number really mean anything, and does it serve a reasonable purpose? Although we began this chapter with a statement of the case economists make for estimating and using a value of life, deep criticisms have been made which are yet to be addressed. I will survey some of these and add a few of my own.

1   Not everything should have a price.

Steven Kelman (1981) has argued forcefully that the mere act of attaching a price to a quality or condition changes it fundamentally. We lose our capacity to experience feelings such as horror and reverence, attitudes which can profoundly change our behavior even though we have no strictly rational account of them. Would we recoil from the Holocaust to the same degree if it were reduced to a monetary sum, however large, representing the lives taken in the concentration camps? Moreover, he adds, people regard *themselves* differently when prices are brought into play. Unpriced values provoke solidarity, since they are directly rooted in the feelings and experiences we share as social beings; by introducing prices we reduce these values to the level of commodities, about which people are socialized to respond individualistically and even competitively (Kelman, 1981). If I learn that you have lost a hand due to an industrial accident, I will immediately experience a sense of empathy, for I too have hands and know what it would mean to lose one. If there were anything I could do to prevent this from happening, or to help you make the transition afterward, I probably would. But if I hear that you have suffered an unspecified loss whose monetary equivalent is $400,000, I would chalk it up to the vagaries of the marketplace and perhaps check once more to make sure my *own* affairs are in order.

Economists, needless to say, are uncomfortable with an argument that opposes the use of prices in at least some circumstances for ethical reasons. They have a reply: whether they recognize it or not, individuals act each day as if these priceless values really do have prices (they trade them off against financial gain), and it would be irrational for people to respond differently to a risk or opportunity just because a number is attached to it. Life may be priceless, they say, but people do accept greater risks of losing it in return for higher pay, and neither their attitudes nor yours or mine should be affected by whether or not economists calculate the actual tradeoffs. This argument has convinced most economists and can be found, in one form or another, in dozens of textbooks, but it fails on three counts. (1) To say that people routinely act as if there were acceptable monetary tradeoffs for life, health, and other values simply begs the question. This is a claim that must be *proved*, and, as this chapter has shown, economists have not yet done this. Of course, individuals may often make choices that can be interpreted as trading off priced for unpriced values, but the real test is whether they do this *systematically*. Unless we hold ourselves to this standard, we have no checks on our ability to falsely attribute motives or behavior to others. (2) Even if we did observe such systematic tradeoffs, we could not automatically assume that they reflect individual preferences. People make decisions, but they also have decisions made for them. This was brought out in the police study, where possible wage/risk tradeoffs were seen to represent not the value that police officers place on their own lives, but their value in the eyes of the local political establishment. The same could be said of the women of the Triangle Shirtwaist Company and the coal miners of the black lung saga; what an economic analysis of their tradeoffs would reveal is ultimately a sociological rather than psychological fact: their employers treated them as if their lives were cheap. This is information of no small significance, but it is not what economists think they are measuring. (3) It is not irrational to devise strategies that limit one's future propensity to make foolish choices; this is called *precommitment*.[50] Suppose we sense in ourselves a tendency to place too much weight on the accumulation of commodities and not enough on less tangible but more enduring values like liberty, community, health, and so on. It would be in our interest to create impediments to our shortsighted urges, and there are various ways we could do this. We could enact a constitution that required protection of these values and that would be difficult to amend on the basis of a transitory whim.[51] In a sense, OSHA regulations serve this purpose for individual businesses and their workers; they are to collective bargaining what a constitution is to ordinary legislation. To put it differently, we could say that, even if workers sometimes choose to trade health for money, we might reasonably question whether this ought to carry any weight. Sagoff (1982) is blunt:

[Consider] a risk, not of death, but of being tortured ... having one's hand cut off, becoming a slave, or undergoing a needless lobotomy. Here the economist may ask, for example, if you would accept $50,000 in exchange for a 1/1000 probability you will be enslaved for the rest of your life. Suppose you take the hypothetical bargain .... What have we learned about regulatory policy? (p. 766)

Consider another example even closer to current practice. Suppose we were to set up a program which monitored workers, recording the name of each individual who is found to have shirked or committed sabotage on the job. At the end of each year the names of the offenders are put in a hopper, one is selected at random, and that person is executed on nationwide television. Now imagine that economists determine that this program is such a powerful spur to productive effort that the economy can be expected to grow by an additional $30 billion even after deducting the costs of surveillance and electrocution. Note that this is precisely the type of case for which estimates of the value of life are intended: each individual bears a small risk of being the unlucky victim, and no one knows in advance who it will be. Once we have accepted the notion that a life can be equated with a monetary value, what prevents us from going through with this grisly enterprise? And, logically, what is the difference between this hypothetical case and the actual, everyday occurrence of occupational fatalities that could have been prevented if firms had been willing to pay the price? The most reasonable response would seem to be to refuse to put a price on lives taken in this manner as a matter of principle.

2   There is more to **homo sapiens** than **homo economicus**

Economists would have us believe that we humans are unitary beings, with a single, all-purpose "self" that expresses itself equally in all roles and capacities. If certain preferences can be inferred from our behavior as market participants, these define us in our entirety. Philosopher Mark Sagoff has challenged this premise in his recent book, *The Economy of the Earth* (1988). It is his view that we have at least two "selves," a private, self-seeking persona represented by our behavior in the market-place, and a public incarnation as citizens who deliberate our shared values with one another. He finds it striking that the choices we make in one realm are often contradicted by those we make in the other. For instance, he gives the example of someone who, as a private individual, would purchase a ski weekend at a mountain resort in what used to be a wilderness area, but who, as a concerned citizen, does not want that resort built in the first place. It is the soul of wisdom, he says, to recognize which type of decision-making, public or private, is appropriate to which kind of situation. It would be wrong to determine what types of bread will be offered to the public through a political or administrative process, since choosing between white, wheat, or rye is a quintessentially private act; instead, we should promote a system of consumer sovereignty. On the other hand, the adulteration of bread by potentially harmful substances violates public values concerning health and honest treatment, and it would be equally wrong to leave this issue to the marketplace. This is true even though many individuals, as consumers, might be willing to absorb a greater risk of harmful adulteration in return for, say, lower prices.

The problem of occupational health and safety takes on a new meaning under Sagoff's distinction. If all the other questions raised in this chapter were resolved – if labor markets worked according to the conventional assumptions and economists were able to estimate wage/ risk tradeoffs with perfect accuracy – any value-of-life calculation would apply only to individuals as workers, not as citizens. Yet when it comes to the public issues surrounding life and death such as environmental and safety regulation, preventive and curative health programs, and the provision of social welfare benefits, what is at stake is the extent of our collective commitment to the values of life and health. Such a judgment is more than the sum of our individual preferences as inferred from market behavior; it is fundamentally *social* and demands public discussion and decision-making. It makes no more sense, for example, to subject air pollution regulations to a cost–benefit analysis, incorporating the value of lives lost to lung disease, than it does to make courtroom judgments of negligent homicide on the same basis. In such a case a jury is not concerned with the preferences of the claimant and the defendant, but with the moral and evidentiary validity of their cases, and these can be determined only through an open, public engagement with the facts and with the opinions of all parties to the dispute.

Perhaps even more telling is the discrepancy between the relatively limited values placed on life in the hedonic wage studies and the virtually unlimited values that emerge in public episodes when coal miners are trapped, sailors are shipwrecked, etc. All possible efforts are made to rescue everyone at risk; no thought is given to the expense.[52] Most economists who have addressed this anomaly, including such influential writers as Mishan (1971), Oi (1974), Zeckhauser (1975), and Viscusi (1983), have attributed it to the fact that rescues involve named individuals, whereas the more mundane, probabilistic threats to life are anonymous: millions are affected to a small degree, while no one knows who will ultimately bear the full cost. Since most of the risks society is concerned with regulating are of this second variety, the argument goes, we can simply regard public displays of unlimited concern as irrelevant.

This line of reasoning does not bear close scrutiny. First, all victims, whatever the cause of their death, will ultimately be named, and there is no *a priori* reason to hold that the values expressed before their identity is known are more valid than those that emerge afterward. Second, and more in the spirit of Sagoff's critique, it is not only that risks of future occupational harm and public life-or-death crises differ with respect to the identity of the victims, but also that they are embedded in fundamentally different processes of social valuation. Occupational risks are faced individually by workers in their capacity as participants in the labor market, while public rescues are just that: public. In discussing the progress of a widely publicized crisis, individuals in their role as citizens explore each other's attitudes, debate their differences, and are held responsible for their judgments.

Proponents of value-of-life statistics who would simply plug them into benefit–cost analyses endorse the substitution of private for public decision-making. Their underlying error is that they assume we can pass directly from private attitudes to public decisions without any intervening role for discourse or even open disclosure. Put this way, Sagoff's argument belongs in the same public-democratic tradition of political theory that includes John Dewey and Jurgen Habermas.[53]

3   Anticipating an event and experiencing it are not the same

What is the value for a film producer of a sweep of the Academy Awards? It would certainly be possible to survey producers in advance and gauge their expectations, but this would not be very efficient or accurate. Why not simply look at the revenues for films that have won awards in the past – that is, use actual rather than anticipated results? By the same token, why should we search for the value of life and health in the expectations of individuals who have little experience with the serious possibility of loss? Of course, economists in this life cannot survey the victims of fatal occupational injuries and diseases, but they can study people who have come *close* to such an end, and they can consult with family and friends regarding their loss. Moreover, there is no impediment to research on victims of nonfatal outcomes. In a sense, this *ex post* approach to the value of life and well-being is implicit in the problem of public rescue episodes mentioned above: many hazards command a far greater public value after they have materialized than before.

In a world of perfect foresight *ex ante* and *ex post* evaluations would be identical; in the real world they will generally differ. This is not at issue; the question is, on which should economists base their studies? For Mishan (1971), the fact that people may not anticipate correctly is immaterial. An ill-informed individual, he writes, "may find himself disabled for life and rue his decision to take the risk. But this example is only a more painful one of the fact that people come to regret a great many of the choices they make, notwithstanding which they would resent any interference with their future choices" (p. 703). This argument, however, confuses self-determination, which is inescapably before-the-fact, with the use of individual assessments in public policy analysis, where reactions to completed events are available. Why would using the sadder yet wiser *ex post* assessments of individuals to evaluate a proposed policy, in preference to their naive *ex ante* impressions, impinge on anyone's freedom of choice? By basing their value of life on the attitudes of people who are generally remote from the actual consequences of catastrophic occupational accidents and illnesses and who have, for the most part, given little thought to them, economists are investing ignorance with the aura of scientific validity.[54]

4 A single value of life, even for a single individual, is a logical absurdity

Contrary to appearances, death is not a homogeneous outcome. There are two reasons for this. First, much of our concern is about dying, rather than death itself. It is one thing to pass abruptly in one's sleep, another to suffer a grueling, hopeless battle with a degenerative disease. Dying in a release of toxic chemicals or in the collapse of scaffolding at a construction site are different from one another and different from other deaths on and off the job. There is no reason to suppose that people regard all of them equally. Second, the significance of death depends mightily on the reasons for it. Some deaths are willingly courted: martyrdom in the service of a religious or political cause, for example, or the risk-taking of mountaineers. At the opposite extreme are deaths which appear to result from the unjust, self-aggrandizing behavior of others, such as criminals, polluters – and corporations willing to cut corners on job safety to make a few extra dollars. Indeed, from this perspective the "disutility" of death is not really the issue:

Economists who believe that much of our behavior under risk is irrational might take another view of it were they to consider that it may be motivated, not by fear, but by resentment. The problem, then, would be to explain, not why we fear some dangers more than others, but why we resent some dangers more than others. One answer is plain. We resent risks imposed upon us, as members of the public, by those who seek, in doing so, to achieve economic ends. (Sagoff, 1982, p. 763)

Strictly speaking, there are two components of this resentment, control and motivation. A death is resented to the extent that it is due to factors, such as chemical and radiological exposures, over which workers have no control, and in response to the drive for private gain. That this latter aspect is largely subjective makes it no less real: if workers believe that particular fatalities could have been prevented by more responsive management they are likely to display a much greater – indeed, a different type of – concern than if they regard the fatalities as acts of God. Nevertheless, the techniques employed in hedonic wage analysis blithely lump together deaths over which workers have some measure of control, such as accidents caused by their own violation of safe working standards, with others, such as chronic toxic exposures, over which they have virtually no control at all, and they make no distinction between hazards workers view as exploitative and those they do not. Worse yet, the numbers yielded up by these studies have no legitimate application, since each public policy issue encompasses its own qualitatively distinct questions of life and death.

In 1984, Viscusi and O'Connor wrote an article for the *American Economic Review* about the effects of chemical hazard disclosure rules on workers' propensity to quit. They titled it "Adaptive Responses to Chemical Labeling: Are Workers Bayesian Decision Makers?," referring to Bayes' Theorem in probability (see chapter 2). The real question that should be asked, however, is whether workers are *Kantian* decision-makers: do they accept or avoid risks on the basis of utility, as economists suppose, or do they value above all their autonomy as human beings in the tradition of Kant's categorical moral imperative? This is an empirical question; we will look for evidence of it in the historical and institutional record (chapter 4), and we will consider its implications for compensating differential theory and labor market analysis in general in chapter 5.

4 The real world of occupational safety and health

One of my favorite cartoons, by Kliban, shows a frumpy-looking professor standing in front of a class. He is pointing to the blackboard, which is filled with inscrutable equations bearing Greek letters and various mathematical symbols. There are many alphas, but on each is drawn eyes, a mouth, and fins. Before him are rows and rows of fish sitting at their desks, busily taking notes. The cartoon is entitled, "Proving the Existence of Fish."

The idea that we could learn more about ourselves by studying our own and other societies is, in the western world, as old as Aristotle. Economics is ostensibly part of this grand project, yet all too often economists narrow their vision to only those ideas or observations that can be quantified or at least be represented mathematically. There is nothing wrong with theoretical and statistical analysis, of course, but slavish adherence to them fails to recognize that most of our collective experience with economic problems is too complex, qualitatively nuanced, and subjective to be captured by the techniques of formalization. Economists, like Kliban's professor, often ignore facts that are right in front of their noses. The consequence, however, may be worse than mere redundant frivolity; refusing to look beyond the blackboard can lead to the twin problems (analogous to the statistician's Type I and Type II error) that economics may fail to identify generalizations that could be supported by this wider array of evidence or may fail to *reject* generalizations that would be refuted by it.

We have already seen the enormous distance that separates the two worlds of occupational safety and health: the commonsense world, based on centuries of experience, that unnecessarily dangerous work is a form of abuse and ought to be regulated on the grounds of justice and decency, and the economic world of competitive markets, free choice, and compensating wage differentials. The views of noneconomists have been little heard in economic circles, since the debates over market efficiency and the value of life have been conducted in arcane terms that only insiders understand. (The past two chapters have been intended as an introduction to this discussion for newcomers to economic analysis.) By the same token, economists have paid little attention to research outside their field; hardly ever, for instance, does a paper or even an entire book on the economics of occupational safety refer to so much as a fraction of the relevant historical, legal, or sociological literature. This chapter confronts the problem of wilful ignorance head-on. I will look closely at the events and experiences that underlie popular perceptions of hazardous work, considering them as evidence every bit as relevant to the evaluation of economic doctrine as the econometric exercises surveyed in chapter 3. At the same time, this review will serve as raw material for a second round of theoretical reasoning, to provide both an adequate critique of economic orthodoxy on this topic and the theoretical insights that can illumine the real world – the subject matter of chapter 5.

A word about organization: I have divided this chapter into eight sections, each concerned with a particular aspect of the history of occupational safety. Each section begins with a presupposition of the theory of compensating wage differentials or a proposition derived from it, followed by a look at the actual evidence. The point of this structure is to emphasize that economic theory is being tested through its direct assertions and its logically necessary conclusions: if either is strongly contradicted by the evidence, the theory loses its claim on our acceptance.

Occupational safety in Anglo-American law

There are just a few perennial themes in slapstick comedy. One of them is the obliviousness of the comic hero to something taking place right in front of him, or occasionally her. Charlie Chaplin was a master of this motif, and so was Chuck Jones, creator of the "Roadrunner" and other cartoons. Wiley Coyote was always a little too clever; he could concoct the most devious schemes, but they would never get off the ground because of some detail perfectly obvious to the viewer but somehow outside the evil predator's narrow field of vision. Even when he was handed a bomb, he always looked at it quizzically (*what is this doing here?*), as if he had no idea that he was about to be blown to smithereens – only to reappear, of course, for his next fiasco. Why do we laugh at this crude, predictable type of humor? Perhaps the truth is that we are secret misanthropes, delighting in the misery of our fellow beings. But let us be more charitable; maybe it is because these pratfalls express an otherwise painful truth about our own condition: we are all at risk of missing the most fundamental, immediate aspects of life, things that should be obvious to us but are not.

Academic economists possess this trait in abundance; when their theories go wrong they often go *very* wrong, due to the all-too-human inability to recognize the assumptions on which their arguments depend. One such blindness is the topic of this section, the unnoticed but critical assumption that workers actually, *legally* accept their working conditions as part of agreeing to take a job. To see what is at stake, return to the year 1776, when Adam Smith was putting his finishing touches to *The Wealth of Nations*. Smith, as we saw earlier, argued that employers would have to compensate workers for accepting work that was more dangerous or otherwise undesirable than the average, with the final result that, when the combined monetary and nonmonetary rewards were considered, all work of a similar type in a given region would be rewarded equally. He stated it as a simple, incontestable truth, as if it were so obvious that any argument or analysis would be superfluous. A modern reader could be excused for thinking that Smith was only describing the world around him: he saw workers negotiating with employers, agreeing to take on their various jobs with all the conditions attached to them in return for acceptable wage payments. And so it has been to this day, according to this view; the conditions and remuneration of work are set in contracts, mutually agreed upon by both parties. If the terms of the contract are not accepted by either side, there is no relationship, in which case both workers and employers have to look elsewhere. To be precise, two assumptions are involved: the terms of employment are determined by contracts freely entered into between labor and capital, and these terms are legally enforceable. Employers must pay the wages they have agreed to, and workers cannot take this money without undertaking the work and accepting the conditions that they have agreed to.

In practical terms, there are two consequences that flow directly from this view. First, workers by agreeing to the risks offered them as part of the employment package waive the right to protest them. If they petition the courts or the legislature to make their jobs safer, the response would be simply that they (the workers) were free agents when they agreed to the employer's terms, and it would be wrong to violate this "freedom." Second, the market-based view of safety leads, as we have seen, to the doctrine of compensating wage differentials. This in turn undermines the case workers might bring under the law of torts (redress for damages) in response to an accident or illness. If workers are fully compensated for bearing risks *before* they are hurt, any additional compensation afterwards would be both unjust and inefficient. If workers are worried about coping with the catastrophic costs of serious threats to health or life, let them take out disability and medical insurance, paying for them out of their extra wages (the compensating differentials). If the insurance is "fair" (the expected value of the premiums equals the expected value of the benefits), and if workers are rational in negotiating the terms of their contracts (demanding wage premiums for risk equal to the cost of insuring against them), workers in both safer and riskier jobs would be on identical footing. What court would then make an *additional* award in response to, say, an accident, thereby making riskier work *more* desirable when all the costs and benefits are factored in? What we would expect to find, then, is that the law in Smith's day and our own would refuse to brook interference with whatever conditions the worker accepts by agreeing to work, and that workers would not be given tort remedies for accident and injury losses for which the employer is responsible.

It will come as quite a surprise to anyone whose knowledge of these things is circumscribed by economic theory that nothing could be further from the truth. Legal scholars have long ago demonstrated that this is a false description of the employment relationship both then and now. Oddly, however, it is a partially accurate account of a period *after* Smith but before the present, which lasted only a few decades before the experiment in free, enforceable contracts was found to be unworkable. How this transpired, and how the legal order both defined and responded to the struggle over occupational safety makes for an interesting story.[1]

The body of common law which, from early modern times, governed relations in England (and later America) between workers and employers was the starkly named Law of Masters and Servants. As its title suggests, its origins were in a society in which different classes had their stations, and it was the function of law to impose rights and responsibilities on each. By as early as the sixteenth century, however, the spirit of individualism was making a significant impact on legal doctrine. People were increasingly being viewed as independent moral agents, capable of entering into and leaving agreements of their own choosing, rather than as interchangeable representatives of the various social classes. In philosophy, this movement produced a succession of contractarian theories beginning with Hobbes, all based in some fashion on the idea that social and political institutions could be justified as agreements free individuals would voluntarily endorse. In law the role of contracts was enhanced, and judges were increasingly willing to let the parties decide on the terms they wanted, rather than those sanctioned by custom or authority. In fact, this movement was so well advanced by the eighteenth century that statutes were passed permitting employers not merely to fire but also to *prosecute* for breach of contract workers who performed inadequately or quit without sufficient notice.

Nevertheless, employment relations in Smith's time were not as strictly contractual as he claimed. Whatever the formal terms of their agreement, both workers and employers could appeal to the courts to enforce obligations that were generally considered fair and appropriate by the standards of the time. If either a worker or an employer felt that their relationship imposed burdens well in excess of the norm, they would have fair prospects of finding a judge who would void this aspect of the contract, despite the fact that it had been voluntarily entered into. This state of affairs was a far cry from the freely contracting utopia painted by Smith.[2] In particular, workers had two important alternatives to compensating wage differentials for excessively dangerous work in the mid eighteenth century: they could appeal in a court of law to have these conditions changed, or they could sue for damages if an accident had actually occurred. In either case it would not be enough for the employer to say that he had followed the contract, and that was that; there would also be an expectation that he would defend his behavior as generally fair and reasonable.

What is so interesting about the relationship between Adam Smith's theory of markets and the world it purported to describe is that it represents a perfect reversal of the usual ordering of reality and explanation. Smith claimed to be providing an analysis of the world he lived in, and later students of economics have largely taken him at his word. But the true causation flowed in the opposite direction: after *The Wealth of Nations* appeared and made a big splash among British intellectuals, judges and parliamentarians actively set out to *create* a laissez-faire system of markets in its image. The greatest strides were made in the first decades of the nineteenth century. The generation of economists who succeeded Smith, people such as James Mill and David Ricardo, were, if anything, even less reticent about the virtues of an economy based on freedom of contract, and they occupied the commanding heights of public life. Their views were actively sought even on issues over which they had little expertise, and for many years most educated Britishers embraced the virtues of a "natural economy" based on free and enforceable contracts. It was in this climate that British jurists embarked on a radical experiment, overthrowing centuries of precedent by treating contracts not as one element to be weighed in a larger and more complex relationship, but as a complete legal relationship in itself: enforceable in all its terms and a shield against intervention even where terms are wanting.

So it was during this period, rather than the mid eighteenth century of

Adam Smith, that the two expectations of the market-based model were satisfied. Between the turn of the century and 1840 essentially no action at all was taken to ameliorate conditions in Britain's "dark, satanic mills." Protests by workers, journalists, and others fell on deaf ears, because it was assumed that, in a free market, workers accepted whatever they got. And after years of cutting back on a worker's right to sue for damages due to employer neglect, the decision *Priestly v. Fowler* (1837) came down decisively in favor of the doctrine that contract implies consent; simply by virtue of agreeing to an employment contract, a worker tacitly consents to all of the circumstances of that employment that he or she knew, or should have known, at the time of acceptance. This, of course, is the view of the employment relationship embodied in orthodox economic theory. In legal terms, it goes beyond the simple freedom of parties to enter into contract; rather, in the name of freedom of contract, jurists and parliamentarians created the legal basis for an economic regime in which individuals could exercise freedom *only* through a contract. Maine's famous mid nineteenth-century aphorism concerning the movement "from status to contract" was in part a description of this state of affairs.

Nevertheless, the experiment in radical contractarianism began to unravel as soon as it was consummated. The development of government inspection and regulation of working conditions will be chronicled in the following section; here I will focus on the evolution of employer liability in the courts.[3] In both British and American law, employers had three defenses against suits by injured workers or their estates: contributory negligence, the fellow servant rule, and assumption of risk. The first has to do with the share of the responsibility to be apportioned to the employer as against the worker, the second with the claim that the employer is not responsible for the actions of subordinates, and the third with the argument that the worker knew what he or she was getting into. Since this final defense is essentially equivalent to the claim of pure worker volition and therefore the likelihood of fully compensating wage differentials, it is of particular interest here.

It is the ironic feature of assumption of risk that it penalizes the worker for being conscious of safety conditions and even for making representations to the employer. The reasoning is: if the worker knew the dangers existed and yet continued to work, this indicates that the worker consented to these dangers as part of a larger employment transaction; had there not been sufficient compensation *ex ante* the worker would have refused the hazardous work. Perhaps the best-known American case in which this defense was raised was that of Sarah Knisley (1913), who lost an arm in a grinding machine. She had previously complained to her supervisor that the machine was unguarded (in contravention of state law); the response was that she should either go back to work or quit. By continuing to work, the court ruled, she had assumed the risk herself, thereby absolving her employer.[4] Fear of dismissal, a counter-argument raised by Knisley and others, was not given much weight; according to Prosser (1955), an essential reference for American tort law, "in the absence of statute the greater number of courts held that a risk is assumed even when a workman acts under a direct command carrying an express or implied threat of discharge for disobedience" (p. 373).[5]

Proposals to restore employer liability arose within both the public health community and the labor movement. In Britain, the belief that liability could be made the cornerstone of public policy in occupational safety and health can be traced to Edwin Chadwick, perhaps the foremost exponent of public health during the Victorian era. Chadwick, whose utilitarian credentials can be inferred from his position as Jeremy Bentham's personal secretary and who later served on the Commission on the Factories (1833) and the House of Commons Select Committee on Railways (1846), repeatedly urged that legislation be passed circumventing the common law and requiring employers to compensate workers for injuries received on the job. His motivation was not support for workers as such, but the establishment of proper incentives and the efficient reduction in accident rates. At the same time, labor and socialist movements in both Britain and the US supplied steady pressure on the courts, for they too thought that the restoration of employer liability would bring about great changes in working conditions. Egregious violations of worker safety and health were highlighted in the press; trials (such as the prosecution of the owners of Triangle Shirtwaist after their catastrophic fire) focused the attention of the public on employer culpability and made judges who ruled in favor of the defense the objects of public outrage and ridicule. In response to all of this agitation, the courts began to waver. They did not repeal the three employer liability defenses outright, but they did chip away at the margins, creating exceptions, limits, and various loopholes.

Employers became nervous. They had to recognize that, should workers be injured or killed on the job, there was now a chance that an unfriendly judge would permit them to be fined for negligence. Their response was to write up disclaimers which workers would be required to sign as part of the employment application, formally renouncing any claim on the employer's responsibility for providing safe working conditions. Typical was this clause in the application form for the American Express company, cited by Fuller (1906):

Now, therefore, in consideration of the premises and of my said employment, I do hereby assume all risk of accidents and injuries which I shall meet with or sustain in the course of my employment, whether occasioned or resulting by or from the gross or other negligence of any corporation or person engaged in any manner in operating any railroad or vessel, or vehicle, or of any employee of any such corporation or person, or otherwise, and whether resulting in my death or otherwise.

This device, known as "contracting out," provided a temporary respite from tort claims, but it also served as a new target of labor and public agitation. Unfortunately, the courts were notoriously eager to uphold the status of these clauses; as late as 1900 the US Supreme Court, for instance, in *Voight v. Baltimore and Ohio Southwestern Railroad Company* ruled, in language the current justices might well endorse, that the worker

was not constrained to enter into the contract whereby the railroad company was exonerated from liability to him, but entered into the same freely and voluntarily, and obtained the benefit of it by securing his appointment as such messenger; and that such a contract did not contravene public policy.

Nevertheless, under growing public criticism and the threat of legislative interference, the courts retreated. In bits and pieces, tort relief for injured workers was restored during the second half of the nineteenth century. In Britain, implied consent was narrowly upheld by the margin of three to two in *Woodley v. Metropolitan District Railway* (1877) over the dissent of Lord Mellish, who wrote, "I think he is entitled to say, 'I know I was running a great risk, and did not like it at all, but I could not afford to give up my good place from which I get my livelihood . . .'" It was finally overturned in *Smith v. Charles Baker & Sons* (1891). The majority decision, authored by Lord Herschell, while recognizing no limitation on the terms that may be assigned by a contract, explicitly rejects the presumption that *only* contracts (or their violation) can be the basis for all subsequent outcomes:

If the employed agreed, in consideration of special remuneration, or otherwise, to work under conditions in which the care which the employer ought to bestow by providing proper machinery or otherwise, to secure the safety of the employed, was wanting, and to take the risk of their absence, he would no doubt be held to his contract, and this whether such contract were made at the inception of the service or during its continuance. But no such case is in question here. There is no evidence that any such contract was entered into. (Atiyah, 1979, p. 707)

Meanwhile, in 1880 the British Parliament passed the Employers' Liability Act which, among other things, restricted the use of the fellow servant defense. (Germany, the leader among industrial countries in this field, had already established extensive employer liability in 1873.) On the other side of the Atlantic, a wave of states, including Wisconsin, Mississippi, Texas, Iowa, Minnesota, Florida, Virginia, Arkansas, South Carolina, Missouri, North Carolina, North Dakota, Mass., Indiana, Oregon, New York, Georgia, New Mexico, Alabama, and Kansas, passed legislation outlawing no-employer-liability clauses in the 1880s and 1890s. In 1898 the Supreme Court, in *Holden v. Hardy* (upholding a mandatory eight-hour day), weighed in with a decision that fundamentally challenged the logic of implied consent and made the case for public regulation of health and safety:

The legislature has also recognized the fact, which the experience of legislators in many States has corroborated, that the proprietors of these establishments and their operatives do not stand upon an equality, and that their interests are, to a certain extent, conflicting. The former naturally desire to obtain as much labor as possible from their employees, while the latter are often induced by the fear of discharge to conform to regulations which their judgment, fairly exercised, would pronounce to be detrimental to their health or strength. In other words, the proprietors lay down the rules and the laborers are practically constrained to obey them. In such cases self-interest is often an unsafe guide, and the legislature may properly interpose its authority ... the fact that both parties are of full age, and competent to contract, does not necessarily deprive the State of the power to interfere, where the parties do not stand upon an equality, or where the public health demands that one party to the contract shall be protected against himself.

Note the intellectual confusion at the core of this opinion: because of unequal power and conflicting interests, workers are not entirely at liberty when they enter into contracts; nonetheless public regulation is upheld *despite* the fact that it overturns the worker's "self-interest." This has all the earmarks of a transitional decision: the rhetoric of freedom of contract continues to reign, but the practical content has begun to shift in favor of the view that employment relations can be coercive.

As all of this was taking place, a fundamental intellectual re-evaluation of the role of contracts was being pursued by legal theorists and economists alike. Various currents of what we now call "institutionalism" were having an impact, and even the economists who would later be known as the founders of the neoclassical school took a dim view of the earlier experiment in laissez-faire. Alfred Marshall, the foremost economic thinker and author of his time, attached little credence to the view that contracts are vehicles for free individual choice; his colleague Jevons publicly supported the regulation of working conditions, even when it might override the explicit terms of employment contracts. Jurists were also questioning the sanctity of contracts and devising alternative approaches which balanced individual volition, as embodied in contracts, against institutional constraints and public standards – "legal realism." In the end, the entire debate over whether workers had implicitly accepted the dangers of their work was rendered moot by the adoption of compulsory workers compensation in Britain (1897) and the United States in the second decade of the twentieth century.[6] By taxing firms to provide for an insurance fund for injured or deceased workers, these programs simultaneously enshrined employer liability while removing the worker's freedom of agency – in the courtroom. (I will look at the evolution of this system in the US in a later section.)

It is important to recognize the larger implications of this story. Adam Smith touted the virtues not of the world he lived in, but of a hypothetical world that would arise on the foundations of free and enforceable contracts. He persuaded a generation of British judges and parliamentarians to fashion this world by holding workers in court to whatever employment conditions they had accepted, and by refusing to adopt legislation that might interfere with this freedom of choice. This perspective spilled over to the United States, where similar arguments held sway through much of the nineteenth century. Nevertheless, this experiment led to undesirable, even outrageous, results, and public pressure to change course became overwhelming. Eventually, intellectual fashions changed; the notion that social institutions could or should be conceived simply as the products of freely entered contracts lost its grip on economics and other branches of thought. Atiyah's epitaph to this episode in legal and social history is worth quoting at some length:

It is true that in certain respects status has become more important as a source of rights and duties than it was when Maine was writing in 1861. For example, national citizenship is today a more important legal status than it was a hundred years ago when barriers to migration were few. But Maine was, anyhow, writing mainly of personal status, matters concerning family relationships ... In this sense, there has been little sign of a reversion from contract to status. It would be more accurate to say that there has been a movement from contract to administration, a movement from private to public law, a movement from bilateral to multilateral relationships, a movement from single, individualized transactions to long-term relationships. There is, however, another sense in which Maine's dictum may be taken. In so far as the incidents of a voluntarily created relationship were generally seen as the result of the parties' own intentions or wills when Maine was writing, it would be correct to say that there has been a movement away from contract and back to status in modern times. For the decline in the role of consent as a source of rights and liabilities has led to a great increase in the number of relationships in which the element of consent is largely exhausted once the relationship is created. (pp. 725–6)

The moral: the theory of compensating wage differentials is based on a model of employment relations in which workers, by agreeing to work, extend their consent to *all* the conditions offered to them. This model was tried and rejected, however, and it no longer describes the real world of employment. Once we drop the assumption that workers accept the risks they face, what basis is there for wage compensation?

Workers compensation

There are two ways workers can be compensated for risk on the job. They can receive compensation in advance (*ex ante*) for taking on the risk, before they know whether or not they will actually be hurt. They can also be compensated after the fact (*ex post*), in which case only those workers who suffered injuries or illnesses (or their estates) will receive the extra money. These two forms of compensation serve the same functions, equity and efficiency, and workers should be generally indifferent over which form is adopted. To see this more clearly, let us return to our simplified world in which workers are equivalent in all respects, labor markets are competitive, and jobs differ only with respect to the risk of an accident. The utility a worker derives from a job can be represented as

$$U = w + \pi(c + p) \tag{1}$$

where w is the wage, π is the probability of an accident, c is the monetary cost of an accident (medical expenses plus lost wages), and p is the disutility of the pain and suffering due to an accident.[7] Now suppose there are two jobs in this economy: each has a different probability of injury, but competitive labor markets require that workers be equally willing to accept either. We would then have

$$U_1 = w_1 + \pi_1(c + p)$$
$$U_2 = w_2 + \pi_2(c + p) \tag{2}$$

But, since competition requires that $U_1 = U_2$, we can set the two right-hand sides equal to one another, rearrange terms, and get

$$w_1 - w_2 = (\pi_2 - \pi_1)(c + p) \tag{3}$$

which is the basic compensating wage differential result.[8] (Note that, on the assumption that $\pi_1 > \pi_2$, the left-hand side is positive because c and p are both negative.)

Now let us introduce the possibility that workers may receive, and *know* they may receive, compensation *ex post*. If this compensation is some fraction, say δ of c, workers in the high-risk job will receive a combination of *ex ante* (wage) and *ex post* (claims benefits) such that their utility is still at the market equilibrating level

$$U_1 = w_1 + \pi_1(c + p) = w_1' + \pi_1[c(1 - \delta) + p] \tag{4}$$

where w_1' is the new wage when *ex post* benefits are anticipated. The difference between these two wages, with and without *ex post* compensation, is

$$w_1 - w_1' = \pi_1(-\delta c) \tag{5}$$

That is, the wage would fall by exactly the amount of the worker's claim, taking into account the likelihood of having an accident for which a claim would be filed. Incidentally, the payment of *ex post* compensation does not interfere with the logic of compensating differentials, since, with settlements of δc, the corresponding result to (3) is

$$w_1' - w_2' = (\pi_2 - \pi_1)[c(1 - \delta) + p] \tag{6}$$

There are two implications that can be drawn from this brief analysis. First, workers should not care whether there are arrangements for paying out benefits in the event of an accident. Each dollar workers can expect to receive in benefits (taking into account the probability of an accident) will simply be deducted from their paychecks. If they worry about surviving the financial impact of a possible future injury they can buy disability insurance with their wage premia and get equivalent coverage. Second, employers should not care about the provision of *ex post* benefits either. Whether they pay the extra wages $(w - w')$ or the extra benefits $(\pi\delta c)$ is not a matter of concern, since they are exactly the same. All of this depends, of course, on the presumption that we are talking about a *system* of wages and benefits that will be reasonably stable, so that workers can accurately anticipate their future disability benefits at the time they settle on a wage.[9]

Workers compensation is just such a system. It provides mandatory no-fault disability and death coverage for injuries and, to a lesser extent, illnesses arising on the job, financed entirely by employer contributions. To the extent that it is experience-rated, each employer's payment into the system is equal to the anticipated claims of his or her workers $(\pi\delta c)$. All of the provisions of workers compensation are well-known; in particular, workers can know with a high degree of certainty with what likelihood and to what extent they will be compensated in the event of an accident on the job. Thus the conventional economic view, predicated on the market determination of wages and working conditions, predicts that neither employers nor workers should care one way or another about the existence of the workers compensation system or the benefits it provides, so long as the benefits do not exceed the cost of an injury and the system is fully self-financed. I doubt that I will be removing much suspense by stating at this point that the history of workers compensation in the United States strongly contradicts these predictions; in fact, the struggle between labor and business interests over workers compensation is heating up even as these words are being written.

Actually, the history of workers compensation is full of surprises, not the least of which is who pushed for it and why. The toll of injury, disease, and death was enormous during the nineteenth century, as nearly every chronicler attests. This was not entirely the fault of employers, since much of the technology was new and little understood, and workers were ill-adapted to the discipline the new methods demanded. Nonetheless, employer negligence was often egregious, and odious working conditions figured at the top of virtually every working-class indictment of capitalism.[10] In this context, the refusal of the courts during the laissez-faire era to hear tort cases against employers was a deeply felt insult, and much of the energies of working-class organizations went into changing this. As we saw, by the 1870s enough progress had been made for employers to feel the need to include liability waivers in their written contracts; by the 1890s these clauses were largely disallowed, and workers were beginning to win significant awards. It was at this point, and not decades earlier when workers had no tort access at all, that the movement for workers compensation took off.[11]

It would be unduly cynical to view this movement simply as an employers' conspiracy to avoid their obligations in court. Disability was a massive problem during this period. Severely injured workers had no recourse: without a large settlement (which was still very unlikely) they were either cast out onto the streets, where they could try to survive by begging or hustling at the margins of society, or they became permanent burdens to their families. Given the high injury rate and the ineffectiveness of popularly available medical treatment, it would be no exaggeration to say that, at any one time, hundreds of thousands or even millions of people found themselves in this situation. Reform-minded activists felt that charity had proved hopelessly insufficient, and only a large-scale public program could provide the solution. Yet the good intentions of reformers would never have been enough to put workers compensation on the agenda, much less see it through to implementation in all fifty states. The decisive push came from the business community; for them workers compensation was a defensive strategy in the face of changing liability laws, less accommodating judicial interpretation, a rapid increase in the number of worker-initiated actions, and a rise in the value of awards. Interestingly, it was *opposed* by workers' representatives, who believed that additional tort reform was likely to yield more ample compensation. It should be obvious that neither business support nor worker opposition makes any sense if the market-based model of compensating wage differentials is true.

What emerged from the political tussle was a compromise typical of American social welfare legislation. The system was farmed out to the states, which could establish their own rules for eligibility and levels of compensation. In each state workers compensation was made mandatory and substituted itself for employer liability: workers were no longer free to sue for negligence, but had to accept whatever compensation the system offered them. Employers, meanwhile, were required to pay into the system, and their contributions were partially experience rated. (Full experience rating has proved difficult to implement, especially for small firms whose accident records can fluctuate wildly from one year to the next – a small numbers problem.) As for the extent of benefits, both workers and employers proved prescient: through most of the twentieth century the evidence has clearly shown that only some of the workers who ought to qualify actually receive benefits, and the benefits fall far short of meeting their direct economic costs, not to mention the less quantifiable costs of pain and reduced functioning outside of work.[12] During the later 1970s and 1980s most states liberalized their programs, but none comes close to full coverage. These reforms were generally supported by unions and opposed by employer groups, once more contrary to the orthodox economic view (Dorsey and Walzer, 1983).

During the 1990s there will be considerable pressure to cut back on workers compensation once more. Due to increasing injury rates and the skyrocketing cost of medical care, workers compensation costs nation-wide doubled (in nominal dollars) between 1984 and 1989 (Gupta, 1991). Worse, this has occurred during a period of falling profits and increasing competition for US firms. Fortunately for employers, however, each state sets its own rules; so they can be played off against each other by the threat of relocation. In addition, employer lobbyists and their political allies have been successful at turning state budget crises to their favor: since spending cuts and tax increases are part of the necessary fiscal adjustment package everywhere, and since it is barely possible to muster majorities for these unpopular measures in the legislatures, it takes only a few resolute politicians to demand workers compensation "reform" as the price of going along with a new budget. This strategy has prevailed in Maine and California this year, abetted by sympathetic Republican governors. The result will be benefits for fewer injured workers and a greater loss of living standards for those who are compensated.

Before closing the book on workers compensation, it would only be fair to mention that there are two studies that purport to show econometrically that workers compensation benefits do reduce wage payments on nearly a dollar-for-dollar basis. Dorsey and Walzer (1983) and Moore and Viscusi (1990) both use essentially the same technique: they conduct wage regressions in which both the risk of occupational injury (as assigned to each worker by his or her industry-average rate) and the level of workers compensation benefits (assigned by state, since each state offers different benefits) are included as variables. The objective is to show that workers in states with more liberal compensation receive smaller wage differentials. Both claim to have done this, subject to qualifications. Dorsey and Walzer subdivided their total sample into union and nonunion segments and studied each separately. They found a nearly perfect tradeoff between workers compensation and wage payments for nonunion workers, which they interpreted as a success for the standard economic prediction, but their unionized sample revealed not only no tradeoff between *ex post and ex ante* compensation, but no wage compensation at all. Moore and Viscusi produce an even more bizarre result: workers compensation more than pays for itself in reduced wages for risk.[13] If this were the case, the effect of the system overall would be a net reduction in total compensation to workers. (This is entirely apart from the question of foregone tort opportunities discussed above.) They recognize that this is implausible and speculate that employers nonetheless come up short because workers compensation induces workers to concoct false injury claims and stay out of work longer than necessary.[14]

These studies would appear to present us with an even more serious dilemma: not only does the history of the workers compensation system contradict economic theory; it contradicts econometric evidence as well. Fortunately (or unfortunately, depending on your perspective), these studies are seriously flawed. As we have already seen in the previous chapter, they assign risk to workers on the basis of industry averages under the expectation that they will then earn the corresponding industry-average wage premium, but this procedure is scrambled by the evidence for industry wage differentials that have nothing to do with working conditions. Thus the econometric studies of the effect of workers compensation on wages are no more reliable than similarly constructed attempts to measure wage compensation generally.

What we are left with is the main historical argument: the origins of workers compensation and the continuing struggle over the extent of its coverage are incompatible with the conventional economic model of market-determined wages and safety. The history is not at issue; it is the theory that must give way.

Not by markets alone: class conflict over occupational safety and health

By focusing on contracts between workers and firms in its analysis of occupational safety, economic theory sidesteps the other channels through which demands can be expressed, such as political and social conflict. But that is not all: conventional theory goes one step further and implies that there should not be any such conflict, because it is not in anyone's interest. This odd claim follows from the properties of compensating wage differentials outlined in chapter 2. According to the equity property, workers in dangerous jobs are no worse off than similar workers in safe jobs, provided they face the same labor market. Thus, we would not expect risk to be associated with conflict within an occupation or industry: why complain when you are fully compensated for the risks you face? Moreover, the efficiency property produced the result that neither worker nor employer would want to be regulated; neither could gain and at least one would have to lose. For a worker to demand through non-market channels that safety be improved would be like trying to regulate herself. If successful she would merely succeed in bringing about a wage reduction that would in all likelihood leave her worse off than when she started. Perhaps the only exception to this conclusion would arise if the worker were locked into a long-term wage contract, so that working conditions could be changed without affecting wages for months or years to come. Yet, as we will see, the connection between class conflict and dangerous working conditions is quite general, and not confined to unionized workers with multi-year contracts.

Reviewing the history of occupational safety and health conflicts in the United States is not like, say, surveying agrarian populism or the development of central banking. There are no more than a handful of historians who specialize in this area, and much of the relevant material emerges as a byproduct of other interests – labor movement history, public health, etc. Moreover, the studies that have been produced are, with few exceptions, narrative accounts of individual issues or episodes; no one has yet attempted a general summary of this disjointed and widely scattered literature. It is not possible, then, to "prove" the existence of general patterns in the history of occupational safety. Nevertheless, anyone who reads a reasonably broad selection of works in this area cannot fail to identify two common themes.[15]

1 Conflicts between workers and their employers over occupational

safety have been frequent and have taken a variety of forms, including strikes, sabotage, street violence, and political mobilization. Both episodes recounted in the Prologue, for instance, are about battles of this sort. The seamstresses of Triangle went on strike to protest the obvious fire hazard in their sweatshop, while the Appalachian coal miners staged wildcat walkouts and organized a massive political movement to demand cleaner air in the mines and compensation for those already victimized. Aldrich (forthcoming) has told this story for the railroad industry, a horrendously dangerous employer during its first century and the scene of many dramatic showdowns between labor and capital. One historical study supplies a statistical test of the salience of safety as a mobilizing issue: Foster (1984), in his study of violent conflict involving the Western Federation of Miners during the first years of the twentieth century, regressed strikes on various explanatory factors including labor turnover and working conditions linked to silicosis, the debilitating miner's lung disease. He found that a term interacting these two was significantly positive, suggesting that workers who faced this hazard and knew about it (were more likely to quit) were also more likely to be involved in the rugged industrial battles of that era.

The connection between risk and protest continues to the present. Robinson (1988), for instance, finds that nonunion workers in more dangerous jobs, just like workers receiving low wages, are more likely to favor unionization, although this relationship is far stronger for women than men.[16] In fact, depending on the sample employed, between 41 percent and 48 percent of workers in hazardous, nonunionized jobs would prefer to be represented by a union, suggesting that there are a considerable number of firms in which an absolute majority of workers favors unionization but is unable to obtain it due, presumably, to management resistance. Meanwhile, bitter struggles over health and safety conditions appear frequently in the newspapers, with datelines from Austin, Minnesota (meatpacking: Hormel) to Geismar, Louisiana (chemicals: BASF). Tactics include sit-ins, "corporate campaigns" to pressure the firm's directors and creditors, consumer boycotts, and coalitions with environmental and other community groups.

2 Workers respond normatively to risks on the job. They appear to have a tolerance level for danger which, if exceeded, becomes the basis for a morally freighted form of conflict. This in turn lends particular drama to struggles over safety: firms that violate worker norms are viewed not simply as adversaries, but as vicious exploiters. Typical in this regard were the campaigns waged by the Western Federation of Miners at the turn of the century; for them, life-threatening conditions in the mines

were acts of war to be opposed by all available means. Industrial disasters in all industries are usually followed by public rituals of accusation: mass funerals and legal action against the corporate officers viewed as responsible are common, as we saw in the Triangle fire and, more recently, in the Imperial Foods fire.

To raise the issue of norms, however, is to suggest that it is not the level of risk *per se* that is at issue in labor struggles, but the level of risk relative to workers' standards and expectations. This is an important distinction, because it indicates that risk does not always lead to conflict.

Consider the relationship between risk and the demand for safety across industries. As figure 4.1 shows, agriculture ranks fourth among the major industries in its occupational fatality rate, behind mining, transportation, and construction, but far ahead of manufacturing, which has been the site of much of the dispute over working conditions. This category includes forestry and fishing as well as agriculture proper, but a detailed look at state fatality rates indicates that tending the land easily holds its own as a cause of death: South Dakota and Nebraska rank third and fifth respectively in this industrial classification, and neither is known for its timber or seafaring trades. According to the National Safety Council, approximately 1,500 farmers and farm hands die each year, mostly from accidents involving equipment, silage, or large animals. Of these, about 300 are children under the age of 16. The single greatest cause of death is tractor rollovers, which are thought to claim about a fourth of all lives lost on the farm.[17] Many of these deaths are preventable; one safety engineer claims that simply by attaching guards to the sides of these enormous factories on wheels the death rate could be cut in half. Yet there is no outcry among organizations representing farmers over this slaughter. On the contrary, farmers have lobbied for decades to *prevent* OSHA and other agencies from regulating farm safety. They have succeeded in exempting the vast majority of farms from OSHA's purview, while resisting another intrusion on their freedom to crush, electrocute, and suffocate themselves and their children. In 1989 less than $1 million was spent to promote safety in agriculture, and, according to one specialist in agricultural medicine quoted by *The Wall Street Journal*, "We [in the United States] really have no policy whatsoever" (Ingersoll, 1989).

A second example permeates all industries: death on the road. Motor vehicle accidents constitute by far the single greatest cause of occupational fatalities nationwide, as figure 4.2 shows. Yet rarely is there any protest among truckers or delivery drivers over their daily bout with fate. (The Domino's Pizza controversy cited in chapter 1 is an exception to the rule.) OSHA has avoided the issues that would have to be addressed

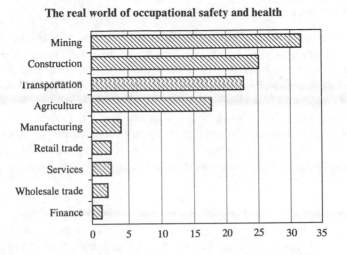

Figure 4.1 Fatal injuries by major industry (rate per 100,000 workers)

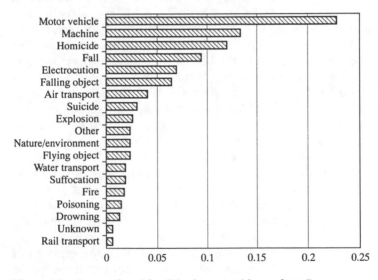

Figure 4.2 Occupational fatalities by cause (share of total)

to reduce this carnage: the ergonomic features of cars and trucks, long, continuous hours on the road, tight deadlines. In this case, however, the cause is not timidity or business pressure; workers simply have not demanded it.

A third setting for the disjunction between risk and response has to do with the nature of the workplace itself: workers in cooperative enterprises appear to accept much higher levels of risk than workers in conventional firms. This conclusion emerges from an interesting study by Grunberg (1991). Taking advantage of the relatively large number of firms in the Pacific coast plywood industry that are worker-owned and -operated, he assembled matched pairs of cooperative and conventional firms similar in all respects except for ownership. He then compared their injury rates under the initial hypothesis that coops would prove safer. In fact, what he learned was the opposite: "co-operators typically have injury statistics that are four to six times greater than those in conventional mills ... [and] even the best co-operative's performance falls short of the worst of the conventional mills" (p. 109). In addition, he found coop injury rates to be much more procyclical; that is, they went up sharply during good economic times and down during periods of slow or negative growth.

Why? One explanation is that coop members appear to be more willing than ordinary employees to report "mysterious" ailments that require time away from work. They are subject to less monitoring, and, in any event, their enterprises are unlikely to discipline them for abusing medical leave and workers compensation policies. As one safety director at a coop mill said, "It doesn't take much of an excuse for members to take a day off" (p. 116).[18] If this were the whole story, the injury statistics would be unreliable, and we would not know whether coop jobs really are more dangerous. But Grunberg took an additional step: he distributed surveys to workers at both types of firms asking how many accidents they had witnessed occurring to *other* workers. Here too, without any incentive to misreport, coop workers indicated that their injury rates were higher. Grunberg accepted the plausibility of this result, noting that few coops had a full-time safety official or in-plant safety program. But now the question becomes, why should plywood coops do less for safety when their members have the ability to establish standards just as strong as those at conventional firms? One potential explanation, consistent with the other examples cited above, is that there is something about working in a cooperative that induces workers to accept less safety – to relax their safety norms. In the following chapter I will explore this possibility in greater detail; for now the plywood study can stand for the more general point that it is not risk as such that promotes worker dissatisfaction (and the propensity for conflict) but risk compared to the relevant norm.

Together, these two principles, the normative response to risk and the diverse forms taken by struggles over occupational safety and health, summarize what we know about the history and current status of these conflicts. The first of these contradicts the depiction of safety as a direct component of worker utility and provides a better framework for understanding both the moralistic tone of worker resistance to excessive risk and, ironically, its absence in situations that would otherwise seem to call for it. The second principle, that workers have many avenues by which to press their claims for better working conditions, undermincs the conventional economic view that the determination of risk and wages takes place only through the mechanism of contracts established in the marketplace. Of course, *any* general pattern of worker resistance to high levels of risk is incompatible with the view that workers receive adequate (strong) wage compensation in these instances, but, in a sense, the real issue is even deeper than this. In light of the evidence for the role of conflict, large and small, in determining the safety of work, how can we attach any credibility to the claim – central to the economic edificc – that the level of safety is the result of an *agreement* between workers and employers?

Government regulation

As we saw in chapter 2, according to economic theory, regulations which make workplaces safer than they would otherwise be cannot make anyone better off but will make at least one party, if not both, worse off. Workers would be foolish to demand such regulations; surely they should anticipate that employers will simply take away their compensating wage differentials, and, because of the uniquely efficient character of a market equilibrium, they may be forced to take away even more to stay in business. This depiction of the standard economic argument may seem too crude to do justice to the perspective of most economists, yet the orthodox literature is peppered with claims that this is in fact how things work. Perhaps the most astonishing example is provided by Smith (1976) in an article intended for distribution to policy-makers in Washington. In "A Safety Fable," Smith, a Cornell professor who is one of the country's foremost labor economists, tells the story of a mythical kingdom in which the gnomes toil away for their employers, the trolls. It happens that the gnomes become upset with the safety conditions of their work, and they petition the king, complaining that the trolls seem concerned only with profits, not with the health and well-being of gnome-dom. The king is something of a softy and goes along with the request, mandating stiff standards for occupational safety. The result is a disaster. Many goods that the gnomes used to buy have become too expensive, since prices must be raised to cover the cost of improving safety. In addition, the thick-witted gnomes (for that is their nature) failed to anticipate that their wages would be cut, since less money was now required to induce them to accept work. As the extent of their predicament slowly dawned, the gnomes returned to the palace, repented their previous ignorance, and beseeched the king to rescind his edicts. They had learned the hard way: gnomes may lack foresight, but the market is always right.

In the real world, those who have had the ill fortune to hold the dirtiest and most dangerous jobs have fought continuously for public regulation of safety. They have done this not because they were slow to grasp economic theory, as Smith would have it, but because this has consistently been the most effective strategy for improving the lot of the worst-off workers. Indeed, the evidence for this proposition is so massive, wide-ranging, and unimpeachable that it raises questions concerning which sector of society should be viewed as gnomeskulls.[19]

Direct government regulation of working conditions has its roots in the reaction to the strong interpretations of contract law promulgated in the early nineteenth century. Edwin Chadwick, whose advocacy of employer liability was recounted earlier in this chapter, was also a proponent of factory inspection as early as 1833 (Atiyah, 1979). His crusade resulted in the Factory Acts of the 1840s and 1850s, reforms which were subsequently copied by other industrializing countries. In this country, Massachusetts became the first state to initiate factory inspection in 1867; ten years later specific safety features were mandated by law. Other states adopted similar legislation until, by the end of the century, most had at least a rudimentary system of regulation (Ashford, 1976).[20] Since it was a pioneer in technology, economic development, and grisly accidents putting workers and riders alike at great risk, the railroad industry was singled out for special attention. State and federal laws mandated specific safety features, such as automatic couplers, under pressure from labor and other progressive activists (Aldrich, 1993). In general, unions preferred industry-wide regulation to company-by-company combat, since this avoided the problem that safety reform in a single company could put that firm and its workers at a competitive disadvantage. Overall, these regulations did in fact improve conditions. Aldrich documents a drastic improvement in railroad safety in response to mandated changes in technology, although a reorganization of work along the lines of greater adherence to rules and standards may have been even more effective. Factory legislation led to the adoption of guards on dangerous machinery, better training and fewer hours for workers doing the most hazardous work, and a reduction in fire hazards, among other improvements.

Nevertheless, safety conditions remained onerous in many workplaces, and the increasing use of toxic chemicals after the Second World War added a new dimension to the problem. After many years of agitation, occupational health and safety regulations were substantially upgraded by the passage of the Coal Mine Health and Safety Act in 1969 (passed, as usual, after a gruesome mine disaster) and the Occupational Safety and Health Act in 1970. The second of these in particular, with its wide mandate and controversial regulations, plays an important role in theoretical as well as policy disputes over the provision of safe working conditions. Those in the economics profession who, like Robert Smith, are prominent defenders of wage compensation theory are also prominent critics of OSHA.[21] This is understandable, since, as we have seen, if market incentives are already appropriate (or nearly so) for the efficient allocation of safety, regulatory intervention will most likely result in deadweight loss. Moreover – and this is a twist – OSHA regulations have frequently been subjected to benefit–cost analysis employing value-of-life measures derived from hedonic wage studies. Of course, the numbers generated by these studies only make sense if workers receive full wage compensation, in which case regulation is unnecessary. The circularity of this argument does not seem to have been recognized; on the contrary, the results of wage regressions are used to "prove" that economic theory is correct and regulation irrational.

In principle it should be possible to study directly whether wage reductions have offset improved safety conditions attributable to OSHA. In practice, however, this is difficult because, as the final chapter will demonstrate, it is not clear whether and to what extent OSHA has actually resulted in reduced injury, illness or death.

It is possible to show that individual industries, such as coal mining, have become measurably safer as a result of regulation, but at this level there is no way to unravel the various factors that affect wages. If coal miners earned more after the passage of the Coal Mine Safety Act than before, how do we know whether this is due to a reduction in compensating differentials, or to some other factor, such as the victory of reformers in the Mine Workers Union that occurred at the same time? Since we cannot put together a convincing statistical case one way or the other, why not accept the judgment of both workers and employers in cases like these, from the beginning of the industrial revolution to the present time? Both sides, in their words and actions, express the view that the net effect of safety regulation is to benefit the workforce at the expense of business profits.

Collective bargaining

In the legendary 1930s film "Harvey," Jimmy Stewart plays an inebriated but genial man of leisure whose inseparable friend is the title character. Harvey happens to be an invisible rabbit about six feet tall, friendly, and a constant source of good advice. Most of Stewart's friends think his obsession with an invisible playmate is more than a little daft, and the viewer is inclined to agree until details accumulate to suggest otherwise. (If nothing else, the film implies that believing in something nice that is not there is better than believing in something bad that is.) Compensating wage differentials have much in common with Stewart's silent companion: economists believe in them, they are nice (efficient and fair), and, above all, they are invisible. True, some economists claim to have found signs that wage compensation really exists, coefficients on risk in wage regressions, but Jimmy Stewart could also point to glasses of beer that were mysteriously drained at his table in the neighborhood bar. We have already seen that the statistical evidence for wage differentials is highly unreliable, yet all is not yet lost. In one critical venue wage compensation, if it exists, will be fully visible to all: collective bargaining. Here workers and employers do not act "as if" particular tradeoffs apply to the combination of wages and working conditions; these items are spelled out explicitly in contracts that can fill up hundreds of pages of fine print. If economic theory is right and workers really have a Harvey by their side, this is where we will find him.

To begin with, it should be noted that unions must overcome many obstacles to raise and successfully bargain over safety issues. First, focusing on working conditions places a larger burden on union officials than does a preoccupation with wages and benefits. Staff requirements are greater, since the problems involve a high level of technical detail, and challenging management on safety can result in an increased flow of grievances, straining the union's resources and shifting the locus of activity to the shop floor (a political problem for some full-time union officials).[22] Second, health and safety issues, because of their ongoing nature, create friction between the union and management, undermining a relationship most unions would choose to promote. Third, unions may increase their own liability for dangerous working conditions if they bargain over them. Drapkin and Davis (1981) cite several cases in which workers sued their unions for inadequate enforcement of health and safety provisions. These have come not under the general "duty of fair representation" mandated by the National Labor Relations Act, but (ironically) under common tort law. Drapkin and Davis believe this problem can be solved by a combination of careful contract language, responsible contract performance, and legislative action to reduce union liability for occupational accidents and illnesses. Finally, the overall structure of labor relations established in the United States at the conclusion of World War II – sometimes referred to as the "Labor Accord" – entailed an exchange of management concessions to unions (wages and union security) in return for, among other commitments, union acceptance of management's right to manage.[23] Insofar as union health and safety demands necessarily impinge on this commitment, union leaders will be reluctant to pursue them.

In spite of these difficulties, unions often assign a high priority to safety issues. Most union contracts contain language pertaining to health and safety concerns (this will be considered in greater detail shortly), and the trend has been for a greater percentage of strikes to involve safety disputes (Gersuny, 1981). Kochan, Dyer, and Lipsky (1977, p. 15) present survey evidence indicating that, while few union officials regard health and safety issues as more important than competing concerns, a majority give them overall parity. Moreover, there is at least some evidence that, when unions fail to give sufficient attention to health and safety, rank-and-file pressure for change increases. As we saw in the Prologue, the movement which ultimately swept away the corrupt leadership of the United Mine Workers was spearheaded by health and safety activists, and Noble (1986) adds the Teamsters (whose reformers have since taken power) to that list as well. Thus a fair generalization may be that union officials are torn between their personal and political interest in advancing safety issues on the one hand, and the structural limits to this type of union activity on the other.

If unions are committed to addressing the safety concerns of their members, there are three general ways they can go about this. First, they can address working conditions directly by including contract language which mandates specific policies and standards to be followed by management. Second, they can follow the indirect path of setting up special committees or other structures through which workers can influence company policy on the shop floor. Finally, they can *accept* dangerous conditions in return for hazard pay – that is, explicitly bargain over compensating differentials. In each case the use of collective bargaining to achieve these goals is supported by existing labor law; Gersuny (1981) cites an NLRB ruling that "safety provisions constitute an essential part of the employees' terms and conditions of employment, and, as such, are a mandatory subject of bargaining" (p. 109).[24] Table 4.1 clearly shows that there has been an increasing tendency for unions to pursue safety in one manner or another.

Increasingly, contracts are incorporating a "right-to-know" clause: the firm is obligated to inform workers of all relevant safety hazards, including the potential effects of chemicals used in the workplace. This trend has been furthered by state laws mandating employer disclosure and a federal regulation promulgated under OSHA requiring that workers be informed of the presence of substances known to cause

Table 4.1 *Percentage of contracts containing selected health and safety clauses, 1954–1981*

Year	Any clause	Firm to take measures	Firm to provide safety equipment	Health and safety committees
1954	60%	38%	27%	18%
1961	65	34	32	28
1966	62	35	28	29
1971	65	42	32	31
1976	82	50	36	39
1981	82	50	42	43

Source: OTA (1985, p. 315).

cancer. How well these stipulations are adhered to in practice, of course, is another matter. Nonetheless, access to information, especially when combined with adequate technical expertise, can be a powerful weapon in the hands of a union that is genuinely committed to promoting health and safety. This observation will play a critical role in the alternative program described in chapter 6.

The next level of protection is provided when unions move from the right to know to the right to say "no" – the right to refuse hazardous work. An ambiguous formulation of this right already appeared in US labor law as early as 1947; section 502 of the Taft–Hartley Act states: "Nothing in this Act shall be construed to require an individual employee to render labor or service without his consent ... nor shall the quitting of labor by any employee or employees in good faith because of abnormally dangerous conditions for work at the place of employment ... be deemed a strike under this Act" (Gersuny, 1981, p. 109). But subsequent court decisions have greatly restricted the scope of this provision, and workers who refuse hazardous work outside the scope of specific contract provisions do so at their own risk. Union negotiators have attempted to provide protection for the right-to-refuse, and one study found 371 agreements covering nearly two million workers in which this right was stipulated under certain conditions. In an additional 42 agreements the union was authorized to refuse work on behalf of its members in the face of an excessive level of risk (BLS, 1976). In practice, however, the right to refuse is exercised only in extreme circumstances and therefore currently represents a targeted response to acute problems, rather than a general health and safety strategy. (In chapter 6 I will consider an approach combining wage compensation and right-to-refuse.)

Grievance mechanisms, as indicated earlier in this section, are not employed as frequently over health and safety issues as worker interest would appear to require. Possible explanations could include the unwillingness of unions to pursue grievances of this sort (for the reasons discussed earlier), the time lag in grievance resolution compared to the highly transient nature of many workplace hazards, and the personal risk of being written up, transferred, or discharged borne by workers who initiate grievances, particularly without union support.

Finally, many unionized firms have instituted joint labor–management safety committees. An extensive study of committees of this type was undertaken by Kochan, Dyer, and Lipsky (1977), who found them to be most effective when addressing areas of common interest. Although there are many potential safety improvements that both labor and management would welcome, and there is therefore much to be accomplished by committees based on a cooperative model, there remain other issues in which conflicts of interest are irreconcilable. These cases – which are central to the concerns of this book – cannot be resolved administratively on the side of greater safety without overcoming management opposition. It is a central conclusion of Kochan *et al.* that using joint safety committees to address this second type of issue is not only ineffective, it also undermines the voluntary cooperation necessary to bring about improvement in the areas of common interest. In their view, joint safety committees are an alternative to collective bargaining, not an extension of it:

the parties must be concerned about buffering the joint committee process from the polemical pressures that surround contract negotiations. The union must guard carefully against allowing the committee to be used as a political stepping-stone for aspirants to higher union office. It must also guard against using safety and health committees as another forum for extending the collective-bargaining process. Although only a few examples of this were found in the cases studied in the sample, such behavior is usually fatal to the committees because of management's fear that the safety committees could simply turn out to be a forum for union harassment, with no benefits accruing to management, and that some encroachment on management prerogatives might occur. (p. 83)

The conclusion would appear to be that labor–management safety committees have useful functions to perform, but determining the provision of *costly* health and safety conditions is not one of them.

These, then, are the mechanisms through which collective bargaining can sometimes influence working conditions directly: embedding detailed standards in the contract, the right to know about hazards, the right to refuse dangerous work, the opportunity to grieve poor working conditions, and the empaneling of health and safety committees. Although each has its limitations, together they can have an impact, provided the union has sufficient bargaining power – an increasingly unlikely circumstance. Of course, workers may eschew any direct attempt to alter conditions and negotiate hazard pay instead; what evidence indicates that they do this?

Two surveys of collective bargaining agreements come to similar conclusions: hazard pay is negotiated by unions but appears far less often than the other mechanisms described above. Each year the Bureau of National Affairs publishes their own study of collective bargaining; their 1992 report, based on a sample of 400 contracts, found these results: 88 percent of the contracts had some form of safety or health language, 60 percent called on firms to take general measures to bring about safe conditions, 50 percent established joint safety committees, 43 percent specified safety equipment to be furnished, but only 13 percent provided hazard pay for *any* workers in the bargaining unit (BNA, 1992). The findings of a second group, led by Mark Erenburg of the Industrial Relations Center at Cleveland State University, were similar: in a sample of 500 contracts, 63 percent had safety language, 24 percent established joint committees, 22 percent enabled workers to grieve unsafe conditions, 15 percent created a right to refuse unsafe work, and only 12 percent created hazard pay (Erenburg, 1989). In both studies, hazard pay was the least common form of collective bargaining over safety; moreover, given the relative frequency of different contract mechanisms, there are probably few if any workers for whom compensating pay differentials are the *only* recourse.

These results, which accord well with the popular view of the role of safety in labor relations, are in striking contrast to the views held by most economists. Recall, for instance, the discussion of union preferences in chapter 2, during the theoretical analysis of compensating wage differentials. The economists surveyed disagreed over which workers' preferences will be represented when unions negotiate over wages and working conditions – young or old, marginal or average – but they all proceeded on the assumption that unions make this tradeoff in some fashion. Yet, as we have already noted, collective bargaining is public and can be studied directly, so we can *see* whether unions really do this. Many volumes have been written on union strategies for health and safety, contract clauses have been tabulated, and major agreements have been analyzed for their strengths and weaknesses, and here is the verdict: compensating wage differentials play at most a minor role in union objectives; bargaining over safety takes the form of seeking a reduction in risk, not more money for assuming it. Where explicit compensation does exist, as in street-level versus upper-story building construction, it is seen as the exception rather than the rule. Of course, a stubborn believer in economic orthodoxy can always reply that wage compensation might be detected in a properly conducted wage regression using a unionized sample, but then we are back once more in the world of invisible rabbits, from which the observation of collective bargaining agreements was intended to set us free.

Internal labor markets and the distribution of risk

The average worker changes jobs often over the course of his or her lifetime, but this does not necessarily mean combing the want ads or setting up employment interviews. A large percentage of these shifts take place within the same enterprise, through transfers, promotions, or other movements up or across the firm's job structure. Unlike the labor markets that govern "outside" job movement, the mechanisms that govern who gets which job inside the firm are not directly responsive to the forces of supply and demand. Economists call them "internal labor markets," but this phrase has more to do with the similarity of function than of process.

The classic study of internal labor markets is Doeringer and Piore (1971). They describe the essential conundrum faced by personnel managers: on the one hand, the wage for each job should be largely comparable to the wages earned by workers in similar jobs in other companies. Workers, after all, compare their treatment across workplaces and would be concerned if, say, clerical supervisors at one insurance company earned substantially more than at another. In addition, personnel administrators are generally of the opinion that the wages set in the labor market are reasonably fair and appropriate, so that the best guide to setting wages for jobs filled within the firm are the wages that would be paid if the job were opened up to outside applicants; and these are presumably the wages paid for similar work by other employers. But there is another constraint: workers within the firm will certainly compare their treatment, and, if it looks as though a particular classification is being favored unjustly, dissension is sure to arise. Alas for those who must devise wage schedules, these two criteria often diverge, and the choice must be made between equity across employers and equity across job titles.

Under these circumstances, personnel officers look to systems that have an aura of fairness about them, so that the inevitable conflicts over pay and status can be muted. The most widely used recourse is job evaluation, a procedure in which professional evaluators – often brought in from the outside as consultants – assign points to each position in the job structure, based on the characteristics of the work, its effect on the work process, the demands made on those who perform it, etc. One thing these evaluators look for is undesirable working conditions, including the risk of injury or illness; workers exposed to them get more points, and more points lead to higher wages. Here, perhaps, is the first visible evidence of compensating wage differentials, although, ironically, it occurs not in the *real* labor market of supply and demand, but in the simulated market operated by administrators within large firms whose purpose is to mollify and motivate their workforce.

There are fundamental difficulties with job evaluation as a basis for compensating differentials, however. First among them is the disturbing fact that it is not workers, but evaluators who make the detailed decisions about how much different working conditions are worth. True, evaluators work for personnel administrators, and these officials must pay heed to the feelings of the workforce, but this is a tenuous connection with many fragile links. Second, the evaluations include a great many factors, and the weights given to particular items may go unnoticed. Third, evaluators view themselves as members of a profession and often resent efforts by outsiders to influence their work, even if the effect of those interventions would be to give voice to the values of the workers being evaluated. Finally, creating a patina of fairness in job evaluation is not the only concern of administrators; they must also keep an eye on the job structure of comparable firms and provide motivation for lower-level workers to try to move up.

But the biggest problem with compensation-through-evaluation is that it usually fails to show up in practice: in most firms the lowest-paid jobs are the most dangerous, and the highest-paid are the safest. How can this be when evaluators give points for exposure to risk? Mendeloff (1979) cites Strauss and Sayles (1967), who point out:

According to worker logic, clean jobs are better than dirty ones. A new man should start at the bottom, at the hardest, dirtiest, least desirable job. Then, as he acquires seniority, he should move up to better, easier, higher-paying jobs. But this is contradictory to the logic of job evaluation, which says that more points should be given for hard work and dirty conditions. Yet people will resist being "promoted" into a higher-paying job that has lower status. In practice, this problem is solved by giving very low point values to the factors of jobs so that there will be little invidious comparison. (p. 567)

What is particularly interesting for our purposes is that at the heart of this conflict lies the unwillingness of workers to accept working conditions and wage compensation as a single, offsetting package. Moreover, there is one general reason why the differentials that seem to reside in evaluations fail to show up in practice: evaluations are often simply ignored. Management frequently hires the evaluators, reads their reports, and then do what they had planned on from the start. The failure to implement job evaluations, in fact, is at the basis of the controversy over comparable worth. Groups representing women workers have filed discrimination suits against employers pointing to the discrepancy between women's point totals in the evaluations and the numbers that appear in their paychecks.

Even if job evaluation were a widespread source of wage compensation, this fact would not rescue economic theories of market performance, nor the doubtful foundations of hedonic wage analysis. But despite the best efforts of professional evaluators, compensation is as scarce within firms as it is between them.

Workers, employers, and compensating differentials: a dance without dancers

W. Kip Viscusi has authored (or co-authored) four lucid, well-argued books which make the case for market-generated wage compensation, *Employment Hazards: An Investigation of Market Performance* (1979), *Risk by Choice* (1983), *Compensation Mechanisms for Job Risks: Wages, Workers Compensation, and Product Liability* (with Michael Moore, 1990), and *Fatal Tradeoffs: Public and Private Responsibilities for Risk* (1992). He offers many pages of analysis concerning the factors that ought to influence the decisions of workers and employers alike, and the reader is left with an image of people on both sides of the labor market making wage/risk tradeoffs that is drawn with such clarity that it is easy to forget that they are only the products of an author's powers of speculation. But what about *real* workers and employers? Do workers actually weigh wages and working conditions when deciding what job to accept, and do employers factor in the wage costs of permitting work to be dangerous? This is an empirical question. There has been little work on the matter, but I will review some of the available evidence.

It is not necessary for the theory of wage compensation that workers be aware of its existence, yet it would help. After all, if risk and pay are tradeoffs in the labor market, and if workers express their preferences by choosing among different types of jobs, it would stand to reason that many workers on many occasions would have a glimmer of this. Yet the historical and sociological literature that describes workers' response to risk fails to disclose this. The most detailed treatment of workers' attitudes on these matters is *Workers at Risk* by Dorothy Nelkin and Michael S. Brown (1984). They interviewed in great detail 75 workers whose jobs put them in potential contact with hazardous chemicals; the book consists of representative comments grouped under different topics. A close reading will reveal no workers who forthrightly recognized the existence of wage compensation, but several who doubted its existence. One theme that runs through the book is the workers' judgment that firms put effort into safety if they are "good," but they withhold it if they are interested only in profits. Typical is one informant who says:

If it's going to cost them money, they don't care ... I think they'd go to any extreme to save money, regardless of whose life it endangered ... They will put up the facade of being safety-conscious, but the reality of working conditions – that is of little concern, because fixing them would reduce profits ... They just want their profit and nothing else matters. (pp. 63–4)

Of course, if firms had to pay higher wages in lieu of cleaning up the workplace, these claims would be false. In one instance, a worker openly considered the possibility of wage compensation and then rejected it:

We're paid quite well, compared to other workers. But I don't think that there's any amount of money you could pay a worker who will contract asbestosis or lung cancer. I don't think any worker would accept a job if he were told that was the price ... Money is essential for survival on this earth, but it's self-defeating when you put your money above your health ... We could force a company to give bonuses for dangerous work. If they did that, at least we'd go in with our eyes open. Now they pay a fellow who's not exposed to anything the same amount they pay the fellow who's exposed to everything terrible. (pp. 164–5)

Once more, the inability of workers to recognize wage compensation is not, by itself, conclusive evidence that it does not occur, since it would be possible for workers to make wage/risk tradeoffs subconsciously to the same effect. The same cannot be said for employer perceptions. For the theory to correspond even loosely to reality, it is essential that those who determine safety conditions be aware that there exists a relationship between wages and risk; otherwise the incentives implied by wage premia would be nonexistent and market-determined outcomes would lose the properties derived in chapter 2. To put it differently, workers can choose jobs in their sleep, so to speak, since this is a strictly passive act: take this one or that one. Firms, as described in the theory, must know what they are doing, since they *actively* set working conditions in light of anticipated labor market consequences.

Unfortunately for partisans of orthodox economic theory, we are better informed about the beliefs of managers than of workers. There is a simple reason for this: professional safety managers, the people who actually make these decisions within the corporate bureaucracy, undergo formal training in the tools of their trade. They learn how to adjust equipment, run safety awareness programs, and gather and analyze accident statistics. They also learn how to measure the economic cost of injuries and illnesses to the firm, so that they can determine whether their work contributes to its overall profitability. The textbooks in safety management, then, constitute a written record of the criteria used by businesses in setting safety standards; it is here we would expect to find an explicit awareness of the wage/risk linkage.[25]

The undisputed founder of modern safety management was H. H. Heinrich. Heinrich was a follower of Frederick Taylor and attempted to apply the theory of scientific management to workplace health and safety. Studying accidents with the same devotion to detail that Taylor had applied to the motions of the human body in production, Heinrich developed both general guidelines for reducing injuries and highly elaborate procedures for monitoring and analyzing a firm's safety record. This work was summarized in his textbook for safety management, *Industrial Accident Prevention: A Safety Management Approach*, which has been in print for more than 50 years. Petersen and Roos, writing in the introduction to the most recent edition of this book (1980), say that it "was and still is the basis for almost everything that has been done in industrial safety programming from the date it was written until today" (p. viii). Among his other achievements, Heinrich also pioneered cost accounting for accidents; he is the author of the famous (among safety managers) four-to-one rule: the hidden costs of an accident are, on average, four times the immediate costs of direct medical attention by the firm and compensation through workers compensation or a parallel system. Here is his complete list of hidden costs, to be ferreted out by the dedicated safety analyst:

1 Cost of lost time of injured employee.
2 Cost of lost time by other employees who stop work.
3 Cost of time lost by foremen, supervisors or other executives.
4 Cost of time spent on the case by first-aid attendant and hospital department staff when not paid for by the insurance carrier.
5 Cost due to damage to the machine, tools, or other property or to the spoilage of material.
6 Incidental cost due to interference with production, failure to fill orders on time, loss of bonuses, payments of forfeits, and other similar causes.
7 Cost to employer under employee welfare and benefit systems.
8 Cost to employer in continuing the wages of the injured employee in full, after his or her return – even though the services of the employee

(who is not yet fully recovered) may for a time be worth only about half of their normal value.

9 Cost due to the loss of profit on the injured employee's productivity and on idle machines.

10 Cost that occurs in consequence of the excitement or weakened morale due to the accident.

11 Overhead cost per injured employee – the expense of light, heat, rent, and other such items, which continues while the injured employee is a nonproducer (pp. 82–3).

To show these guidelines in action, Heinrich describes six instances in which he provided a full cost accounting to firms for on-the-job injuries. What is most interesting to us, of course, is not what he says but what he does not: *nowhere does Heinrich mention compensating wage differentials as a cost firms must consider when deciding how much to invest in safety.* This point is so important that its implications are worth considering one more time. According to economic theory, firms actively take wage compensation into account when deciding on working conditions; this is the meaning of the employer cost minimization embodied in equation (2) of chapter 2. In practice they would rely on their expert staff to gather the relevant information. Heinrich is laying down the rules for assigning costs to injury rates, but he does not incorporate any wage effects at all.

Subsequent books are just as silent on the concept of a wage/risk tradeoff. DeReamer (1958) – this is quite a name for an industrial safety expert – begins his work by proselytizing for safety; for him this means, among other things, convincing businesses that it is in their interest to keep accidents down. He stresses that accidents imply a breakdown in production, and "anything that slows production and increases cost should be the concern of all supervisors" (p. 11). DeReamer also brings up the importance of goodwill in the surrounding community and general ethical considerations, but, like Heinrich, he has nothing to say about increased wages. Similarly with Blake (1963) and Gilmore (1970): whole chapters are devoted to identifying accident costs but not a word to wage premia.

By themselves, these books provide disquieting evidence against the existence of wage compensation for risk. Still, they might be understood as products of a period in which the classical, Smithian theory was in eclipse. Recall that, by the turn of the twentieth century, intellectual currents had drifted away from the view that markets automatically compensate workers for risk on the job, and this was even true for the economic giants of that period, such as Marshall and Jevons. There is little positive mention of Smith's theory in the economic literature between 1900 and 1970: having ceased believing in it, most economists stopped thinking about it. But it reemerged, as we saw, with the modern renaissance in mathematical theory, since the case for it in a system of equations seems far more compelling than in a study of actual behavior and institutions. During the 1970s a growing body of work argued that Smith was right all along and that, properly measured, wage compensation should be recorded as real. Perhaps, then, the most recent textbooks in safety management will reflect this new orthodoxy and alert corporate officials to the wage effects of a substandard safety record.

No such luck. The books published since the study by Thaler and Rosen (1976) are just as oblivious to the possibility of wage compensation as their predecessors. For a representative sample, see Follman (1978), the revision of Heinrich by Heinrich, Petersen, and Roos (1980), and, especially, Grimaldi and Simonds (1984). Simonds is the most prominent figure in this field since Heinrich, making particular contributions to accident costing. His is the only book, for example, that employs an explicit benefit–cost framework for analyzing safety programs, and his theory and case studies are nothing if not meticulous. Moreover, the entire approach bespeaks a broad familiarity with economic reasoning and literature, and by the time this book was written the body of research on compensating wage differentials was large and highly visible. But his work, like the others, makes no mention of it. Finally, Biancardi (1987) contributes a chapter entitled "How to Consider Cost–Benefit Analysis in Occupational Safety Practice." It contains a review of the relevant literature on the direct and indirect costs of accidents from Heinrich to the present, and, once more, compensating wage differentials are not even considered.

This section, and those before it in this chapter, have gone to great lengths to demonstrate the obvious: neither the Triangle workers, nor the coal miners, nor the millions of other workers facing dangerous working conditions have received compensation they would regard as adequate, nor do employers consider wage compensation when deciding whether safety is worth it (to them). Neither group, moreover, acts as if the properties of Smithian compensation – equity and efficiency – are real; they struggle over *ex post* compensation, government regulation, and safety clauses in contracts that would serve no purpose in a Smithian world. The fact that this evidence is widely accessible to the general public and largely low-tech (subjective and impressionistic, not statistically rigorous) does not invalidate its message: workers in dangerous jobs are worse off for that fact, and there is no reason to believe that safety conditions in a market economy are set at their most efficient level.

5   Alternative theories of risk, wages, and the labor market

Settled habitation is a relatively recent phenomenon in human history. For countless millennia before the discovery of agriculture, societies moved constantly in pursuit of their sources of food and fuel. When the local supply of wild fruits and cereals was exhausted or when game migrated to other regions, our ancestors would pack up and find a new, more productive home. Even today there are a few cultures that rely on regular migration; because of their ancient pedigree they are sometimes called "primitive," but it is important to remember that they are the ones who have continued to survive. The *really* primitive cultures never made it: presumably they remained stuck to a familiar spot in the forest or a drying oasis, unwilling to venture into the unknown even as supplies grew increasingly scarce.

If the preceding chapter is correct, economics is at risk of meeting a similar fate. Its well-crafted models of rational choice in a world of free, enforceable contracts have become unproductive, and continued growth depends on the flexibility to strike out in new directions. Fortunately, the theoretical environments that can prove hospitable to migrating economists already exist, and the journey is not too far. This chapter will discuss alternative approaches to the analysis of risk, the structure of labor markets, and the nature of the employment relationship. In the end, I will try to show that, together, they can largely explain the broad historical and institutional facts of risk, reward, and conflict.

New perspectives on risk perception

Let us begin with the depiction of worker choice in conventional economic theory.[1] Workers are like powerful computers with a vast database of safety information. For each potential risk on their jobs, they calculate the probability of an accident or illness and its associated cost. Then they discount depending on how far into the future the event may take place, and they sum all the products

$$E(r) = \sum \pi_i c_i, \quad \sum_i \pi_i \leq 1 \tag{1}$$

where $E(r)$ is the expected disutility of risk, π_i are the probabilities of each of the i possible events, and c_i is the cost (monetary and otherwise) if the event occurs.[2] The result of this computation is that, in the aggregate, workers correctly anticipate the number of injuries and illnesses and their total cost. This will be the same number and severity predicted by equally rational and well-informed employers, and it will also be validated in published health and safety statistics, if they are accurate. It makes matters much simpler to suppose that workers think this way, but do they? Do we?

A good starting point would be the notion of bounded rationality, pioneered by Nobel laureate Herbert Simon. Human beings are *not* powerful computers. They have many remarkable talents, but the systematic calculation of a vast number of variables is not one of them. Simon's insight is that, in order to make the best of their limitations, people reduce the complexity of the problems they face by imposing simple rules of thumb. Instead of strictly maximizing over their options, for instance, they tend to "satisfice" by choosing the first option which gives them a targeted level of results – that is, they settle for "good enough" rather than holding out for the very best, as economic theory often requires. In fact, the implications of bounded rationality are significant for many areas of economic research, including not only utility theory but the analysis of organizational structure and behavior – Simon's specialty.

Here we are concerned with the application of bounded rationality to risk perception. Immediately, we can see from equation (1) that our initial model of risk evaluation is too demanding for any mortal to live up to. In most work situations there are likely to be a vast number of potential risks, more than it would be possible to identify and calculate. Individuals must *choose* which ones they will take into account and discard the rest. However this is done, some risks, the ones that are ignored, must effectively carry a zero weight. Most students of risk analysis agree that the prime candidates for nonrecognition are extremely low probability events. As reasonable as this seems from the vantage point of individual decision-making, it is fraught with significance for occupational safety and health, since many of the risks imposed by modern work methods are highly improbable for any given worker, but likely for the workforce as a whole. It is not unusual, for instance, to find discussions of hazardous chemicals whose use may result in an extra ten or twenty fatalities per year – out of the hundreds of thousands or even millions of workers exposed to them. To the extent that workers screen out these risks, however, the market mechanism is rendered inoperable.

On the other hand, the filtering process of bounded rationality can lead to workers *overweighting* low probability events. This paradoxical result follows from the fact that the few such events not discarded will stand out in a reduced field of vision. Suppose, for example, that workers pay attention to the slim but catastrophic possibility of contracting lung cancer from airborne benzene. If as a result of bounded rationality this is one of only a half dozen or so job characteristics they register, they are likely to attach even more importance to this one risk than it deserves.[3]

Another way to reduce the complexity of decision-making is to ignore consequences beyond a certain point in the future – in other words, convenient myopia. This would have seriously distorting consequences for worker perception of health risks in particular, since many occupational diseases have long latency periods. There is some evidence in Nelkin and Brown (1984) that workers react myopically to the threat of future health impairment.

Finally, people often reduce the complexities of life by setting up a system of mental categories. Events are assigned to their proper box, and decisions are made on a category-by-category basis; this is sometimes referred to as a "mental accounting system," analogous to the financial accounting systems used by firms to keep track of the many sums that flow in and out each day. The logic of this procedure is clear: by subdividing large questions into many smaller ones and tackling them individually, we can manage more pieces of information. The price we pay is also apparent: such a system impedes analysis and decision-making *between* accounts. This has particular significance for workers' response to dangerous work. Conventional economic theory predicts that workers would trade off greater risk in return for greater money income, but if the mental accounting model is correct, workers might weigh risks against one another, incomes against one another, but not income against risk. Economists might regard this behavior as irrational, but only because they assume that we humans actually have the capacity to compute equation (1) *and* incorporate the result in an even more complicated formula for total utility.

There is considerable empirical evidence that supports the notion that

people actively evaluate risks but balk at making risk/income comparisons. Economists and other policy analysts, for example, have
repeatedly attempted to measure communities' willingness to pay for
having a hazardous facility placed in their midst, generally to no avail.[4]
In one typical enterprise, Kunreuther, Desvousges, and Slovic polled
two samples, one drawn nationally, the other taken from the state of
Nevada, to see whether they would be willing to accept a radioactive
waste repository in their locality in exchange for substantial monetary
compensation. Nearly three-quarters of both samples refused to make
the tradeoff; astonishingly, it made no (statistically significant) difference
for this result whether the proposed payments were tripled or even
quintupled. Geographical proximity to the hypothetical site had a small
effect on the national sample (the closer, the less willing to trade off),
but none for the Nevadans, who have actually given serious thought to
the issue since their state has been tentatively selected as the site for just
such a facility. Here, then, is a different way to look at the spotty
evidence for compensating differentials examined in chapter 3: instead
of poor evidence for Smithian wage compensation, it may be good
evidence for mental accounting and an unwillingness to trade off
income for safety. From a theoretical standpoint, the practice of
keeping separate mental accounts challenges the fundamental premise
of hedonic analysis, the notion that all outcomes of a choice are
evaluated using the same hedonic calculus. Without this presumption,
there is no basis for apportioning an individual's willingness to pay or
be paid for a complex good (such as employment) into its constituent
elements (such as safety).

An entirely different approach to the problem of risk evaluation
emerged in response to the growing literature on utility "paradoxes,"
especially the phenomenon of *preference reversal*. It was found that
individuals might prefer A to B when starting with A, but B to A when
starting with B, even when both A and B are well-known and easily
understood. Clearly, individuals respond differently to gaining and losing
identical amounts (of money or whatever is being measured), but this
insight implies a very different type of analysis from that contained in
equation (1). Up to this point, we have assumed that utility calculations
are in absolute terms; that is, people evaluate their situation by
considering their absolute level of income, their absolute level of safety,
and so on. This is the meaning implicit in the algebra of the utility
function. But psychologists and others associated with *prospect theory*
claim that our true calculations are conducted relative to a reference
point – a standard for comparison often related to the initial status quo
(Kahneman and Tversky, 1979). The question is not, what is our level of

utility *per se*, but our utility relative to this standard. One way to illustrate the difference is to revamp equation (1) in light of prospect theory

$$V(r) = v(V - \sum_i \pi_i c_i), \quad \sum_i \pi_i \leq 1$$
$$= v[V - E(r)] \tag{2}$$

where $V(r)$ is the individual's relative valuation, v is a function that treats positive and negative quantities asymmetrically (such as, "multiply a positive quantity by 1 and a negative quantity by 2"), and V is the value accorded to the reference point. Only in a formulation such as this is it possible to portray decision-makers as analyzing their gains or losses as they look forward to a potential change in their situation – hence the label "prospect theory." Note, moreover, that relative rather than absolute evaluations generally require much less information, since the same probabilities and costs that enter into both the initial and the prospective outcomes effectively cancel out, leaving only the differences for consideration. This economizing on information makes sense in light of bounded rationality.[5]

If this view of our mental processes is accurate – and it is supported by a fair amount of experimental evidence as well as simple introspection – it challenges the logical foundations of wage compensation theory, at least as depicted in chapter 2. Workers will generally have different reference points for safety (and wages as well), making economy-wide or even firm-wide utility comparisons impossible despite the assumption of identical preferences (the same v and c_i from equation (2)). In fact, even if the reference points are identical, valuations will differ because some workers will be above and others below this point, and potential gains are not viewed the same as losses. Thus, none of the three propositions of chapter 2 will hold: (1) The allocation of wages and safety need not be efficient, since there is no uniquely preferred distribution (potential preference reversal). (2) Workers may not be equally well off in absolute terms if they base their choices on relative changes in utility à la prospect theory; some employers, for example, can cater to workers at low initial positions, providing they can accept the turnover that may result when workers adjust their reference points to their new status. (3) Clearly the hedonic property is lost, since it is explicitly based on the notion that workers perform absolute, not relative, evaluations of safety and income. This much is easy to determine; what is far more complex is the problem of explaining just where these reference points come from – why they might differ from job to job, for example, and how they might change over time. I will return to these questions later in the chapter as more pieces in the puzzle become available.

Up to this point we have considered what might be called "computational" wrinkles, the different techniques people adopt when performing a global maximization over all possible options and outcomes is inappropriate. Now let us turn more directly to the *attitudes* toward risk and reward that also conflict with the conventional theory of preference and choice. The first of these has become a staple of the risk perception literature since it was introduced by Chauncey Starr more than twenty years ago (Starr, 1969): people tend to fear more acutely those risks they believe are beyond their control. It is not uncommon to find people who smoke cigarettes, drive at top speed on the highway without using a seatbelt, and engage in other high-risk behavior who will nevertheless be outraged by the prospect of a nearby incinerator that might increase their risk of serious illness by a mere fraction of a percent. This attitude is often labelled "irrational" by specialists in the field (Camerer and Kunreuther, 1989, p. 578 call it "emotional"), but it makes sense if we shift our criteria from "utility" to "fairness." Lung cancer is just as deadly whether it results from one's own lifestyle or from breathing polluted air, but why should this be the only concern? Just as death itself may be regarded quite differently depending on its cause (chapter 3), the "why" is as important as the "what" in evaluating any health impairment. Once again we face the conflict between Bentham and Kant, between the view that health is an end in itself versus the claim that each individual has a *right* to choose his or her own level of risk. It could be argued, of course, that people are often irrational in their choice of which imposed risks to take a stand over, but the proper comparison is between similarly involuntary risks, not risks overall.

It is possible to take this line of inquiry one step further. Among involuntary risks, people tend to be most distressed by those which result from the self-seeking behavior of others. Consider the example of alar, a chemical sprayed on apples to prevent their dropping prematurely. When public interest groups protested this spraying a few years ago, there was a nationwide crisis in the apple industry. Consumers refused to buy tainted fruit, and growers lost millions of dollars. Defenders of the chemical derided what they saw as public ignorance; people willingly accept, they said, much greater risk in their daily life than that posed by alar. This comparison misses the point, of course, since it fails to distinguish between voluntary and involuntary risk, but consumers were also responding to their perception that they were being exploited by growers willing to cut corners to make a profit. Had the episode been framed simply as one of ignorance – "gosh, we didn't know it was that bad" – there would have been less concern. The very effort to defend the spraying, however, was perceived as further proof that the growers cared more for their bank accounts than the public welfare; consumers were being "violated." The use of alar was now no longer, if it ever was, a health crisis; it was a *moral* crisis of greed and victimization. And, while the public might have been mistaken about the technical issues involved, its moral judgment was correct in Kantian terms: prospering at the expense of the larger community is wrong even if the public cost is not "large."

Clearly, the same story can be told of occupational safety and health, and the history of conflict over working conditions is replete with examples in which ethical questions far overshadow narrowly utilitarian ones. This distinction is the key to our finding that many of the most dangerous occupational hazards are *not* opposed by workers – the risks involved in driving, in operating a farm, and in working for cooperative enterprises. In all of these cases, workers either believe the risks they face to be under their own control and/or for their own benefit. (That this may be objectively false in the case of driving does not lessen the force of the perception.) Nelkin and Brown (1984) also found many expressions of the role of personal autonomy and its violation among workers exposed to toxic chemicals; for example:

The supervisors [on my job] are researchers who have complete autonomy, and some of them feel that regulations are laughable. You know, some of these professors, I honestly believe, are willing to die for their experiments. They are more interested in not disrupting the time schedule of their experiments than in the safety of the workers who fix the stuff. (p. 55)

All the company cares about is bucks. They don't care about the people like me who make their bucks. They use people; they kill people. There's nine or 10 people who've died there, and they didn't give one rat about it. All they care about is bucks. (p. 65)

Occupational safety remains a public health problem, of course, but it is also a human rights problem.

A second problem, genuinely on the border line between rationality and irrationality, is that of *cognitive dissonance*. This phenomenon, familiar to psychologists for generations, induces people to ignore or even alter their perceptions in order to avoid unpleasant conflicts with their maintained beliefs. Lovers often do not want to know the shortcomings of their loved ones; patriots would rather not hear about the misdeeds of the governments to which they pledge their allegiance;

and workers may systematically filter out disconcerting facts about the risks they face at work. A simple model will make the issues more explicit.[6] Extending the risk valuation process in equation (1), we can write

$$U(p) = \sum [(\pi_i - p_i\delta_i)\,c_i + p_i\,d_i], \quad p = \{1, 0\} \tag{3}$$

where p_i represents the choice whether to perceive the ith risk (yes = 1, no = 0), δ_i is the reduction in the likelihood of i occurring if the risk is perceived, and d_i is the cost of perceiving i due to cognitive dissonance. If the vector p is chosen to maximize (3), the first order conditions will be

$$|p_i\,d_i| \leq |p_i\,\delta_i\,c_i| \tag{4}$$

or, for those risks that will be perceived

$$|d_i| \leq |\delta_i c_i|, \quad p_i = 1 \tag{5}$$

(These take the form of inequality constraints, since the variable p is discontinuous.) What is happening? An individual faces a set of risks whose initial probabilities and costs (if they eventuate) are given. By perceiving any particular risk, she can reduce its likelihood by δ but incurs the psychic cost of d. So we ask the question, when can she increase her utility by permitting herself to consider a risk? Answer: when the cost due to cognitive dissonance is less than the benefit resulting from the greater ability to avoid the adverse outcome. This seems rather obvious, but (5) makes it perfectly clear which variables govern the willingness to perceive in this simple model. Greater susceptibility to cognitive dissonance (d) is a negative; the greater cost of a harm occurring (c) and the greater opportunity to change the likelihood of harm (δ) are positives. We could make one additional assumption: suppose, as seems plausible, that c and d are proportional: we dread thinking about something to the extent that it would be unpleasant if it actually happened. Then the entire decision of what to perceive would depend on the single variable δ, the individual's ability to translate awareness into change – her power in the situation, if you will. This insight can help illuminate many real-world instances of cognitive dissonance.

Many of the classic experiments in cognitive dissonance involved the unwillingness of subjects to entertain information that called into question decisions they had made in the past. According to equation (5), this should be a fertile approach, since the ability to alter the "like-lihood" of the past is zero. In fact, given any level of d, the only psychic justification for awareness would be the expectation that similar decisions might have to be made in the future for which the information could come in handy. Experimenters, however, frequently concocted exotic situations that subjects would regard as one-of-a-kind in order to get their results. Closer to our concern in this book, workers would have little incentive to dwell on the hazards of their work if they thought them to be beyond their control. This provides an unexpected counterweight to the argument about voluntary versus involuntary risk above. On the one hand, both theory and evidence indicate that workers are more likely to be concerned about risks they view as imposed without their participation; on the other hand, precisely because these risks may be uncontrollable they may prefer to disregard them. For now, let us simply admit this as a quandary; I will return to it at the end of the chapter and propose a resolution.

A final point that ought to be made about attitudes toward risk does not have an academic literature to support it, but occurs nonetheless in real life. Many men view physical risk-taking as a sign of manhood, and concern about health and safety as effeminate, "sissy" behavior. I encountered this variation on machismo many years ago when I worked a collection route for the US Postal Service. Post office regulations stipulated that no parcel could weigh more than 70 pounds, but clearly some were much heavier. I brought the issue up to my union representative, but he simply took this as a sign that I lacked the manly stature of a true postal worker. (What is so macho, I thought, about a slipped disk? Talk about Mr. Zip ...) Of course, there *is* something heroic about taking risks for the benefit of the community, if – and only if – those risks are truly necessary. Perhaps the inability of many male workers, such as offshore oil-riggers, long distance truck drivers, and others in risk-glorifying occupations, to see the line that separates saviors from suckers owes more than a bit to cognitive dissonance.

Labor market segmentation

The view that the labor market, rather than being a single, competitive entity, is composed of many layers, with workers in each more-or-less trapped for life, has its roots in the nineteenth century, but its modern form is strikingly different. The older version of segmentation theory was based on workers' personal characteristics: some were just more reliable or productive by nature and could command higher wages and better conditions; others were the living detritus of industrial society. We have already seen this prejudice in Mill (see chapter 2); consider now this turn-of-the-century explanation by Marshall (1948) of why we fail to find compensating wage differentials:

the disagreeableness of work seems to have very little effect in raising wages, if it is of such a kind that it can be done by those whose industrial abilities are of a very low order. For the progress of science has kept alive many people who are unfit for any but the lowest grade of work. They compete eagerly for the comparatively small quantity of work for which they are fitted, and in their urgent need they think almost exclusively of the wages they can earn: they cannot afford to pay much attention to incidental discomforts, and indeed the influence of their surroundings has prepared many of them to regard the dirtiness of an occupation as an evil of but minor importance.

Hence arises the paradoxical result that the dirtiness of some occupations is a cause of the lowness of the wages earned in them. For employers find that this dirtiness adds much to the wages they would have to pay to get the work done by skilled men of high character working with improved appliances; and so they often adhere to old methods which require only unskilled workers of but indifferent character, and who can be hired for low (Time–) wages, because they are not worth much to any employer. (p. 558)

It seems as though we might somehow be able to translate this analysis into modern, noninvidious language and preserve the plausible kernel of the argument, but how?

The modern revival of segmentation theory is based on a single, giant leap: instead of looking to the individual characteristics of workers as the cause of labor market layering, economists have turned to the different ways workers are treated by the firm. The classic work of Doeringer and Piore (1971), for instance, focuses on the presence or absence of internal labor markets, paths of upward mobility within the firm. These are important not only for their direct effects, but also because workers will be treated differently if the firm regards them as candidates for future promotion. More time and effort will be invested in their training, and this in turn will provide them with a measure of bargaining power, since it will now be costly for the firm if they choose to leave. Moreover, as the relationship between worker and employer becomes more permanent, the "love it or leave it" method of resolving disputes is replaced by a measure of due process – grievance mechanisms, arbitration boards, and other restrictions on arbitrary management power. Instead of good workers and bad workers, then, we have good jobs ("primary") and bad jobs ("secondary").[7] The persistence of segmentation results from the unfortunate fact that there are not enough good jobs to go around.[8]

From this perspective, the association between workers' characteristics, such as their race and gender, and their position within the occupational hierarchy stems not from their individual or group qualities, but from discriminatory sorting. Women are paid less, for instance, not because they are less productive (as human capital theory implies), but because sexist hiring practices disproportionately consign them to dead-end, secondary jobs. There are many unresolved problems with segmentation theory, not least of which is why there should be a large gap rather than a smooth continuum between labor markets, but it is attracting increasing attention among economists in Europe and Japan as well as the US.

Everyone knows that some jobs pay better than others, but on what basis can we determine whether there is really an underlying process of segmentation taking place? In a useful survey of the empirical literature, Dickens and Lang (1991) suggest that two hypotheses ought to be tested: (1) that a two-sector model of the economy with the broad characteristics of primary and secondary employment offers a better account of the data than a one-sector model, and (2) that workers who would like to be employed in primary jobs are stuck in the secondary sector instead. They claim to have done this in a series of studies which show that the first criterion is met overwhelmingly using a procedure that guards against the circular logic of classifying workers as secondary because (for whatever reason) they have low wages and little return to human capital, and then using this to demonstrate that this sorting "explains" the data; while the second is met by demonstrating that workers (such as blacks) with no objective reason for preferring secondary work are nonetheless employed in those jobs, earning wages below what one would expect for their personal characteristics. In addition, they point out that the literature on interindustry wage differentials, which was briefly discussed in chapter 3, also supports the notion of segmentation: the wage determination mechanism differs greatly across industries, and workers in lower-wage industries appear to be stuck in bad jobs. Finally, there have been numerous case studies (some mentioned by Dickens and Lang) which describe phenomena that can only be called segmentation: the role of luck in getting a choice job, the radical differences in technology, productivity, and the structure of work between different industries, and the perceptions of both workers and managers that segmentation actually happens.

Recalling that Mill claimed that only the most favored workers would receive compensation for assuming risk, we can consider the two published attempts to combine labor market segmentation and hedonic wage regression. The first of these was conducted by Robinson (1984), who began with the hypothesis that the labor force is segmented into "noncompeting groups" of undetermined number. Wage differentials will exist for variations in occupational risk within these groups but not between them. His prediction was that regressions that fully specify group status would yield positive differentials; otherwise they would vary insignificantly from zero (offsetting effects) or even be negative if noncompeting effects predominated. Believing group status to be related to occupation, he regressed wages against BLS data on three-digit occupational (not industry) injury rates and other variables and found, as expected, a significantly negative coefficient on risk – compensation in reverse. He concluded: "The average risk level of the occupation serves as a proxy for an entire constellation of job characteristics which are not caught by the variables describing the individual workers within those occupations" (p. 11). He then proceeded to examine wage differentials in industry cross-sections, finding weak evidence for positive differentials (interpreted as offsetting effects), which became negative when industry averages of unionization, race, sex, and other worker characteristics were added as independent variables. This suggested to him that industry-based distinctions fail to sort out the underlying labor market segments. Here his analysis ended, leaving him with the negative conclusion that studies which fail to incorporate the effects of segmentation will not identify compensating differentials. This is rather too much to infer, however, since, as we have seen, the combination of measurement error in the BLS data (it leaves out most illnesses) and the absence of important explanatory variables – particularly industry affiliation itself – renders his results unreliable. Moreover, his study could not distinguish between segmentation and other potentially confounding effects of occupation, such as unmeasured skills or other productive attributes.

More recently, Graham and Shakow (1990) tried to demonstrate the effects of segmentation directly. They divided the 1977 University of Michigan Quality of Employment Survey sample into three groups, primary, secondary, and unknown, based on such factors as job skills, the opportunity for promotion, unionization, race and gender, and (principally) wage income. Discarding the middle group, they ran separate tests on the primary and secondary samples. To measure the extent of dangerous working conditions, they used two sources, fifteen working conditions variables from the QES and the Society of Actuaries data on occupational mortality described in chapter 3. Each needs a bit of clarification: the QES variables were condensed into two "composite" measures using principal component analysis, while the actuarial data were adjusted by controlling for occupational averages in racial composition and workers' physical condition.[9] Graham and Shakow then made two predictions: first, that the secondary workers would face more hazardous working conditions than the primary workers, and, second, that they would receive less compensation for it. The first was tested by a simple comparison of means, the averages for each group of the different risk variables. Here they found what they expected, that in nearly all respects primary work is safer – corroborating, incidentally, the information presented in chapter 1 concerning the distribution of risk across the workforce. The second prediction was tested by running separate wage regressions for primary and secondary workers; here the evidence was only partially supportive. Both groups received statistically significant wage compensation for risk as measured by the first principal component, although the amount was two-and-a-half times as large for the primary segment; neither received significant compensation for the second component, with the sign of the coefficient positive for primary workers, negative for secondary. (Actuarial risk was not employed in the regressions.) They took this as modest support for the hypothesis of segmentation, since it appeared that compensation was greater for primary workers, while secondary workers might even face an element of negative compensation (the sweatshop effect).

This study is suggestive, but falls short of supplying reliable evidence. First, the use of actuarial data raises the ghosts considered in chapter 3, and the adjustments of Graham and Shakow are not sufficient to dispel them. Waiters have diminished longevity because of the social position of people who do this work for a living; controlling for race and a few physical characteristics may capture some of this, but it is unlikely to capture most of the relevant personal differences. Since this measurement was not included in the wage regressions, however, it is not the source of the most troublesome difficulties. More serious is the bias introduced by sorting workers into primary and secondary largely by income. There will be a tendency for primary workers to *appear* to receive more income in exchange for risk since they receive more income generally. This is not offset by the fact that they have safer jobs on average (as Graham and Shakow argue), since the amount of wage compensation measured in their study falls far short of explaining the large difference in total wages.[10] Worse yet, the dependent variable in their regressions is the actual wage, not its logarithm, so that the coefficient on risk measures total dollars rather than a percentage of the worker's income. The difference in compensation they report on the first principal component is approximately consistent with equal percentage compensation. If we assume that people value money in relative rather than absolute terms (10 percent of my income means about as much to me as 10 percent of yours means to you) they may have actually disconfirmed their second hypothesis.

The overriding problem, however, is theoretical, not empirical: why should we expect differences in wage compensation *within* labor market segments? According to the theory, primary workers are better off generally; they have higher wages *and* better working conditions. Studies which lump all workers together will tend to underestimate whatever wage compensation for risk exists, because the positive relationship between wages and safety *between* segments will offset the supposedly negative relationship *within* segments and be falsely attributed to worker preferences. Thus the prediction of segmentation theory is that dividing samples into primary and secondary pools and then testing each separately should increase compensation in *both* groups. Indeed – and this is the key point – there is nothing in labor market segmentation *per se* which challenges the logic of compensation for risk. Employers still supply workers with wages and working conditions, and they must still take into consideration worker preferences between these two. If by switching a sum of money out of wage compensation and improving safety, or *vice versa*, they can increase worker satisfaction at no cost to themselves, why wouldn't they do so? Analytically, each segment could be viewed as its own mini-economy, representable by the model of wage compensation presented in chapter 2. We might decry the injustice of making one whole category of workers better off than another, but within each group the same three properties of efficiency, equity, and hedonic imputation would still apply. Empirical researchers would have to take pains to control for segmentation, but they should otherwise expect to see robust wage compensation.

There is, actually, one sense in which labor market segmentation might alter compensation for risk: wages in the primary sector are not set according to supply and demand in the market (since there are more workers who want these jobs than there are openings for them), but according to an institutional process of rule-setting and negotiation loosely denoted by the phrase "internal labor markets." A more precise account of this process may suggest either greater compensation or less, but this analysis must wait for yet more theoretical ingredients to be added to the stew.

Efficiency wage theory

Let us return once more to the two worlds of occupational safety and health – the world of conflict, regulation, fairness and unfairness as seen by the general public and that of compensating wage differentials, efficient and equitable, as seen by most economists. Perhaps the fault line that separates these two views more decisively than any other is this issue of unemployment. For critics of safety based on pure employer discretion, the fundamental problem is that workers are rendered vulnerable by the fear of losing their jobs, and, in the absence of regulation, this prevents them from demanding and achieving safe working conditions. This was apparent in the passage from John Stuart Mill criticizing Adam Smith which was cited in chapter 2; it is also implicit in Marx' writings on factory conditions, although, as we have seen, he did not employ it to challenge directly the doctrine of compensating differentials. Modern writers outside the mainstream of the economics profession never fail to raise the issue of unemployment; for recent examples see Ashford (1976), Glyde (1984), the report of the Office of Technology Assessment (1985), and Noble (1986). Typical is Ashford, who underlines the importance of potential job loss by pointing out:

Job security, a dominant real-world concern of working people, has no place in this abstract [labor market-clearing] model. Recent findings, however, indicate that job loss ranks as the third most serious form of stress which people experience during their lives, surpassed only by death of a loved one and the stress associated with family breakup and divorce . . . . Working people faced with the prospect of serious economic harm in the event of job loss are willing to tolerate a too heavy burden of workplace hazard rather than "rock the boat." (p. 353)[11]

Workers themselves often argue this way. There are many references to the deterrent effect of unemployment in Nelkin and Brown (1984); one example is the chemical operator at a food processing plant who bluntly asserts, "You never balance the wage against the risk; you balance the wage against the alternative. And the alternative is starving when you're put in this situation. That's what's so phony about this cost/benefit analysis" (p. 91).

Astonishing as it may seem, economists do not even try to counter this argument: *there is no mention of involuntary unemployment in any of the conventional economic literature on compensating wage differentials.* This is apparent, for example, even in the policy-oriented writings of Smith (1976), Viscusi (1983), and Zeckhauser and Nichols (1978). In fact, every formal model of compensating wage differentials which has appeared within the past twenty years implicitly assumes full employment; this is enshrined in the assumption that employers must satisfy the market-determined level of worker utility.[12] Although noneconomists can only marvel at what appears to be an act of collective self-delusion, there is a fairly simple explanation for it: until recently, there was no satisfactory account of involuntary unemployment in micro-economic theory. (Even today, many conservative economists argue that involuntary *anything* is an oxymoron in a market economy.) Fortunately, however, acceptable models of unemployment, consistent with rational behavior by both workers and firms, now abound in the literature. I will turn to perhaps the most widely accepted of these, efficiency wage theory.[13]

Like most ideas in economics, efficiency wage theory has its roots in the classics. The term itself originated with Alfred Marshall, who noted in his *Principles* (1948) that the productivity of work, figured apart from its application to varying stocks of capital and other factors, may differ among individuals and entire populations. These differences will, he argued, call forth differences in wages such that it is not the actual wage which will be equalized for labor of a particular type (such as stitching garments), but the "efficiency wage" – the actual wage adjusted for differences in work efficiency.[14] In this view, then, otherwise unexplained differences in wages can be attributed to differences in worker "efficiency." The reverse causation was proposed by Leibenstein (1957), who observed that malnutrition can affect output in societies characterized by widespread subsistence incomes. Better paid workers will be better fed and therefore more productive. It was in a formalization of this second approach that Stiglitz (1976) reintroduced the phrase "efficiency wages," but now attached to wages that *produce* a given level of efficiency.

A second path to this concept begins even earlier with Marx. He distinguished between "labor power," the potential ability to perform work, and "labor," the work actually performed. Employers hire the first, but they require the second. Thus they must engage in every stratagem known to management science to motivate, cajole, or threaten workers to yield up their labor. Here lies the essential distinction between the market, that "Eden of the rights of man" in which labor power is purchased, and the domain of production, characterized by chicanery and outright coercion. But what weapons does the employer have to make workers work harder than they would choose on their own? Under particularly repressive regimes, the power of the state, with its police and dungeons, can be used to enforce work discipline; this has been the case under such disparate orders as the USSR under Stalin (where failure to fulfil the economic plan was a crime against the state), South Africa under apartheid, and the death squad dictatorships on the outposts of the "free world." In general, however, employers cannot count on this type of assistance, and capitalists must also be aware that the guns trained on workers today could be turned on them tomorrow. Under liberal regimes the most serious reprisal for unsatisfactory work is dismissal. If there were actually full employment in the economy, of course, this threat would lose much of its force, since dismissed workers could simply take another job at the going wage, but Marx hypothesized that there would always be a pool of unemployed workers – the "reserve army of the proletariat" – so that almost any job would be viewed as a valuable commodity. In truth, Marx was not very clear on the forces that would govern the extent of unemployment; at times he saw it as the result of insufficient investment (due to lack of profits) relative to the expansion of the labor force; at others it appeared as the strategic ploy of the capitalist class as a whole, acting on their own or through the instrumentality of a subservient state. What was never pinned down was the incentive that individual capitalists would have to sustain the reserve army, since the existence of involuntary unemployment means that at least some employers are paying higher wages than they have to.

The solution was postponed for a century; then Gintis (1976) published the first model of Marxian unemployment consistent with rational choice on all sides. In outline, it goes like this: the employer loses money directly by raising wages but gains money indirectly by making it more costly for the worker to be fired, which in turn increases work discipline and output. Thus wages are raised until the marginal cost of doing so exactly equals the marginal benefit from greater discipline. This profit-max-imizing wage will necessarily be higher than the market-clearing wage (otherwise, as we have seen, dismissal is costless); when all employers act this way simultaneously, the result is involuntary unemployment. There is no need to invoke worker ignorance or capitalist conspiracy; every-one's behavior is strictly rational and fully informed.

This Marxian model is evidently a variety of efficiency wage theory, since it provides an explanation for why it might be profitable to pay out more money to workers than the bare minimum, but there are other approaches. Higher wages may reduce worker turnover, for example, with savings for firms that employ on-the-job training, or it may improve the employer's applicant pool by attracting the best-qualified workers. It may also operate directly on morale: if workers believe they are being treated more fairly they are likely to volunteer a greater level of commitment to the job. Perhaps all of these are true to some extent, but for the sake of simplicity I will stick to the simple model of labor discipline attributable to Marx (via Gintis).[15]

We are now in a position to ask whether workers will receive compensating wage differentials in the presence of unemployment. The following model suggests some surprising answers.[16] As in chapter 2 we will assume that all workers are identical in both preferences and abilities, while firms differ only in their costs of providing safety. Workers have three things to consider about any job – wages, working conditions, and how hard they will be working. Call these w, s, and i for wage, safety, and the intensity of work respectively

$$u = u(w, s, i) \quad u_w > 0, u_{ww} < 0, u_s > 0, u_{ss} < 0, u_i < 0, u_{ii} < 0,$$
$$u_{ws} = u_{wi} = u_{si} = 0 \tag{6}$$

Now assume that the monitoring of effort is imprecise and that dismissal is the only incentive mechanism available to the employer. The probability π that the worker will be dismissed is then a function of work intensity

$$\pi = \pi(i) \quad \pi_i < 0, \pi_{ii} > 0 \tag{7}$$

In a one-period model the worker maximizes expected total (on and off the job) utility by choosing a level of intensity according to the program

$$\max U = \pi(i)v + (1 - \pi)u(w, s, i) \tag{8}$$

where v is the worker's level of well-being if dismissed. Workers cannot control w, s, or v, but they can control i. Holding v constant, their optimal level of intensity can be expressed as a function of w and s

$$i = g(w, s, v) \quad g_w > 0, g_s > 0, g_v < 0 \tag{9}$$

(We can also assume the "normal" properties of diminishing marginal returns to w and s.)

Now to the employer. Let us suppose the employer knows equation (9) for each worker and can therefore calculate the effects of changes in wages and working conditions with perfect accuracy. This equation then becomes the constraint in the profit-maximization function, replacing $u = u_0$ as in equation (2) of chapter 2. Assuming, for the time being, that the firm is not concerned with varying its level of employment, this function is

$$\max \Pi = f(i) - (w + cs) + \lambda[i - g(w, s, v)] \quad f_i > 0, f_{ii} < 0 \tag{10}$$

where f is a production function in i, c the constant unit cost of providing safety, and the price of the good being produced is normalized to equal 1.

First-order conditions are

$$\Pi_\lambda = i - g\,(w, s, v) = 0 \tag{11a}$$
$$\Pi_i = f_i + \lambda = 0 \tag{11b}$$
$$\Pi_w = -1 - \lambda g_w = 0 \tag{11c}$$
$$\Pi_s = -c - \lambda g_s = 0 \tag{11d}$$

Dividing (11c) by (11d) we get

$$\frac{1}{c} = \frac{g_w}{g_s} \tag{12}$$

This is an interesting result. It states that when both the worker and the employer are acting in their best interest, a situation will occur in which the ratio of the marginal costs of supplying wages and safety (1 and c) will equal the ratio of their marginal contributions to worker intensity and therefore output (g_w and g_s). This is an efficiency result comparable to the one obtained in chapter 2; it is not possible to reallocate the employer's spending between wages and safety in such a way that workers will be more committed to the job. But that is not all. By examining the comparative static properties of (11) we can find out what happens when either of the parameters beyond the control of the parties, c and v, changes. Without going through the derivations (which can be found in Dorman [1991b], cited earlier), these are

$$\frac{dw}{dc} > 0 \tag{13a}$$
$$\frac{ds}{dc} < 0 \tag{13b}$$
$$\frac{di}{dc} < 0 \tag{13c}$$
$$\frac{dw}{dv} > 0 \tag{13d}$$
$$\frac{ds}{dv} > 0 \tag{13e}$$
$$\frac{di}{dv} < 0 \tag{13f}$$

Note (13a) and (13b) in particular. The second says that if the cost of providing safety increases the firm will provide less safety, but the first says that it will also increase wages. Thus workers in industries with high safety costs will receive more money in return for worse working conditions – compensating wage differentials.

If we were to stop here we might conclude that Adam Smith's theory works as well under efficiency wages as it does under supply-and-demand, and that unemployment, at least as it is generated by an efficiency wage process, does not interfere with wage compensation. But it is not so simple. In the model presented in chapter 2 we knew that all workers received the same level of utility; $u = u_0$. Here, however, the constraint specifies only that workers select their optimum level of intensity, whatever it might be – and it might be different for different workers. It is possible, then, that workers might receive unequal levels of utility from their jobs even though wage compensation exists and is efficient.

To determine whether this is the case we need some way to identify worker utility in this model. Fortunately, it can be shown (although I will not do so here) that, for any level of i, w, and s satisfying equation (9) and provided that v is held constant, the worker's optimal intensity and the utility derived from the job (including the disutility of intensity) are positively related; whenever one is higher, so is the other.[17] This gives us a way to check on the equity property of wage compensation. Returning to the comparative statics, we can see from (13c) that equilibrium intensity falls when the cost of safety rises; this means that workers in unsafe jobs are, in fact, worse off. In other words, they get wage compensation for greater risk, but not enough. How can we understand this result? Recall that in the efficiency wage story, firms "purchase" work effort by providing more desirable wages and working conditions, with the amount they buy depending on the costs and benefits (to them) of the transaction. As the cost of safety rises it becomes more expensive to buy work intensity, and so, just like any other good, they buy less of it. But this means they reconcile themselves to lower productivity which, as we have seen, represents a lower level of worker utility as well.

Oddly enough, the literature on compensating differentials is entirely unprepared for this result. The debate has been framed entirely as one of compensating differentials versus the complete lack thereof, with no middle ground. Any finding of a positive coefficient on risk in a wage regression has been interpreted as *fully* compensating for the workers involved; hence the extrapolation to a value of life. From a semantic standpoint this is understandable. My dictionary defines "compensation" as either a "counteracting variation" or an "equivalent" – one word fits all. Almost imperceptibly, one goes from the claim that workers receive *some* compensation for risk to the claim that they receive *complete* (or "equalizing") compensation, and evidence of the first is taken as a demonstration of the second. Another source of confusion is economic theory itself. So long as it is assumed that markets clear, so that firms are "utility-takers" – unable to vary the amount of utility from the combination of wages and working conditions they offer their workers – any compensation must necessarily be complete. It is only now, with a different understanding of the possibilities open to workers and their employers, that we can justify making this distinction. We can therefore put it this way: workers can receive *strong* compensation that fully offsets the disutility of added risk, *weak* compensation that provides a partial offset, or no (or even negative) compensation. Under the simple version of efficiency wage theory sketched above, compensation is strictly weak.

Weak compensation directly undermines the equity and hedonic properties of market-based risk. Workers will not be equally well-off; those in dangerous jobs will suffer more, just as the popular view contends. Moreover, the coefficients on risk in wage regressions will understate the true utility value workers place on safety, since their compensation still leaves them worse off than those in safer jobs. Remarkably, this is true even though the efficiency property continues to hold, as we saw above.[18]

The comparative statics also indicate that both w and s are positively related to v in equilibrium: workers who can expect to be better off if fired get both higher wages and more safety.[19] There are two ways we might think about variations in v, either as differences across time or between different groups of workers. The first approach brings to mind the business cycle: as unemployment rises during a slump workers face a greater cost of job loss; then, as the economy recovers, their cost of job loss subsides again. Assuming that employers are willing and able to exploit the temporary ups and downs of v, we might suppose that both wages and safety will be procyclical. In fact, this is broadly true of wages (although there are many complicating factors), but it is not true of injury rates, our basic short-run measure of on-the-job safety. On the contrary, all available evidence indicates that occupational injuries increase during periods of economic expansion.[20] Two possible explanations have been given for this relationship. First, firms raise output more than employment during a boom, with the resulting speed-up causing an increased accident rate. Second, the hiring of new workers as businesses expand may itself result in a temporary reduction in safety practices. Of course, the bare-bones model of wages and safety sketched above is too abstract to incorporate either of these effects.

More promising is the interpretation of changes in v as representative of the different prospects of unemployment and re-employment faced by different groups of workers, as proposed by Stiglitz (1987). For example, consider two workers, one black, the other white, performing the same job. If both are paid the same wages and receive the same working conditions, the black worker will have a higher cost of job loss – lower v – because he or she can look forward if dismissed to both a longer period of unemployment and the expectation of lower pay when rehired, at least to the extent that this particular worker's prospects are consistent with the overall averages. Now the results of the model suggest that employers, if they can identify which groups of workers are most disadvantaged, will profit by reducing their wages and their safety conditions. This is a plausible prediction, but it fails to address a prior problem: if equally productive workers can be paid less simply because they are women, minorities, or otherwise discriminated against in the labor market, why not hire *only* these eminently exploitable employees? Once again, the simple model at hand has nothing to suggest in reply, since it does not consider the employer's decision of which workers to hire, but at least in this case the problem is that the model is incomplete, not that it is directly contradicted by the evidence. It should also be borne in mind that all labor market models stumble over this issue and must resort to *ad hoc* arguments, such as discriminatory employer attitudes, the morale of the remaining higher-paid workers, and so on. Clearly, this is an area in which more research is needed.

At last we have at least the initial features of a criticism of wage compensation theory that Marx could and should have made against Adam Smith. It is based on concepts that Marx himself pioneered: the firm's task of controlling and motivating the worker (for Marx the problem of extracting labor from labor power), the presence of involuntary unemployment (the reserve army of labor), and the threat of dismissal held over the workforce (the role of coercion within the production process). It generates a result which, by invalidating the strong version of Smithian compensation, is sufficient to deflate the theoretical case made for *laissez-faire* and freedom of contract in Marx's own time. True, it does not capture by itself the larger points Marx wished to make about exploitation, alienation, and class relations, but he did not help his cause (nor, of course, those of the workers at the mercy of the courts and legislatures) by making no point at all about the inadequacy of markets for health and safety.

For all its virtues, however, the efficiency wage approach has serious shortcomings. Since efficiency wages must be higher than market-clearing wages in order to preserve a positive cost of job loss, employers are absorbing extra costs. They have an incentive, then, to find some other, cheaper way of motivating their work force if one is available. At first glance it might appear that the threat of cutting a worker's pay would work just as well as that of firing her to get her to do the firm's bidding. This is not true, however, because such a threat lacks credibility. Suppose a worker is found to be acting against the company's interests and is given a pay cut. Now her job is even *more* undesirable; she will start looking elsewhere and further threats from the firm will have little meaning. This in turn means that she will be even more recalcitrant on the job. In the typical fashion of economists, we can assume the firm knows all of this in advance and therefore concludes that the threat to reduce wages would damage the company's interests if actually carried out. Of course, they could try to bluff, but threats really do have to be executed sometimes, and, in any event, once workers get wind of the firm's reluctance to go through with threatened wage cuts, they will be inclined to challenge the firm's authority that much more.

Wage increases, on the other hand, may succeed where wage cuts do not. The firm could hire workers at initial wages *below* their outside options, but promise them a pattern of regular pay increases so long as they are not found to be violating company policy (Becker and Stigler, 1974). This would solve the motivation problem, while permitting the firm to offer a multi-year wage profile whose overall value (its present value at the moment workers are hired) is no greater than the market-clearing wage. For example, workers could be hired at $5 an hour and receive annual pay increases of $1 an hour for the next twenty years – provided the firm remains satisfied with their performance. Suppose that at the going discount rate, which applies to both workers and firms, this is equivalent in value to a constant wage of $12 an hour for each of the 20 years, which happens to be the market-clearing wage. Firms have solved their motivation problem, since a worker has an incentive in each year to stay on for the next, rather than leaving and starting all over again at the bottom.[21] Moreover, they have done this at no added cost; the present value of their initial wage offer is no more or less than the standard-issue market-clearing offer, since only the timing of the benefits has been altered.

Could this be a general alternative to efficiency wages? Probably not. Above all, it assumes that employment will be long-term, that the firm will want to keep the same workers year after year, and that stable demand for their products will enable them to actually do so. This may be the case for so-called "core" or "primary" employers – large firms with secure market positions – but these represent an ever-shrinking minority of jobs. In addition, it is unlikely that a steep enough wage profile can be reconciled with the market-clearing stipulation. There are limits below which initial-period wages cannot fall, and this ratchets the entire wage profile upward. Moreover, to the extent that long-term employment relations and steadily rising wage commitments entail the construction of internal labor markets, we are really describing a different model of employment altogether, with potentially costly investments in training offset by increases in productivity. In other words, the efficiency wage story applies best to the truly *bad* jobs in our economy: low skill, high supervision, perpetually uncertain. The alternative of rising wages and long-term commitments, even though it was developed as a "cheap" substitute for efficiency wages, represents a higher stratum of the labor market.[22] This observation, in turn, largely rehabilitates efficiency wage theory as an explanation for the inadequacy of wage compensation for risk, since, as we have seen, secondary jobs governed by the ever-present threat of dismissal are also the most dangerous.

There are other shortcomings of efficiency wage analysis, however. It assumes, for instance, that worker behavior on the job can be represented entirely by its effect on productivity. Thus, a high level of worker intensity means higher production; a lower level presumably means that the worker is enjoying leisure on the job. The result is that management is essentially acting as society's agent by cajoling the labor force into doing its proper job. The underlying vision is one in which the firm devises the most efficient set of tasks and then tries to get workers to perform as many of these as they can afford to pay for. This bears a striking resemblance to Frederick W. Taylor's doctrine of "scientific management," in which all decision-making is concentrated in the front office, and a combination of sophisticated monitoring and compensation techniques is used to induce workers to follow the program. While it is true that many firms have *tried* to implement Taylor's strategy, it is generally conceded that it is something of a management utopia; there is no way to eliminate in its entirety the role for workers' on-the-job knowledge and planning.[23] In political terms, efficiency wage theory, as generally expressed, denies any potential legitimacy of workers' resistance to company authority. By making worker obedience (intensity) nothing more than a simple input into production, and production the only purpose of the firm, the theory weds social welfare to an authoritarian vision of working life.[24]

A second issue has to do with the reduction of industrial relations to simple contract enforcement. Recall that in the previous chapter I briefly presented the view of Atiyah regarding the inability of contract-based models to capture the economic, social, and legal implications of employment. This criticism applies to efficiency wage models as well and has particular relevance to the analysis of occupational safety and health. Safety, after all, is not simply a "thing" transacted by two parties in the marketplace, the way a sweater is purchased in a clothing store. It is, at least in part, *constitutive* of the relations between worker and employer, a product and a component of the way in which different individuals, often with divergent interests, relate to one another as they engage in the common tasks of production. A different set of theories – a different metaphor, really – is needed to convey this aspect of the problem. That is the purpose of the following section.

Cooperation and conflict in the workplace

One of this country's greatest perennial quandaries is where to draw the line between "public" and "private." Should freedom of speech apply to leafletting and demonstrating at shopping malls? Should prohibitions against discriminatory hiring practices extend to churches and other religious organizations? Can landowners in prime coastal areas be forced to provide public access to beaches and boat launches? In a sense, these and similar issues reflect a central contradiction in our laws and institutions: on the one hand, we value the right of individuals to decide for themselves what they want to do with the things they privately own, beyond the reach of public scrutiny; on the other, we recognize that many of the ostensibly private realms of life are truly public, since they provide a location and a set of rules for the interactions that bind us together as a society. No institution is more riven by this contradiction than the private corporation. Legally, a firm such as General Motors could fire all of their workers and managers, sell off all of their factories, invest all their money in theme parks and video games – *and they would still be exactly the same legal entity as they are today*. This is because GM and all other corporations are viewed simply as private investment funds under the control of their respective boards of directors; as long as there is continuity in this ownership structure, the firm remains the "same." At the same time, it is obvious that GM is *not* just an ownership structure. It is also an association of thousands of individuals: the policies they follow and the rules they obey or disobey. It is equally a fund of skills and experience, a legacy of the struggles and achievements of millions of our forebears with a prodigious effect on our collective economic future. In other words, it is very much a *public* institution whose members do all the things with one another that citizens of any commonwealth generally do, and in which society as a whole has a vital stake.

The private aspect of economic life is captured fairly well by market analysis. The finance literature is replete with sophisticated models which would be useful to anyone contemplating buying into or selling out of corporate equity. The labor market literature offers a detailed treatment of the choice faced by a worker who must compare multiple job offers, self-employment, continued education, and other personal options. Optimal stockpiles of inventory, hedging against currency fluctuations in international transactions, pricing strategies in segmented markets – all of these and more can be illuminated by conventional economic theory. But what about the public aspects of private institutions? Is there a body of economic theory that can shed light on the internal, *political* dimension of corporate life?

Today we can answer that question, mostly yes. The theory of games – of strategic decision-making in response to material incentives – has much to offer to students of institutional mechanisms and morcs. Of course, game theory is not exclusively an economic bailiwick, but its close relationship to economic analysis has been transparent since its beginnings nearly 50 years ago in the minds of John von Neumann and Oskar Morgenstern. Because game theory is not restricted to the mechanism of exchange (as is market analysis), and because it explicitly takes into account the strategic dimension of human affairs (behavior directed toward changing the behavior of others), it offers a reasonable starting point for the analysis of cooperation and conflict *inside* the corporation. In this section I will set out a few relevant concepts from cooperative game theory and suggest how they might be applied to the problem of occupational health and safety.[25]

First some definitions. A *game* has two aspects, a set of potential outcomes (*payoffs*) for its players and a set of rules governing the selection and distribution of those outcomes. In this general sense, chess is a game with three outcomes (winning, losing, and drawing), and a complex set of rules governing the movement of the pieces, the alternation of moves, the definition of checkmate, possible time controls, etc. But informal social situations can also be considered as games. Consider the problem faced by drivers on a crowded highway in which construction suddenly requires that two lanes merge into one. The rewards have to do with the amount of time each motorist will lose due to the delay; the rules are the rules of the road, as well as the physical requirements and capabilities of the automobiles themselves. The players (drivers) must quickly decide when to cut in, when to yield, and so on.

A *strategy* consists of *all* the contingent choices – called *moves* – a player must make in the course of the game. That is, by choosing what she will do in each situation that might arise, the player has devised a single strategy. Perhaps the most useful comparison is to chess. A strategy in game theory is essentially what chessplayers call "tactics." This is an actual calculation of the form "if she does this, I will do that, and then if she does that, I will do this." Chessplayers often calculate all significant possibilities for several moves in advance before deciding on the one move that makes all the rest possible and relevant. (The most powerful chessplaying computers use this method almost exclusively; it is referred to as the "brute force" algorithm.) In our terminology, once a chessplayer has decided what she will do in all potential future situations, she has adopted one strategy.[26]

There are two general types of games, cooperative and noncooperative. A cooperative game is one in which the players would do best by cooperating with one another rather than seeking their own individual advantage, if – and this is a big if – the cooperation is sufficiently universal. The highway construction scenario above is this sort of game. If each player attempts to cut in front of the other, the result will be a massive traffic backup that makes the problem much worse than it needs to be. I have actually seen this type of behavior on urban highways in rush-hour (Chicago and New York to be exact). Each approaching pair of cars would enter a slow, ominous battle of position, much like a sumo match. Drivers would inch forward, threatening outright contact, hoping to intimidate their rivals. Eventually, in a burst of power and bravado, the "winner" would squirt ahead, leaving the ring for the next pair of contestants. Of course, *any* rule that clearly indicated which car should go first would be better for everyone if everyone would follow it. (The most likely contender is "alternate lanes one car at a time," for reasons I will explain later.)

Noncooperative games usually involve the division of a "pie" of some magnitude. For instance, bargaining over the price of a used car is a noncooperative game. A dollar more for the seller is a dollar less for the buyer, and strategy consists of trying to outfox or outmuscle the other player or players. Chess is clearly a noncooperative game. I will not pursue this approach here, but there is a large and interesting literature that considers bargaining-type behavior with the firm.

A game can be played once or many times. The most interesting and lifelike games are those that are played over and over: *repeated games*. A strategy for a repeated game consists not only of all the contingent decisions one might make in one running of the game, but in the whole sequence from beginning to end. Each repetition is called a *stage game*, and it is generally assumed that the stage games are identical except for their history. As you would expect, when the analysis moves from single, one-time-only games to repeated games, the possibilities for strategy become deeper and more complex. Players must calculate not only the direct outcome of their moves in the game they are playing at the moment, but also how it will affect the choices made by other players in future games.

Two general assumptions are made about the behavior of players.

(1) Players are assumed to be strictly self-interested, in that they consider only their own payoffs when deciding on a strategy; that is, they take the payoffs of others into account only insofar as they affect the behavior of others, and then, in turn, their own payoffs. This unflattering view of human motivation can be defended on two grounds. First, in many real-world situations people do act selfishly, or at least close enough to it that a selfish depiction is not too far off the mark. Second, making this assumption greatly simplifies the analysis, and it may be better to be able to say a few things about an unrealistic model than nothing about a realistic one. The model can always be employed selectively or introduced as one aspect of a larger, qualitative analysis. ("To the extent that individuals in this situation are self-interested they will choose x, but we should temper this conclusion by taking into account sympathy, resentment, and other motivations based on the outcomes of others.") (2) Players are assumed to be rational in the sense that they make the best choices available to them based on their options and information. Here, too, those with a penchant for realism might object, for who among us is truly rational? But the same defenses apply as well: the rationality assumption may be nearly true in many instances, and even if it is not results derived from it may be interesting all the same.[27] As for the information on which the players rely, we can assume, unless specified otherwise, that it is perfect (complete and correct) and common (everyone knows the same thing). An example of this is chess: both players know all the rules, all the history, and the current state of the board. The highway example is close but not quite: drivers can see the road, know the rules, and know what their "adversaries" are doing, but they do not know the true value of each potential outcome to the others. They do not know who is in a hurry, nor which cars' insured value exceeds their market value; so they cannot anticipate accurately who will be defensive and who will not.

Finally, it follows from the previous assumptions that only those strategies will be adopted that are *individually rational*. It cannot be the case that a strategy is adopted, yet the player, with the information then available to him, could have chosen a different strategy with better expected outcomes. This holds *a fortiori* for each component of a strategy; that is, for each move. This stipulation has important implications for what is permissible in a rational strategy. It may be necessary as part of a strategy to issue threats. A threat says, "If you do x then I will do y and you'll be sorry." But if your opponent really does x you are still in the game and your next move must be individually rational. If retaliating (doing y) is not the best move at this point you will not do it. According to our information assumptions, however, your opponent knows this fact,and your threat is therefore not credible. This credibility constraint is called *subgame perfection* by game theorists. In many analyses, including the one which follows, it plays a crucial role.

Now we can take the next step and establish the model that will characterize relations within the firm: repeated cooperative games. A two-person, two-choice matrix of payoffs for each stage of our cooperative game can be depicted as shown in figure 5.1.

The players are A and B; they can either cooperate C or defect D. In each cell are the payoffs to the two players based on the corresponding pair of choices; the first payoff is A's, the second is B's. To make matters simple, we can assume perfectly symmetrical payoffs; A and B could trade places in this matrix and nothing would change. (We will not maintain this assumption later in the analysis.) The classic Prisoner's Dilemma game is characterized by these conditions

$$a > d, d > b, c > a \qquad\qquad (14)$$

If both players cooperate they will do better than if they both defect (it is a cooperative game, after all); but if only one player cooperates, she will do worse than if she had defected, while the defector will do better than if he had cooperated. Thus there are benefits to mutual cooperation, but at least temporary benefits from opportunism (taking advantage of the cooperation of others) and costs to unreciprocated beneficence. Two important variations suggest themselves: (1) The other conditions may hold, but there may be no benefit from opportunism

$$a > d, d > b, c = a \qquad\qquad (15)$$

This is an *assurance* game. There is no reason for anyone to cheat, but players must still be reassured that cooperation will be mutual, so as to avoid the cost of unilateralism. (2) The Prisoner's Dilemma could be modified by reversing the consequence of unilateral cooperation

$$a > d, c > a, b > d \qquad\qquad (16)$$

This is the game of *chicken*. Each player has an incentive to intimidate the other into passively accepting her own aggression, but to punish the aggression of your opponent is to suffer at least a transitory loss yourself.

We will use all three of these in the following analysis, but in the context of a repeated game. Thus, a distinction must be made between strategies that would be rational if the game were played only once and

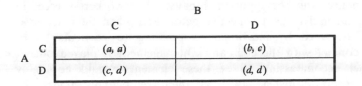

Figure 5.1   Two-person, two-choice payoff matrix

those that could be selected as part of a larger sequence. It would never be rational to play D in a chicken game (16) if your opponent had already committed to D, and if the game were to be played one time only. But if the game is repeated you might choose to retaliate even though it punishes you as well as your opponent, since doing so might elicit a return to cooperation in the future.

Consider the following stylized account of occupational safety and health. A firm consists of workers and management. Workers face potentially dangerous working conditions, in part due to the conscious decisions of management, in part by accident or technical necessity. If management imposes a hazard, workers as a group have two options: they can either adjust passively to the new risk, perhaps requiring a partially offsetting wage differential as market forces take effect (see the section above on efficiency wage theory), or they can actively resist the hazard. Resistance must begin with the individual worker or workers immediately affected by the management's action and can take the form of filing a grievance, refusing to perform certain duties or performing them very "cautiously" (slowly), protesting to supervisors, or calling in for an OSHA inspection. Management can respond to resistance by either launching a counteroffensive, such as reassigning or even dismissing workers, or by remedying the objectionable working condition. (They could do both, of course, but I will restrict the problem to two mutually exclusive options.) If management issues reprisals the workforce as a whole must determine whether to back up the protesting individuals. Should they do so, management can either back down or issue reprisals against *them*. Conflict continues until workers accept the risk or management chooses to provide safety, and these interactions are then repeated indefinitely as new issues arise.

Several overlapping strategic interrelations can be identified in this account. First, workers must determine whether to act individually or collectively in response to risk. Second, even if they agree to act collectively individual workers must decide whether a response to their specific risks will trigger the support of the group, since not all individual risks or responses will be supported. Finally, when workers succeed in constituting themselves as a collective actor, and when their action is successfully triggered by individuals responding to particular work hazards, a conflict with the company's management is played out. A single model encompassing all of these elements would be highly complex; I propose instead to treat them sequentially under the assumption that their main features would not be altered in a simultaneous approach.[28]

1   Forming a coalition in the workplace

It is well known that collective action over worker concerns frequently assumes the form of a Prisoner's Dilemma.[29] Assuming for now that collective action can actually be effective, it is clear that worker solidarity (universal cooperation among workers) is better than everyone going his or her own way (universal defection). A united effort can win improvements in wages and working conditions beyond the reach of individual negotiation. Unfortunately, solidarity is difficult to sustain. Each worker has an incentive to free-ride off the efforts of the others. After all, if everyone but you struggles to win a collective improvement, you will enjoy the benefits without assuming any of the costs. This reflects the attraction of opportunism. On the other hand, if only a few workers coalesce to make demands on management, they are vulnerable to retaliation, while it is unlikely that their demands will prevail. This is the cost of unilateral action. Together, these conditions are summed up in (14). Note, however, that this game is being played among a large number of players, and the above characteristics depend on how many are cooperating at any time. Thus, the benefit of opportunism applies with greatest force when cooperation is otherwise nearly complete, since withdrawing your individual contribution is unlikely to have much effect on the overall effort. Similarly, unilateral cooperation is most dangerous when the overall level of cooperation is low. The implication is that worker solidarity is vulnerable to free-riding when it is abundant and to fear of reprisal when it is scarce; it is difficult to get to and difficult to keep. Indeed, if the game were played only once – equivalent, for instance, to a day-labor job in which a largely new workforce assembles each day – cooperation could never arise or sustain itself under the assumptions of game theory. In such a situation it is *always* individually rational to defect, since for each player, given whatever the others do, the payoff is greatest from defecting. If others cooperate, fine – take advantage of them. If they defect you had better do the same.[30]

Fortunately (for workers), this is not necessarily the case for a stable group of workers who find themselves facing similar issues over and over. The so-called Folk Theorem holds that, in a repeated game in which mutual cooperation is better than mutual defection, there is always an individually rational strategy by which the players can attain the cooperative outcome.[31] The intuition behind this result is that, as a general strategy, free-riding can bring workers only temporary benefits. Once it catches on, solidarity collapses and everyone ends up in the undesired state of fend-for-yourself. *Knowing this, they have an incentive to avoid it.* It is enough for each worker to anticipate that she will react to the noncooperation of others by breaking off cooperation herself, and that others will do the same to her. Note that it remains true that universal noncooperation remains an individually rational solution; if everyone else defects you can do no better. But the Folk Theorem demonstrates that this does not have to happen: mutual cooperation is *also* individually rational when we take into account the future response of others to our own free-riding.[32]

Whether workers succeed in overcoming their collective action problem and constituting themselves as a cohesive force depends on four general factors: (1) How great is the potential gain from unified action? In positions involving little skill or experience, where workers can easily be replaced by outsiders, or where the company itself has few resources available for improving working conditions, even the most disciplined show of unity by the workforce may have little effect. Relative to the costs of collective action, cooperation may just not be worth it. (2) How large are the transitory benefits of opportunism? If solidarity is expensive – if it requires substantial contributions of time, money, or other personal resources – individuals will have an incentive to free-ride. On the other hand, if people have internalized social norms of solidarity the attraction of opportunism will be diminished; in fact, *not* doing one's part could be experienced as personally costly (Elster, 1991). (3) How great are the risks of unilateral action? It has been estimated that approximately one in twenty workers who so much as *vote* for union representation will be fired in reprisal; active union organizing under current labor law and practice is practically a guarantee of dismissal in nonunion enterprises (Freeman and Medoff, 1984). In the absence of unions, workers have even less protection against management reprisals. In most workplaces they can be demoted, transferred, or dismissed without even a charge being entered against them, much less being given a procedure with any resemblance to due process. The threat of dismissal, of course, carries added weight in an economy with widespread un- and under-employment. Still, there are some workers who, because of valuable personal skills or solicitous management, may find the risks of taking action on the job bearable.

(4) How effective are formal and informal networks among workers in promoting solidaristic strategies? Remember that the Folk Theorem established that universal cooperation is only one of the potential outcomes of a repeated cooperative game; there are no guarantees. In many cases workers begin in a state of extreme disunity and must find their way to collective action. This is the task of a labor movement, whether it takes the form of a conventional trade union, a caucus or other political group, or simply an understanding among friends. Getting to solidarity and staying there requires persuasive leadership and strong internal communication to convince workers that cooperation is morally compelling and materially rewarding, and that everyone else has already made this commitment. At moments of crisis, such as strikes or other risky actions, when the temptation to defect is at its maximum, organizations need particularly strong resources to prevent a break in the ranks.[33]

Safe and healthy working conditions are a collective good. If pressure from an aroused workforce brings about an improvement, everyone who shares the same working environment will benefit whether they helped bring it about or not. It therefore bears the hallmarks of a Prisoner's Dilemma. Labor organizations must try to convince workers to pass up the temptation to free-ride, while encouraging those who would protest to take action despite the risk of reprisal. If the game were played only once their task would be virtually insurmountable, but in work situations where these issues arise day after day, game theory suggests they may succeed.

2   Deciding which hazards to resist

Worker solidarity must be nearly universal to be effective, but most occupational risks are local and transitory: they affect only some of the firm's workers, or they do not last long enough for the workforce as a whole to come to a decision about them. Moreover, most of the strategies for resisting on-the-job risks are local or spur-of-the-moment: complaining to supervisors, refusing to carry out a dangerous assignment, and filing a grievance are actions that individuals or small work teams must initiate, often without an opportunity to consult with the wider group. Supposing that the fundamental collective action problem outlined above has been solved, individual workers still face uncertainty over whether the risks they might react against will be "validated" by the group as a whole, so that local or spontaneous acts of rebellion will be backed by the solidarity of all. This backing can obviously make the difference between a futile protest that results in personal defeat and a powerful challenge for which the initiators are protected from reprisal.

How can individual workers know whether the group will be behind them? One solution, of course, is for the entire group to commit itself to backing all protests against all possible risks, but this puts the credibility of the entire community at the mercy of its most adventuristic members. The only alternative is to establish standards that individuals will feel confident applying in their own immediate circumstances.

The problem of establishing such standards can be represented by the assurance game, whose conditions are summarized in (15). The group benefits from cooperation and its members have no temptation to free-ride (if the workers directly involved in a local safety episode fail to act, no one will do it for them), but if individuals take action and, for any reason, the group fails to support them they are exposed to serious harm. To a large extent, this problem can be solved by communication; the types and intensities of risk which the whole workforce has given its commitment to oppose can be reiterated and interpreted to each local group. A practical application, for instance, is the safety and health committee which moves through the firm, evaluating local conditions and alerting individual workers to potential hazards that meet the entire group's standards for collective action.

Yet information alone is not enough. The standards themselves must have the characteristic that each individual, despite her unique personal outlook or the pressure of events, can determine how it should be applied. This is referred to by game theorists as the "bright line" quality of an assurance solution. For a simple example, consider once more the merging traffic story. It is in the interest of all drivers to commit themselves to a cooperative strategy (assuming that roughly the same group will find itself in this type of situation repeatedly), but they must also agree on the *same* cooperative strategy. For instance, one strategy might be that the left lane enters freely for one minute, then the right lane, and so on. If everyone were to do this, the traffic would flow very quickly through the obstruction. Unfortunately, it can be imposed only by police or traffic lights, since it is unlikely that drivers on their own would simultaneously arrive at exactly the same rule. The simplest cooperative strategy is one-by-one alternation: a car from the left lane, a car from the right, and so on. This is much slower than one-minute alternations, but it is so easy to identify in an unplanned situation that drivers are usually able to adopt it without coercion. It is this "bright line" quality which enables individuals to ascertain whether or not their cooperation will be reciprocated. By analogy, safety standards in the workplace also need distinctive characteristics. Workers will find it useful to spell out in advance certain easily observable types of problems, such as poor heating or ventilation, slippery surfaces, or particular well-known chemicals that might leak or spill, so that a clear demarcation can be drawn between protected and unprotected acts of protest.

It is important to recognize the consequences of this form of standard-setting. The types of risks to which workers will be alerted may not be the most dangerous or even the most remediable. Exposure limits to a chemical will be emphasized not because that chemical is the most hazardous, but because workers can readily determine when they are being exposed to it and can generally agree on the dividing line between "safe" and "unsafe" exposure. Of course, the most toxic chemicals are usually candidates for the "brightest" standards, since safety can be equated with no exposure at all – the simplest of all demarcations. Perhaps the most important implication of this assurance game has to do with the importance it attaches to government health and safety standards. Simply by promulgating these standards, public health authorities establish bright lines, and this in turn determines which risks workers will respond to in workplaces across the country. Workers might even disagree with those standards, but they will still tend to fall back on them in the workplace, since they can at least be confident that if they are violated in a local episode the solidarity of the entire workforce will be triggered.

3   Deciding when to confront management over safety and health
Thus far we have considered games that take place only between the workers themselves: whether to work together in solidarity and how to come to a decentralized understanding over what issues in the work-place are actionable. Once labor's own affairs are in order, however, it must still deal with the company. Each day management makes decisions which can affect health and safety on the job. Managers are not sadists – they do not enjoy making work more dangerous for its own sake – but they often find it profitable to impose a higher level of risk. Workers can complain, but if a hazard is particularly expensive to eliminate, management will comply only if workers threaten to impose an even greater cost. (This could take the form of direct costs, such as strikes or other obstructions to production, or the opportunity cost of lost cooperation over other issues.) But such threats are not costless for workers either. Giving supervisors a hard time will usually lead to some sort of reprisal, and certainly refusing to work, whether individually or collectively, is almost certain to create enormous problems for workers. It is reasonable, then, to view conflicts over health and safety as a variety of the chicken game, summarized earlier by the conditions listed in (16). From the standpoint of workers, the

goal is to induce management to cooperate by improving working conditions. If management expects workers to passively accept these conditions (not protest), it has no incentive to do so; but if workers wish to retaliate against this practice they must accept at least a transitory cost.

More precisely, assume that the game takes the following form. Management reveals its choice concerning safety (where Safety and Risk represent safe and unsafe conditions respectively), workers then respond (where Accept and Resist represent passive acceptance and protest respectively), each side receives its corresponding payoff for the duration of one period, and the game is played again. The move histories of both sides are common knowledge, but each player has only imperfect knowledge of the payoffs received or anticipated by the other.[34] The payoff matrix for one stage is shown in figure 5.2.

Note that the cell representing resistance to safe working conditions is shaded out, since it will not arise.

In this game we drop our earlier assumption of symmetry, so that $a_L = a_M$ and $d_L = d_M$ could arise only by coincidence. Since this is a variation of chicken, the following condition holds for worker payoffs

$$a_L > b_L > d_L \tag{17}$$

For now, assume the corresponding condition for management

$$c_M > a_M > d_M \tag{18}$$

If the game were played only once, it is obvious that management would defect and workers cooperate. Why? Because it would not be individually rational (subgame perfect) for workers to retaliate against management defection, and management knows this. But when the game is repeated the outcome is indeterminate. We cannot rule out the rationality of worker retaliation, since their temporary loss can be offset by the gains that would accrue in the future if management chooses to back down. Knowing this, management might choose to not reduce safety at all, *provided the threat of worker retaliation is credible.* Everything in this game hinges on the conditions for making credible threats.

To keep matters simple, restrict the focus to two time periods. (Since next period's payoff could represent the then present expected value of all subsequent payoffs, the problem is not qualitatively altered.) For labor's retaliation to be individually rational, the following condition must hold:

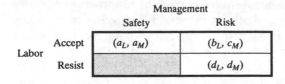

Figure 5.2   Payoff matrix for the occupation safety stage-game

$$p_R \delta (a_L - b_L) \geq b_L - d_L \qquad\qquad (19)$$

where p_R is the change in the likelihood of management cooperation in the next period due to retaliation today and δ is a discount factor between 0 and 1 (since next period's payoffs have less value than today's). The viability of worker retaliation depends quite simply on the costs of taking action $(b_L - d_L)$, the benefits of winning the struggle $(a_L - b_L)$, the willingness of workers to trade off current costs for future benefits (δ), and worker perceptions of management strategy (p).

Correspondingly, management finds it individually rational to introduce or maintain an occupational risk if

$$(1 - \pi_R)(c_M - a_M) \geq \pi_R(a_M - d_M) \qquad\qquad (20)$$

or equivalently

$$c_M - a_M \geq \pi_R(c_M - d_M) \qquad\qquad (21)$$

where π_R is the likelihood that workers will resist. Their decision rests, then, on the cost of eliminating the risk $(a_M - c_M)$, the cost of worker resistance $(d_M - c_M)$, and the probability of resistance π_R.

These conclusions seem obvious without the apparatus of game theory, and they are, but the simple model sketched above makes it possible to ask, and in some cases answer, questions of greater detail and interest.

(1) The rational options available to labor and management are in part functions of their relative power. The cost that workers can impose on the firm if they resist dangerous working conditions depends on their role within the production process – their skill, their opportunity for discretionary judgment, and the extent to which their consent must be

honored in the firm's internal social structure. The cost that this resistance imposes on the workers themselves depends on their rights under labor law and the procedures of the firm, as well as the strength of their labor union or other collective organization.

(2) A worker always has the option of quitting and accepting the consequences of re-entering the labor market. If we regard the value of this "outside" option as the worker's reservation wage (v), it follows that $a_L, b_L \geq v$. In the special case in which $a_L = v$, it must also be true that $b_L = v$, since it can neither be greater nor less. This is the case of perfectly compensating wage differentials. It is not a very desirable case for workers, since they are completely indifferent between working and quitting; they do not feel they are doing any better by staying with the firm than they could if they left. Since this is rarely true, however, we can accept as the more common situation $a_L > b_L \geq v$. Here workers receive a "rent," a surplus in excess of their likely payoff in the open market.

(3) If workers settle for individual adjustments to increased risk, they are choosing compensating wage differentials as their best option. In the no-rent situation, as we saw, they are just as well off whatever management's decisions regarding working conditions. Once there is a rent, however, they cannot do as well under passive adjustment as they could if the risks were rescinded. (This is corroborated by the results derived from the efficiency wage model.) A different way of putting it is that, if workers have more leverage with management under collective than individual action, $a_L > b_L$ and compensation is weak, not strong. Why then would workers content themselves with wage compensation? This would happen either if the balance of power were sufficiently against them, or if the game were played just once (or a small, finite number of times). In fact, the logical structure of the compensating differentials model bears this out. As we saw in chapter 2, the theory considers a market "game" in which the employer offers a wage/safety package, and the worker either accepts or rejects it. This continues until a package has been offered which the worker will accept, or a worker has been found who will accept the offer. The pattern of such agreed-upon packages can be shown to exhibit full wage compensation for risk. It is obvious that this is the description of a one-shot game, since neither party acts with the intention of affecting the other's *future* behavior. And as we have seen, when the game is played just once, b_L is the worker's only rational response. Thus an additional criticism of the wage compensation model is that it considers only one instant in time,

the moment of contract, and therefore neglects the wider range of possibilities that emerge in repeated games.

(4) Could the players in this game simply bluff to get their way? Certainly, although they may not get away with it. Effective bluffs create their own credibility: suppose, for example, that management enjoys only a small cost saving by making the workplace more dangerous and is highly vulnerable to worker resistance ($c_M - a_M$ is small; $c_M - d_M$ is large). Nevertheless, if they can convince workers that this is not the case, but rather that $d_M - a_M$ is even positive, π_R falls to 0 and the viability condition expressed in (21) is met. Of course, labor may try to call this bluff by resisting. On its next turn, management can either maintain the bluff or fold, much as in a poker game. The actual course of events depends on the beliefs of both sides, as well as on the power relations that determine the costs of guessing wrong. Even if a threat is not a bluff – if the threatened reprisal would be individually rational even if the adversary had complete knowledge of all relevant variables – it pays to adopt the same intimidating posture. For instance, it may be the case that $d_M - a_M$ really is positive for the firm (it is invulnerable to resistance), yet it would still do better if workers declined to resist ($c_M > d_M$). There are two expectations the firm would like to instil in its workforce: that resistance will not cause it to change its policies, but also that it plans to make the workplace safer even without any worker response at all. This is because p_R represents not the likelihood of improved safety in general, but improved safety due specifically to the strategy of resistance. This suggests one explanation for the fact that firms everywhere proclaim their commitment to a high level of safety even though it is often demonstrably untrue.

(5) Workers and managers have incomplete information regarding the others' incentives and strategies. Because of this, acts of cooperation and resistance serve two purposes. They are concrete acts with direct consequences, and they are also pieces of new information that can alter prior judgments concerning the true values of p_R and π_R. For example, suppose management introduces a new risk into the workplace. If workers respond with resistance they impose costs on management and themselves. They also send a message saying, "You have underestimated our p_R. We plan to protest until you back down." If management believes this, they must back down according to the assumption of individual rationality. On the other hand, they may feel that the workers are bluffing. The only way to find out for sure is to maintain the risk and see what happens. By doing so, they are sending a message of their own:

"We think you are bluffing. If we hold firm, you will see that you cannot afford to keep this up, and *you* will back down." Given the structure of the game, if workers are convinced then it is rationally necessary that they give up, since $b_L > d_L$. What we have described is a scenario for conflict: it is a test of each player's ability to sustain its own message and doubt that of its adversary. The formal analysis of the game does not reveal any particular "theoretical" outcome. This is a truly open struggle: it can go either way.

(6) Thus far we have assumed that all risks in the workplace are consciously imposed by management. However, suppose, as seems reasonable, that this is not true. Many risks are simply "there": they result from the unalterable technical requirements of production, the ineradicable traits of workers, or other factors beyond management control – including blind chance. Now π_R depends not only on the choice of management strategy, but also on the nature of the risk under dispute. If workers know with certainty which risks are controllable and which are not, they will simply play the game over the controllable risks and adjust to the others as best they can. For some risks this distinction may be obvious, but there will certainly be many whose true cause cannot easily be inferred. Practically speaking, on what basis might workers distinguish risks that can be reduced by protest from those that cannot? In the absence of more precise information it makes sense to regard risks as likely to be controllable by management if they exceed those at other, similar workplaces, if they are higher than they were previously in the same workplace, or if they violate publicly disseminated safety standards. Once more, then, we come upon an argument for normative responses to risk, quite apart from any justification of the standards embodied in these norms.

We have now surveyed three aspects of what we might call the social relations of occupational safety and health: the problem of mobilizing the workforce to act collectively around health and safety issues, the identification of safety standards that workers can count on for triggering collective action, and the actual conflict between labor and management over working conditions. Putting all three of these games together, we can draw two general conclusions:

1 The balance of power between labor and management affects the likelihood of worker response to risk in two ways. First, it enters into the likelihood that workers will overcome their collective action problem to behave solidaristically. This is a precondition for almost any effective worker influence on working conditions. Second, it

determines where workers will draw the line between the risks they will choose to respond to and those they will passively accept.

2 Workers will respond to risks not on the basis of their absolute disutility, as in an expected utility model, but in relation to more-or-less fixed standards. These standards therefore take on the function of *social norms*, patterns of judgment and behavior that, to an outside observer, may appear to reflect identical preferences on the part of each individual, but which, at least in this analysis, simply arise spontaneously in the process of rational collective action. In particular, these norms tend to be comparative rather than absolute, and they depend to some extent on perceptions of intent. The normative selection of risks to be regarded as actionable strengthens the bright line aspect of solutions to the assurance game, while the perception by workers that a risk is deliberately imposed on them by management increases the likelihood that it will be resisted.

Game theory does not offer a comprehensive guide to the inner life of corporations, but it does address much of the strategic tug-of-war between workers and their employers. After the vicissitudes of the labor market have been weathered, after the negotiations over a contract and an agreement on its terms have been brought to a conclusion, life goes on. Where market analysis ends, a new model of social interaction within the employment relationship must begin, and game theory fulfils this role. What it suggests in the case of occupational safety and health is that safe working conditions are not simply "purchased" by workers at the moment of contract, but must be fought for within the daily life of the firm. Because of the social context within which this struggle takes place, there will be no simple mapping from individual worker preferences to actual workplace conditions. The calculus of power – law, ideology, and the distribution of economic resources – intervenes from the outset, and the organizational skills of workers and their movements determine the scope for change. And in the crucible of conflict, individual preferences are melded into social norms, the collective "preferences" underlying collective action.

The elements combined

Each eye observes separately, and through parallax their joint perception fixes the object of vision in three dimensions. To conclude this chapter, I will attempt a theoretical parallax, using the different vantage points developed in the preceding pages to explain the multifaceted history of occupational safety and health.

1   Social norms and the anomalies of risk perception

Perhaps the most striking departure of the real world from the theoretical construct of conventional economics is the predominance of "irrational" perceptions and evaluations of risk. Of course, on closer examination the standard account of rationality is so narrowly circumscribed that it excludes a considerable amount of perfectly reasonable behavior.

Attitudes toward risk tend to be normative. Sharp distinctions are made between risks above and beneath the normative level, and individuals appear to be more conformist in their preferences than they really are. Given the constraints of bounded rationality – the inability to identify and assess each risk individually to our own satisfaction – we often rely on the views of others. This economizes on time and attention, and, providing we listen to the right voices, is a reasonable response to our cognitive limitations. From game theory, meanwhile, we have seen that attention to safety norms increases the likelihood of worker success in disputes over working conditions.

Because the physical dangers posed by occupational risks are mediated by our ability to identify and then act collectively to mitigate them, it should not be surprising that there is seldom a perfect correspondence between "objective" risk and the norms that trigger action. In particular, we do not have to resort to accusations of neoprimitivism among modern-day techno-sectarians (Douglas and Wildavsky, 1982). The risk of x may be greater than that of y, but if the elimination of y is potentially achievable while x is not, establishing a public x-norm can only dissipate the resources for collective action while adding to the burden of cognitive dissonance. As is so often the case, the geography of power imposes its map on the terrain of perception and belief. A powerful demonstration of this effect was provided by the black lung movement. Opposition to coal dust remained "underground" for decades until workers believed they could bring the operators, the government, and their own union to account; suddenly a risk that thousands of miners had quietly "accepted" became unacceptable.

In addition, risk norms are founded on comparative, not absolute criteria. Workers evaluate the hazards they face not on the continuous scale of expected utility described in chapter 3, but in relation to an agreed-upon reference point. The relevant standard of comparison may be drawn from the workers' own history, from the conditions of other workers, from public health regulations, or from imagined alternatives that workers have come to believe *could* exist. We know that this type of behavior is widespread from the evidence accumulated by prospect theory, and we know that it is consistent with the strategic dictates of collective action. What it implies is that objectively lesser risks may face greater opposition if they exceed their reference points – a justifiable response if the reference points themselves are justified. Moreover, if the reference points change the perceived risk may increase, even if it remains objectively the same. From a political standpoint, a principal role of health and safety activists is to agitate for higher safety norms, thereby lowering the threshold for discontent and resistance.

Another shortcoming of conventional utility theory is that it fails to distinguish between qualitatively different types of risk, in particular between risk that does or does not violate the worker's personal autonomy. It can be said that, in practice, most individuals are Kantians; they resent small risks that they attribute to their being exploited by others more than large risks they impose on themselves or believe to be imposed by chance. This is why negligence suits filed in the wake of occupational atrocities have such symbolic meaning for workers and the general public alike: they represent a moral claim against those who have harmed others for personal gain. Whatever one may make of this preoccupation with autonomy as a basis for judgments of personal well-being, it makes considerable strategic sense. Autonomy-violating risks are precisely the discretionary kind that game theory predicts players will focus on; after all, their cost is not only their direct potential for injury or disease, but also the costs of *future* depredations if their imposition is not resisted. If your trash blows on to my lawn I will pick it up and soon forget all about it, but if I think you *deliberately* dumped it and are likely to keep on doing it day after day I would have to be crazy – or completely intimidated – to give it the same casual response. And, to complete the analogy, it does not matter very much if more trash is blown than dumped; within limits, how much is not the issue. Finally, given the predisposition of most people toward resisting autonomy-violating risks, the quality of abusive or exploitive intent serves efficiently as the type of bright line workers and other actors look for when they want to assure themselves that their responses are normative.

To summarize, risk is not risk. The principal distinction is between normative risk, the risk workers will usually accept passively (much as the theory of market choice claims they have already done at the moment of accepting employment), and extranormative risk, which becomes the focus of workplace and political conflict. The characteristics of unacceptable risk are its "excessive" level relative to a widely recognized standard, its apparently "deliberate" origin, and the conviction of most workers that it can realistically be reduced. The experience of occupational safety and health in all industrialized societies consists of the emergence, evolution, and struggle over these workplace safety norms.

2   The incompleteness of compensating wage differentials

Dangerous working conditions are most likely to arise in secondary jobs, but these are also the least likely to provide adequate wage compensation, as we saw in the discussion of efficiency wage theory. Moreover, the very acceptance of wage compensation as a sufficient response to risk constitutes worker accommodation to management in the strategic environment of the workplace. Thus, the game-theoretic analysis predicts that compensation will most likely be paid for *normative* risks, those that workers are not attempting to redress through collective action.[35] For example, long distance trucking is an intrinsically dangerous occupation and probably pays a wage premium, but few drivers would accept even more money to drive trucks that were intentionally left in a state of disrepair (extranormative risk). This observation is reinforced by the evidence from other social and experimental contexts that few individuals are willing to accept money in return for agreeing to be the target of someone else's potentially harmful behavior. Finally, as we saw in the game-theoretic look at the workplace, employers have an incentive to claim that they are taking every conceivable precaution to make the environment as safe as possible. Since paying wage premiums for added risk appears to contradict this display of concern, their strategic interest militates against it.

3   The role of labor market segmentation

Secondary jobs pay lower wages, offer more hazardous working conditions, and use a wage-determination mechanism that further diminishes the well-being of workers in high-risk jobs. Moreover, since employment in most secondary jobs is unstable, workers face much higher barriers to collective action and are therefore poorly placed to agitate for greater safety. A thread running through many of the great occupational disasters has been the short-term status of the victims – the immigrant women working on a contract basis at Triangle Shirtwaist, the black day-laborers at Gauley Bridge, the fly-by-night employment at Imperial Products in North Carolina. This is not to suggest that there is no room for improvement in higher-paid, more stable jobs; as Nelkin and Brown (1984), among others, have demonstrated, even many of the "best" jobs are unnecessarily dangerous. Yet the good news about even the most hazardous primary jobs is that the workers have the potential, if they can mobilize themselves, to bring about significant improvement. By contrast, the tragedy of secondary employment is not only that poverty is compounded by ill-health, but also that those most in need of health and safety reform have the fewest resources to struggle for it.

4   *The role of government regulation*

Neither worker nor employer would invoke the regulatory powers of government under the pure compensating differential model presented in chapter 2. In the real world, however, workers have historically fought for more stringent regulation of occupational safety and health in every country that has undergone industrialization. The theoretical perspectives offered in this chapter suggest rational motives for this history. (1) Since workers do not receive fully compensating differentials, particularly for extranormative risks, safety regulation makes them better off. (2) Since workers, due to universal cognitive limitations, are generally unable to identify and evaluate risks as rapidly as firms can create them, they may benefit by permitting a specialized arm of government to regulate the workplace on their behalf. A similar conclusion would be reached by arguing from cognitive dissonance that workers might rationally delegate the regulation of safety to a public body so as to avoid the psychic distress of self-monitoring. (3) The promulgation of workplace standards helps workers solve their collective action problems by providing them with a clearer basis for solidaristic mobilization. Within reason, tighter standards promote greater worker militancy by increasing the amount of risk viewed as extranormative. (4) The existence of standards adds credence to the moral claims of workers. These in turn reinforce belief systems conducive to collective action. (5) The powers of the regulatory authority can be invoked by workers, giving them more leverage in their workplace struggles with management.

Overall, the strategic view of employment relations developed in this chapter recognizes the rationality of worker demands for occupational safety regulation. It does, however, provide an ironic twist: since many of the motives for advocating regulations stem from their usefulness in workplace conflicts, it is primarily those workers who *can* struggle for safety on the job who are the most vocal in support of favorable government intervention. The truly powerless, workers trapped in the most dangerous secondary jobs, are all too likely to remain silent. This means that public policies to improve the quality of working life must do more than respond to immediate pressure if they are to address the most acute needs.

6 New policies to promote safety and equity in the workplace

In the opening chapter I documented the failure of America's system of occupational safety and health regulation to achieve its objective of a safe workplace. The rate of injuries has increased during the 1980s, while occupational disease silently takes, in all probability, an even larger toll. The burden falls most heavily on those who can least afford it: minorities and those with the lowest pay and fewest opportunities for advancement. Above all, the cost of this intensifying injury, disease, and death is *unnecessary*; other countries facing the same economic constraints do achieve higher levels of safety.

What then should we do to bring about reform? How far-reaching must the changes be, and in what direction? Before investigating these questions, we need to know just what it is we want to accomplish and how we will measure our progress. This is more difficult than one might think. The naive approach would be to aim for minimum risk; this, after all, would have the virtues of simplicity, ease of assessment, and apparent fairness. Unfortunately, it does not stand up to scrutiny: (1) The simple minimization of risk fails to recognize that risk often has rewards. If a small reduction in risk requires a substantial loss in the quality or affordability of the products labor is producing, it may not be worth it. Building an urban subway system, for example, may be inherently dangerous, but not to build it, or to set such high standards for workers' safety that the subway becomes too expensive, may impose a higher cost in air pollution, increased traffic accidents, and so on. Workers' safety is only one aspect of a larger economic and social problem. (2) Risk minimization fails to take into account the fact, stressed in the previous chapter, that risks are not all of equal importance. *Why* risks exist is just as important, from workers' perspectives, as what they are. Are they the result of cost-cutting, so that the company's owners can make more money? Are they primarily the responsibility of workers themselves, through the care they exercise in their work? Are they above the existing norm for work of this type? If the purpose of occupational safety regulation is to make workers better off, attention must be paid to their own values and responses.

A second approach, one which most economists would endorse, would set as its standard an *efficient* level of risk, one for which the marginal cost of making a job a little safer is exactly equal to its marginal benefit. What is intended is a solution like s^* in figure 6.1. Clearly each increment of safety prior to this amount produces positive net benefits (marginal benefit in excess of marginal cost); above this level additional safety improvements cost more than they are worth. Note, incidentally, that a formulation such as this assumes that the incremental cost of providing safety rises as the job becomes safer, while the incremental value of it (to the worker, presumably) falls.

At its face, this economic perspective on safety policy seems to address the first objection to simple risk minimization, since it compares the benefits and costs of potential improvements. Moreover, it is not necessarily at odds with the goal of greater safety, since a strong case could be made that the United States is well to the left of s^* at present. Finally, it has the potential advantage of being able to incorporate the subtleties of worker evaluation, so long as by "benefit" those formulating the policy understand "benefit perceived by workers themselves." Such an interpretation, of course, would preclude the technocratic approach to cost and benefit calculation practiced by much of the risk assessment industry. Nevertheless, there are two critical flaws in the cost–benefit framework: (1) It is virtually impossible to provide quantitative measurements of the benefits to safety regulation, particularly if the cognitive dimension explored in the previous chapter is taken seriously. In practice, policy analysts have used hedonic values of life and health, such as those discussed in chapter 3, when calculating the benefit side of the ledger, but we have seen that these numbers are unlikely to bear much relation to workers' true evaluations. (2) The economic approach reduces the social dimension of the workplace environment, with all the complications considered in chapters 4 and 5, to simple quantitative values. What gets left out are the connections between safety, social relations at work, and the larger balance of power between workers and employers in society. A technical "fix" that targets a certain level of safety but does not alter the social or strategic environment within which risks arise and are contested will fail to nourish the climate of care and reciprocity required for truly humane work – and, as Noble (1986) has shown, will even fail to enforce its own strictures.

So what ought to be the objectives of occupational safety and health or, better, *workplace environment* policy? In part, both of the above

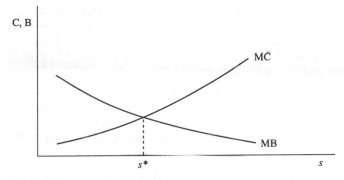

Figure 6.1

approaches have merit: risk should be reduced overall (if not minimized) and it should be done with an eye to efficiency, particularly insofar as the preferences of workers themselves are taken into account. But it is also important to consider the *process* by which these outcomes are determined – the effect of public policy on how decisions are made. Workers are neither the passive consumers of their own working conditions envisioned by advocates of technocratic management, nor do they possess fully formed, unchangeable views on what is safe and what is not. The truth is more complicated: workers, like all of us, form judgments on the basis of their learning, and there is no magic moment at which learning is complete and the "right" preferences are established. Moreover, learning is a social process; the direction it takes and the speed at which it occurs depend on the nature of the communication that takes place among individuals. This implies that an effective workplace environment policy must promote a *discourse* on safe and healthy working conditions: while respecting the judgments of those who actually face the risks each day, it must also spark a movement to increase workers' awareness of these issues. Second, if workplaces are too dangerous, it is largely because workers have too little power; so an effective policy must give explicit attention to democratizing industrial relations. This is not separable from the first objective, however, since a compelling discourse (one which ordinary people would be stimulated to join) must have a chance of bringing about real change.

One way to describe this approach to policy is to see it as a practical application of the type of democratic theory that emphasizes communication and collective self-development.[1] In general terms, democracy of this sort is based on substantive equality of individual participation in decision-making (democratic elections, civil liberties, equal access to the levers of political influence), a "public space" for popular discussion of important issues (intermediate institutions – social but nongovernmental – that provide a forum for public debate), and a commitment to providing sufficient resources for each member of society to gain the ability and opportunity to join the democratic conversation. No simple formula emerges from this approach, but its values are easy to identify: complete political equality, a free and active exchange of ideas extending through the entire society, and policies that are effective both as implementations of existing preferences and as vehicles for challenging and changing them. Of course, there may be tradeoffs between these objectives, especially when the initial state of public opinion is so at odds with objective reality that no decision-making process can be both democratic and effective. An optimist might counter, however, that the information on which effective policy must be based is nearly always widely diffused, since its bits and pieces take the form of everyday life for the majority of people. With a strong mechanism of public communication these bits can be pieced together to form a reasonable approximation of the true state of affairs; thus a democratic public has the potential to make better decisions than a small body of experts.[2]

In the field of occupational safety and health this bias toward democratic procedures is well-founded. In general, workers are potentially the best-informed individuals concerning what risks actually exist and how serious they are. They are on-the-spot and therefore well-placed to monitor transitory hazards, unique circumstances, and the like. They are also privy to their personal reactions, physical and psychological, to the risks to which they are exposed. Their active participation in identifying deficiencies in occupational safety is therefore analogous to the patient's role in participating in health diagnosis and care – the contributions of local and tacit knowledge. This is not to say, of course, that workers know everything; clearly their personal information, even if pooled and publicly discussed, must be augmented by the expertise of safety and health professionals, just as in the medical analogy. Nonetheless, there is reason to believe that, at least in this area, the democratic involvement of workers in the making of health and safety policy is not only a moral imperative: it is also directly practical.

In this chapter I will consider what such a policy might look like. Before doing this, however, it will be useful to survey the current system and its shortcomings, and to compare it to its foreign alternatives. Since this is not a treatise on law or public administration, the discussion of US safety policy will necessarily be rather general. This approach would be a liability if the flaws of the existing regime, OSHA and workers compensation, could be removed with small, carefully targeted adjustments. They cannot.

OSHA: regulation and its discontents

In one of his best-known parables, Franz Kafka tells the story of a man who travels to the city to gain access to the Law. Passing through the gate, he approaches an outer chamber guarded by a doorkeeper. The man asks the doorkeeper for permission to enter but is turned down. Simply dodging the doorkeeper and racing into the building occurs to him, but he is told, "If you are so drawn to it, just try to go in despite my veto. But take note: I am powerful. And I am only the least of the doorkeepers. From hall to hall there is one doorkeeper after another, each more powerful than the last. The third doorkeeper is already so terrible that even I cannot bear to look at him" (Kafka, 1946, p. 3). The man spends the rest of his life waiting in this first chamber and never gains admittance to the Law.

For many workers the Occupational Safety and Health Act of 1970, with its broad promises and convoluted implementation, is equally frustrating. No one can accuse this law of not setting a bold objective: "to assure so far as possible every working man and woman in the nation safe and healthful working conditions ... [and] assure insofar as practicable that no employee shall suffer diminished health, functional capacity or life expectancy as a result of his work experience." If simply passing a law calling for these results were equivalent to achieving them, this study would not need to be written.

Unfortunately, there are many links in the chain between promise and fulfilment, and all of them are problematic. First, research must be conducted on health and safety hazards; to do this the act created the National Institute of Occupational Safety and Health (NIOSH) in the Department of Health and Human Services. Then actual standards must be set by the Occupational Safety and Health Administration (OSHA). These may be challenged by employers, however, and so a protracted period of litigation and deal-making may ensue. Once the standards are finally in place, inspectors visit workplaces to check for compliance. If they see violations they *may* write up the offense, and if higher management within OSHA approves cases may be referred to the Justice Department for prosecution. Once more the matter is in court, with predictable delays and opportunities for further compromise. Finally, even if every step in the enforcement process is vigorously pursued, the possibility remains that regulation simply will not work: employers will continue to impose old hazards or replace them with new ones. As we will see, every one of these links – the doorkeepers to safe and healthy workplaces – has served to prevent the goals of the OSH Act from being realized. Indeed, as we saw in chapter 1, we are in some respects *further* from achieving these goals than we were when OSHA was instituted. While the extent of occupational illness is difficult to measure, the evidence indicates that the rate of occupational injuries continues to rise. What went wrong?

First, NIOSH was never adequately funded, with the result that research lags far behind the introduction of new techniques and substances in the workplace. Worse, federal regulators are forced to rely on industry studies, with their built-in biases and incentives for misreporting. Epidemiological work is stymied by the inadequacy of record-keeping, and as simple a matter as informing workers that they are being studied for possible health risks has been bitterly contested.[3] In general, this is not attributable to NIOSH employees, who are dedicated and well qualified; rather, they have not been given enough money to do their job properly and are not backed up by higher levels of government when disputes with industry emerge.

If the shortcomings of NIOSH have not attracted public attention, it is probably because the real bottleneck occurs at the level of standard-setting. The process by which OSHA generates new standards for workplace safety has proved to be unbearably slow: one by one, standards governing specific hazards have been proposed, challenged, reconsidered, and litigated. Even during its best years, under the Carter administration, OSHA never came close to its original mandate (Mendeloff, 1979), while progress virtually ceased under Reagan. The history of its activities in the field of hazardous substances (an area where much was expected) is particularly disappointing. Noble (1986) sum-marizes the record as follows:

The agency adopted only 15 major health rules between 1971 and 1984; only 11 of them actually set exposure levels. Two rules, the labeling standard and the access-to-medical records rule, dealt with worker rights to information; a third, the cancer policy, established a framework for health standard setting; and a fourth, the 14 carcinogens standard, established work practices for the safe handling of the substances. Moreover, all but two of the new health rules revised existing TLVs [threshold limit values] from the original standards package. Thus the total number of toxic and hazardous substances covered by OSHA exposure limits remained slight – less than two dozen – despite the fact that there are approximately 2000 suspected or known carcinogens in use in the workplace. (p. 179)

To take but one example: a standard for exposure to benzene, a known carcinogen, was delayed for more than ten years (1977–88). During that time the *low* estimate for the number of excess deaths likely to have resulted from this delay was 275; the upper estimate was

1,100 (Moure-Eraso and Tsongas, 1990). Once set, OSHA standards themselves tended to be weak, dictated far more by political pressure from business interests than objective public health considerations (McCaffrey, 1982).

But the promulgation of standards was just the beginning of OSHA's problems. Funding was never adequate to the task and became even less so during the Reagan administration. Figure 6.2 shows the inflation-adjusted budgets for NIOSH and OSHA, expressed in the form of dollars per privately employed worker in each year, over the period 1976–94. Expenditures rose during the years following the passage of the OSH Act, reaching a peak in the final two years of the Carter administration. The decline under Reagan reflects the successful political campaign waged against not only OSHA but most other forms of "social" regulation. Note that expenditures for OSHA and NIOSH track each other closely until the second year of the Clinton administration. Since then, NIOSH has received a modest funding increase (still leaving it below its 1976 level, measured in constant dollars per worker), while OSHA has plumbed new lows. One upshot of OSHA's underfunding has been its inability to hire enough inspectors to see that standards, as few as they are, are enforced. It is a commonplace to note that the federal government employs more game wardens to protect wildlife from illegal hunting than safety inspectors to safeguard the lives and health of American workers.

After slashing the size of its inspectorate, OSHA under the Reagan administration devised new procedures for improving the "efficiency" of its remaining force: beginning in 1981 it became OSHA policy *not* to respond to worker complaints over safety, while firms with above-average safety records were exempted from on-site inspections (Abel, 1985). Rather than encouraging firms to reduce injuries and illnesses on their own, however, the policy created an incentive for firms not to *report* them. As a result, many large firms, including Union Carbide, Chrysler, General Motors, and USX (formerly US Steel), have been issued fines for willfully underreporting accident data (Risen, 1987a; Karr, 1987). Because of the shortage of inspectors, of course, it is likely that many more firms have done the same but avoided detection. One result of this policy, incidentally, is the reduced quality of the government's own safety statistics. This casts a shadow over the BLS data discussed in chapters 1 and 3; the problem is compounded in all likelihood by the continued growth of off-the-books production during the 1980s. This unreported activity, including the employment of undocumented immigrant workers, probably contributes to BLS undercounting, since work in this sector is significantly more dangerous than work in regulated sectors.

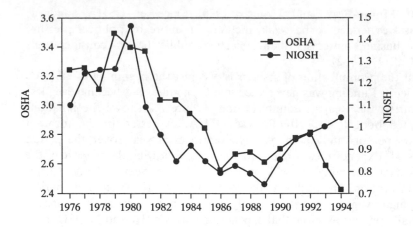

Figure 6.2   Expenditures per worker (in 1994 dollars)

These two handicaps – insufficient standards and not enough inspectors – would be enough to defang OSHA, but even if a standard has been promulgated, and if an inspector has found a violation, it is still probable that little if anything will be done. It is OSHA policy to encourage inspectors to reach voluntary compliance agreements with violators, even though the record demonstrates that this approach usually results in more agreement than compliance (Lofgren, 1989). Indeed, by OSHA's own records, the number of serious violations alone (half the total violations) exceeds the number of penalties issued (Gray and Scholz, 1991). Not that the fines matter much anyway: the majority have been under $100 (Serrin, 1991), while for 1985 the average was a mere $34 (Weil, 1991).

It is hardly surprising, then, that OSHA has been unable to fulfil its mission of safeguarding the lives and health of American workers. The question remains, however, whether OSHA could succeed even if it were properly funded and administered. It is important to consider this carefully, since the answer will determine whether we need a change in fundamental policies or only in political leadership.

First, it should be noted that the political and administrative failure of OSHA is not independent of the regulatory strategy it embodies. (1) It relies heavily on the performance of a public bureaucracy, but the preponderance of evidence, both at the level of the government as a whole and at the level of OSHA in particular, indicates that business interests always have enormous leverage in this arena (Noble, 1986). They alone have the resources to contest every issue at every stage of the process; they provide the lion's share of money for electoral campaigns and can call in their IOUs when and where they choose; and their ability to withhold or relocate investment is the ultimate weapon against the public sector. Despite political leaders' best intentions (when they have them), the day-to-day operations of the apparatus of government will bend toward business interests when not actually captured by them. (2) It fails to mobilize workers as a countervailing power to business. As we have seen, the level of risk in the workplace is determined to a considerable extent by the balance of power between workers and employers. While OSHA does offer some opportunities for greater worker influence, its primary effect is to *replace* this influence with its own. (3) Poor working conditions exist precisely because firms resist expensive safety improvements. It is the mission of public policy to overcome this resistance; so the opposition of employers cannot be used as an *excuse* for regulatory failure.

Second, the centralized regulatory model incorporated in OSHA is inherently ill-suited to the demands of workplace regulation. Empirical studies have shown at best a modest relationship between OSHA activity, such as standard-setting, investigations, or complaints, and subsequent safety improvement. (See the studies cited in the following paragraph.) Why? A reasonable conjecture would be that the tools of OSHA are ill-matched to the nature of the problem they address: (1) Centralized rule making for thousands of workplaces is a formidable bureaucratic task at best; the pressure of political cross-currents renders it virtually impossible. (2) Most occupational risks are transitory. This is true of slick floors, loose scaffolding, leaky seals. Safety features mandated by law may be unavailable or malfunctioning from time to time, but inspectors are not likely to know this. (3) Workplaces are so different in their production processes that perhaps no two are effectively regulated by the same set of rules. Worse yet, ineffective rulemaking breeds apathy and disrespect, not only among employers but among workers as well. (4) We still lack information concerning the health effects of different levels of exposure to different chemicals, environmental conditions, sources of stress, etc. Indeed, individuals frequently vary in their susceptibility to these influences; under these circumstances, public health officials, aware only of laboratory experiments and epidemiological data, may actually be less informed of the health risks undertaken by a particular worker than that worker herself. In addition, even if an "acceptable" level of risk could be ascertained for each worker, regulation provides no incentive for reduction of risk below the statutory threshold. This is particularly undesirable where dose-response thresholds are either unknown or unlikely. Taken together, these problems suggest that even an aggressive, well-funded OSHA would make only modest headway in the real world of the workplace.

This judgment is borne out in empirical studies of OSHA effectiveness. The first generation of studies, conducted in the late 1970s, found little evidence of any relationship at all between OSHA inspections, citations, and subsequent safety improvement (Mendeloff, 1979; Smith, 1979; Viscusi, 1979). As new data became available and research techniques became more sophisticated, however, some effect was uncovered. A second generation of research, beginning in the mid 1980s and continuing today, is more favorable to OSHA. Typical is the work of Gray and Jones (1991). Using OSHA's own database, they tracked firms that had been inspected more than once for exceeding exposure limits for dangerous substances. Their conclusion: "Our best estimates indicate that the average plant in our sample experienced a reduction of 50 percent in citations and 42 percent in overexposures, compared to the hazards found on the initial inspection of the plant" (p. 507). This might be because there really are fewer violations, or because firms learn how to hide them better. The problem with this study, however, stems from the use of paperwork indicators (citations) rather than actual health out-comes to measure safety. Further work with this database, focusing on occupational injuries (Gray and Scholz, 1991) at 6,842 manufacturing plants between 1979 and 1985, was more explicit. Here actual injuries (albeit reported ones) were examined. The analysis is complicated because the more dangerous a workplace is, the more likely it is to be inspected, while the purpose of the study is to see if inspection *reduces* the subsequent danger. After disentangling these opposing effects, the authors found, on average, that the net effect of an inspection leading to a penalty is a 20 percent decline in the firm's injury rate over the following three years. Taken together, these new results portray an OSHA with unfulfilled potential for improving working conditions: by underfunding this agency and restraining its aggressiveness, political leaders are permitting thousands of workers to be killed and maimed unnecessarily. At the same time, however, even the most optimistic reading indicates that a revitalized OSHA is but one piece in a larger program; more vigorous enforcement alone cannot close the gap between US safety conditions and those in other OECD countries.

But focusing on standard-setting, inspection, and citations gives us a one-dimensional view of OSHA. To its credit, the OSH Act provided for more than regulation as an antidote for dangerous work. Two additional provisions are worth mentioning, plant-level safety and health commit-tees, and the right to refuse dangerous work. (1) The statute embodying OSHA encourages but does not require firms to set up safety and health committees. On the other hand, individual states are authorized to set up their own OSH systems, provided they meet federal standards, and six of those which have done so require at least some employers (certain sizes, industries, or risk levels) to set up at least some type of committee. Preliminary surveys by the General Accounting Office suggest that making OSH committees mandatory nationwide would have a positive influence on working conditions (Morra, 1992). We will have more to say about such committees later in this chapter. (2) The OSH Act authorizes workers to refuse to perform work if they reasonably believe it to be life-threatening and if they have exhausted alternative channels. In this extreme situation, workers are not to be penalized by their employers in any way, and the right to refuse is not lifted until an OSHA inspection determines that the work is safe. In practice this provision is almost invisible. First, how dangerous is dangerous? After all, many jobs are dangerous all the time, and there is no magic line separating too-dangerous from not-quite-dangerous-enough. Second, OSHA is very far and the foreman is very near. Few workers know their rights and even fewer employers can be counted on to respect them. Even if OSHA is summoned the company can stall, stonewall, and litigate. Finally, nearly all workers are in a permanent state of vulnerability. They are at risk of being written up, short-timed, passed over for a promotion, or otherwise subjected to employer retribution. Even an elaborate system of monitoring and enforcement for the right to refuse would find it difficult to protect workers against companies bent on punishment, and OSHA provides no such apparatus at all. Nonetheless, there has been a rekindling of interest in the right to refuse in recent years; we will return to it shortly.

Workers compensation: an incentive for safety?

Workers Compensation (WC) was developed because employers' liability defenses were being overturned in court (chapter 4), and it won acceptance because workers needed a financial safety net in view of the human toll of work. It was not intended as an instrument for making work safer. But functions attach themselves to organs, and we have come to rely on WC to steer employers in the direction of injury and illness prevention.

In principle, the incentive effect of WC depends entirely on experience-rating. If all firms paid the same premiums into the system, or even if firms paid standard amounts based on industry, location, or other factors, there would be no payoff to improving working conditions. The ideal, of course, would be the opposite, a system in which the employer's premium would depend entirely on the firm's safety record; then safety would truly pay. The actual structure of WC is a compromise. Experience-rating (basing premiums on the firm's claim history) plays an important role, but it is modified, particularly for smaller firms, since their fluctuation in claims from year to year is likely to be large in percentage terms (due to fewer employees), and wild swings in WC costs would interfere with efficient economic planning. (The actual rules differ across states.)

Several studies have attempted to measure the incentive effect of WC, mostly with an eye to assessing the importance of experience-rating. Since each state has its own WC program with its particular financing and benefit rules, the general strategy is to look for correlations between state-level WC features and safety records. The problem is complex, though: after all, higher benefits – and therefore higher premiums – might make firms more safety-conscious, but they might also change workers' incentives to *report* illnesses and injuries. This latter problem is almost universally described in the literature as "workers' moral hazard"; the assumption is that as benefit levels rise workers will try to cheat the system by filing spurious claims. As an example, consider the analysis of Dionne and St-Michel (1991). Workers, according to these economists, would like to make false WC claims, but face two costs – the difficulty of finding equally corrupt doctors to collude with and the risk that their scam will be revealed and benefits will be denied. So they "optimize" by equating the marginal benefits and costs of cheating, and in this formulation the effect of increasing benefits is to raise the equilibrium level of false claims. To test this model, they compare the recovery periods of different ailments for which WC has been filed. Since back ailments are more difficult to diagnose, and are therefore a potential bonanza for scam artists, they check to see whether increases in WC benefits have a differential effect on these claims. Their empirical results corroborate this hunch: when benefits rise workers claim a longer recovery period for back problems, but not for other, more easily diagnosed ailments. This is taken as evidence that worker moral hazard really exists.

What is wrong with this story? Behind the entire argument lies the unspoken assumption that, in a world of perfect information (no opportunity for cheating), workers would make all their legitimate claims and only their legitimate claims. Yet anyone with even a modest familiarity with working-class experience knows this is not true. WC pays only a portion of lost wages – generally about two-thirds. For someone living month-to-month, trying to make car and house payments, that may not be enough. More subtle, but perhaps even more important, is the pressure from the employer. Filing the extra claim or adding the extra week of recovery could jeopardize a promotion or even the job itself. Few supervisors will say openly that they penalize workers for filing under WC, but, all else being equal, a worker who simply sucks it in is more likely to be viewed as a "team player." Thus, when benefits rise and claims follow suit, it may well be that fewer legitimate claims are being *suppressed*. (Of course, with any increase in benefits claims will rise for both legitimate and illegitimate reasons; without additional information there is no way to know which effect predominates.) It is easy to see how this logic applies to Dionne and St-Michel: back pains are not only difficult for doctors and claims adjusters to diagnose; they are also difficult for *workers* to diagnose. It is all too easy to continue working, hoping that the pain will go away by itself. The incentive to tough it out will depend on the costs and benefits of filing. Increase the compensation, and stoicism becomes less attractive.[4]

However the relationship between benefits and claims is interpreted, it rules out the use of claims as an indicator of workplace safety. Instead, researchers have tried to match WC features with BLS injury data to determine whether WC has an impact on risk. The results have been inconsistent; changes in time periods under study, explanatory variables, and techniques for converting diverse state benefit and rate structures to simple one- or two-dimensional measurements can make the relationship appear or disappear. For now the conclusion must be that we simply do not know whether or not WC, experience-rated or not, makes a difference.[5] To an extent, this is puzzling. Surely increasing the financial penalty for a covered injury or illness should instil a new respect for safety in the hearts of corporate managers. A partial answer may be found in the fact that a firm may respond to increased WC costs, not by improving safety, but by attempting to reduce the generosity of the system. On a local level, greater efforts can be made to dissuade otherwise qualified workers from filing; statewide and nationally, firms can pool resources to make campaign contributions, finance conferences, and otherwise apply pressure for WC "reform." Of course, these strategies are not mutually exclusive – a firm could send an army of lobbyists to the statehouse *and* an army of ergonomists to its factories and offices – but it is also true that a profit-directed firm would not spend for safety promotion if the same dollars could be used more effectively for benefit restriction. (In reality, firms have responded to the explosion in WC rates by spending more money on lobbying in California, Maine, and other states, while injury and illness rates have continued to trend upward.)

A more general question is whether WC could be reformed to play a larger role in bringing about safe working conditions. There are at least two reasons to believe that its potential is limited. First, from an economic standpoint, efficiency requires that employers pay the full cost of preventable injuries and diseases, where the cost is determined by the workers themselves. As with the tort system WC was intended to replace, however, there is no mechanism for determining this. On the contrary, since claims are adjudicated on a no-fault basis, features must be introduced to guarantee that workers will be *undercompensated* in order to insure that carelessness remains costly. In practice this has meant that workers are limited to a fraction of their lost earnings. Since lost earnings constitute only a portion of the true losses from injuries, the goal of full compensation remains far beyond reach. Second, since experience-rating can never be complete, both because of the small numbers problem (too much fluctuation in premiums) and the nature of no-fault insurance itself (inability to contest claims), incentives must be based at least in part on projected future risk rather than past performance. This in turn would require a system of inspection and evaluation of workplace conditions – but then we are back in the world of safety regulation à la OSHA.

As long as workers rely on wages to maintain their standard of living, and as long as work remains a dangerous activity, we will need a system that guarantees all of us adequate compensation in the event of injury or illness. Properly devised, this system can even make a modest contribution to providing incentives for safety. But the main components of occupational safety and health policy will have to be found elsewhere.

Small world: occupational safety and health in other industrialized countries

Good ideas are scarce; that is why an entire career can be based on just one of them. A famous example in the history of economic thought is the "relative backwardness" hypothesis of Aleksandr Gerschenkron, the influential Russian emigré and Harvard development economist. It was his insight to observe that the economic fortunes of a country depend mightily on its level of development *relative* to that of its neighbors. Gerschenkron is remembered for little more than his elaboration of this insight, but it was more than enough. In the best of cases, he argued, simply being bordered by more advanced economies can give your own a big boost through the importation of better technology, copying successful laws and policies, and generally learning from the leaders. Eventually, of course, a successful economy closes this gap and must learn to grow on its own initiative.

From a social perspective, the United States enjoys a veritable bounty of relative backwardness. Our public and private institutions do a terrible job of safeguarding equality, health, and other social values compared to other countries at a similar level of economic development. In fact, we share a 2,000 mile border with one country, Canada, that towers over us in nearly every phase of social policy. This presents us with a wonderful opportunity: we can make great strides without ever having to think an original thought. Hence the purpose of this section, to describe the institutions and policies that have enabled other advanced capitalist countries to achieve safer workplaces. In the interest of not merely closing the gap, however, but actually leapfrogging our partners in the global economy, I will consider their approaches critically. As we will see, their systems of occupational safety and health policy have serious shortcomings – even their own architects admit this. To put it differently, we can learn both positive and negative lessons from the experiences of other countries, and these can be put to use to create the most effective set of programs we can devise.

Certain features of public policy are common to all the OECD countries, including government standard-setting, workplace inspection, and some form of workers compensation. Naturally, these take somewhat different forms from one country to the next, and the level of commitment – funding, aggressiveness, and the willingness to stand up to powerful corporate interests – varies widely, differences that matter greatly for outcomes at the workplace level. Yet this is not very interesting for our purposes, since we do not need to travel the globe to know that commitment counts. More useful, on the other hand, are the laws and policies that differ in kind from those in the US, and these will be the subject of the following survey.

Social reform tends to happen in waves; most industrialized countries, for instance, experienced a wave of reform around the turn of the century, at the time of our own Progressive Era. The hard decade of the 1930s ushered in another wave, as did the end of the Second World War and the later upheaval of the 1960s and 1970s. In the United States, the first two of these periods corresponded to the development of Workers Compensation and the Fair Labor Standards Act; the last gave us the Occupational Safety and Health Act. In Europe, Canada, and Japan the 1970s was a period of enormous interest in new initiatives in the workplace; virtually every industrial country revolutionized its safety and health system. The guiding philosophy behind these efforts, however, differed widely from those in the US, Gevers (1983), describing this last European reform wave, summed up the new approach with these words:

The single most important feature of these reforms is the shift of emphasis from national to enterprise level: the individual undertaking has to develop its own health and safety policy and devise the protective measures it deems best. (p. 411)

To put it differently, governments in the EC and other countries have backed away from the direct command-and-control strategy of regulation, preferring to regulate (or, in the case of Japan, guide) the *process* of safety enforcement, which is delegated to the workers and firms directly concerned.

Of course, standard-setting and regulation continues in all industrialized countries, but the latest wave of innovation centers on local decision-making. An example is the enterprise action plan, a document drawn up by the firm that includes both an inventory of safety and health issues and a set of proposals for addressing them. Although the details of this approach differ from one country to another, action plans are mandated in France, Belgium, the Netherlands, and the Scandinavian countries. Regulators, at least on paper, scrutinize them for their adequacy and demand proof of implementation. Of course, these plans are held to higher standards in countries with social democratic traditions: an employer who does not file or does not implement is far more likely to be cited in Norway than in France.

Action plans are intermediate forms, taking their marching orders from government regulations and answerable to public officials, but formulated locally. A more far-reaching departure from the command-and-control model is the autonomous safety and health committee that sets its own standards and monitors its own results. In nearly all industrialized countries, joint labor–management committees play a central role.[6] They are seen as so valuable to the larger goals of public and occupational health that their existence is not left to chance: most workplaces are required, or at least strongly urged, to have them. Of course, the specific implementation of this approach varies from one country to another. Some of the most important differences are:

Structure

Joint oversight of working conditions can take many forms; a plant-level safety committee is just one. Committees at the level of the work group (below the enterprise level) play an important role in Sweden, Norway, Canada, Japan, Italy, the Netherlands, and Denmark, while works councils – worker-elected committees concerned with a full range of on-the-job interests, including safety – are mandatory in Germany, the Netherlands, and Luxembourg, where they possess full codetermination rights. France, Belgium, and, to some extent, Denmark make use of both safety committees and works councils, with both structures participating in a measure of codetermination.

Voluntarism

Should the government require firms to have safety committees (and/or works councils), or should they only encourage them? These measures are mandatory in the Scandinavian countries, Canada, Germany, the Netherlands, France, Belgium, Ireland, and Luxembourg; they are voluntary in Italy, Greece, and Japan. Japan, however, is something of a special case, since moral suasion, particularly when it emanates from a higher-level authority, is very effective: if the government wants firms to set up committees, they will generally do so.

Coverage

A central paradox of safety and health policy is that conditions tend to be more dangerous at small firms, but government regulations are more burdensome to them as well. Most countries respond by exempting small employers from the requirement or informal expectation that they establish safety committees. (Sweden and Norway are exceptions: they mandate committees at all firms, whatever their size.) On the other hand, some have attempted to extend workers' rights to participate in safety management to small firms in other ways. Belgium, for instance, deputizes unions to perform the function of safety oversight in firms with fewer than 50 employees, although this obviously works only for the unionized sector. In the Netherlands the right to participate devolves on the individual worker in small firms, but this does not settle the information and bargaining power issues that necessitated committees in the first place. Japan's approach reflects that country's unique industrial structure: most small producers occupy a position in the web of subcontracting relationships that establish major employers, first-tier satellites, second-tier subcontractors, and so on. Thus, while the Industrial Safety and Health Law of 1972 applies only to larger-scale enterprises, these firms are held responsible for safety conditions at their suppliers. Unfortunately, this responsibility, mostly effective for first-tier contractors, attenuates rapidly down the chain of subcontracting, with the result that workers in small firms have very little protection (Wokutch, 1992).

Extent of participation

Safety committees can be toothless advisory bodies, or they can have a measure of real control over the conditions of work. In most European countries they have significant power, although in the peripheral regions where social policy is less developed (Ireland, England, Italy, and Greece) they are primarily consultative. On the other hand, even without statutory reinforcement these bodies can influence conditions in unionized firms, and this effect is noticeable in all these countries. (Of course, it is the nonunion firms that are most in need of improvement.) In Canada matters are somewhat more unsettled, since the laws at the provincial level leave open the amount of power safety committees can wield. Their scope is therefore a matter for bargaining, and firms naturally resist most vigorously those proposals which would give workplace safety committees authority in plant decision-making; they are viewed as assaults on "management rights." Japan is, once more, a special case. Its safety committees would appear to have little formal power, but social pressures for consensus decision-making and the ideology of harmony of interests (employers are expected to share workers' interests in health and safety) give these committees significant force[7] (Wokutch, 1992).

Role of unions

This is a difficult issue. Health and safety committees are supposed to embody a *joint* concern for reducing risks in the workplace, while unions exist to press workers' interests *against* those of the employer. Of course, in practice there are many shades of grey: safety committees can be instruments of consensus-building or arenas for nose-to-nose bargaining; unions can be aggressive champions of workers' separate interests or submerge those interests in an alliance with the employer against the outside world. So it is not impossible to combine these two structures, although there is likely to be at least some residual tension. In Sweden, for example, unions operate within a joint committee structure from a position of comparative strength, since the overwhelming majority of the work force, public and private, is unionized. In Britain, on the other hand, the law formally supports unions that want to establish safety committees, but the weakness of labor makes safety a much more contentious issue. In Japan, worker representatives to joint safety committees are selected by unions in unionized firms (primarily the larger ones), but the collaborative nature of Japanese company unions guarantees that there will be little role conflict. Ultimately, the relationship between unions and joint committees depends on both elements: not only the rules governing worker participation in safety within the enterprise, but also the strategic course workers have taken in their own organizations.

While it is difficult to generalize, most observers credit joint safety and health committees with significant advances in working conditions. Their advantages include making use of local and specific knowledge, enlisting rank-and-file workers to supplement official inspectors, strengthening elements of management that value better conditions, disseminating important but often complex (and unpleasant) information about hazards, and raising the level of safety consciousness generally. But their contribution to a better working life also depends, as we will see, on the other components of safety policy – particularly those that increase the decision-making power of the workforce.

A critical ancillary to the right to participate, whether by unions, joint committees, or some other means, is the right to know about the hazards posed by work. This is particularly important as technological change has revolutionized not only production but risk. The requirement that firms disclose all potentially hazardous substances and techniques was introduced throughout Europe and Canada during the last wave of reform; if it has not been formally codified in Japan, this is primarily because the norms of personal responsibility would make it unlikely, at least in larger firms, that managers would misrepresent dangers to their workers.[8] It is only in the United States that this right, so obviously fundamental to a participatory system, has been successfully contested by business interests.

Perhaps the central component of a decentralized safety and health strategy is the right of workers to refuse hazardous work: without this crucial guarantee committee meetings and company disclosures can remain stuck at the level of good intentions. As we have seen, the OSH Act provided for a limited right to refuse, although it was accorded so little statutory support that it has remained a peripheral aspect of the system. Other countries such as Canada, Sweden, Norway, Denmark, and the Netherlands, however, have placed great emphasis on this right. In most cases the right to refuse is vested in worker representatives, such as union reps or worker members of safety committees, although allowance is usually made for individual action pending investigation. Detailed rules prohibit reprisals against workers who exercise their rights, and the protection of refusers is an important function of unions and safety committees.

There is widespread agreement that the right to refuse dangerous work has had a powerful impact on working conditions where it has existed and been utilized, both because of its direct effects (workers avoid the most hazardous situations) and because it lends force to workers' claims for safety across the board. It is not a panacea, however. By its nature it is a response to exceptional circumstances and is unlikely to be invoked over the potentially deadly threats posed by low-level, chronic stresses and exposures. Above all, it is only as effective as the safeguards for resisters, and the fundamental condition of workers in all capitalist enterprises is subordination. Unions and other collective structures can mitigate this condition, but the problem is most severe in unorganized firms, where workers who refuse face retaliation alone. It is not surprising, then, that the right to refuse has had the greatest success in the predominantly unionized economies of Scandinavia, whereas Canada, with its progressive laws but largely unorganized workforce, has fared less well. In Ontario, for instance, fully 93 percent of all refusals are by unionized workers – yet two-thirds of all workers are not unionized and face the most extreme risks.

A decentralized strategy, relying on the participation of rank-and-file workers as well as line managers to monitor and enforce safety standards, requires an ambitious program of research and training. All participants need to become "barefoot" industrial hygienists in order to do their jobs effectively; in particular, the right to refuse depends on a radical democratization of expertise. At the same time, enterprise- and unit-level committees will uncover problems that call for professional investigation. They need a safety and health research system that is designed to respond to their concerns, one whose agenda is set by the requests flowing in from workplaces throughout the country rather than directives from political authorities. In fact, many countries have experimented with restructuring their public occupational health systems in this direction, and professionals in the field have been mostly supportive. The real limits are political: is the government willing to let researchers respond freely to the needs of the workplace and let the chips fall where they may?

The range of alternatives can be seen by comparing two countries. In Japan the government funds a wide variety of research and training activities including a University of Occupational and Environmental Health (established 1978). Much of the funding, however, is channeled through an industry-based organization, the Japan Industrial Safety and Health Association, a counterpart to America's National Safety Council. Workers have little input into the content and direction of the research program. Sweden, by contrast, operates a system whose main function is to respond to requests emanating from worker-dominated safety committees. At the same time, Swedish health professionals provide the open-ended training in toxicology and ergonomics necessary for rank-and-file workers to identify the problems that need to be investigated. The result is a cutting-edge program whose advances are followed closely around the world. An example: Americans have recently become aware of potential hazards from high-emission computer monitors. New, healthier low-emission monitors are now being marketed with the claim that they meet the more stringent Swedish health standards. But Sweden developed those standards only because workers who stare at terminals all day were able to bring their concerns to public health professionals, and the system was set up to give these professionals the time and money they needed to do their job.

All of the above innovations concern *how* to improve working conditions, but the most far-reaching development, thus far confined to Scandinavia, redefines the goal of workplace reform itself. The work environment movement, centered in Sweden and Norway, views health and safety as parts of a larger whole which includes the social organization of work, the role of skill and judgment, and the adaptation of production to the human being – not the other way around. From this perspective, hazardous working conditions are symptomatic of deeper problems: authoritarianism within the firm that prevents people from taking needed protective measures, monotony from work drained of craft and variety, stress from the devastating combination of too many demands on the job and not enough control, and, above all, technologies designed without sufficient consideration for the people who will have to work with them.[9] Thus, the Norwegian Work Environment Act states that all workers have a right to a healthy and humane work environment; work environment committees at the enterprise level are empaneled to enforce it. A similar law in Sweden makes work environment matters a mandatory topic for collective bargaining. There are no miracles in Scandinavia, however: the main result thus far from these initiatives has been a flourishing of research on the technology/organization/health nexus. A true humanization of work, in reality as well as theory, will require yet more radical changes in organization and authority in the workplace, as we will see in the following section.

This has been a whirlwind tour around the industrialized world, hopping back and forth to gather the shards of safety policy. I have made no attempt to demonstrate the ways these pieces fit together to form distinctive national approaches: that would require a very different type of study. My main purpose has been to demonstrate that the menu of alternatives is much broader than one would realize by examining only the US experience. Other countries have moved increasingly in the direction of decentralizing authority, delegating varying measures of standard-setting and enforcement to workers and managers on the front lines. The United States, which has been such a voracious importer of goods and services from these other economies, would do well to import more of their ideas as well.

In fact, the recent OSHA Reform Bill, introduced in the Senate by Edward Kennedy and the House by William Ford, incorporates two of the many policy devices outlined above. First, it requires all firms to adopt an action plan on occupational safety and health and to make it available to workers and outside inspectors. Second, it mandates joint health and safety committees for all employers.[10] As we have seen, these are both worthy emendations and would no doubt save many lives. As proposed, however, they still fall far short of what has been achieved elsewhere, and, given the extreme weakness of the US labor movement, they are likely to work less well here than in Europe or Canada. Congress would do well to approve OSHA reform quickly and then take up the urgent task of creating a new, more effective system.

Rights and regulation: a new direction in safety policy

Now that we know that markets alone will not ensure an adequate level of safety and health in the workplace, and that simply passing a law commanding workplaces to be safe will not do the job either, where do we go from here? In this section I will outline what I believe to be the general principles that should govern an effective system of occupational safety and health and suggest specific steps to implement them.

The first broad principle is that of local control, participation, and empowerment. Those most directly affected by working conditions, those who actually live these conditions each day, should be at the center of safety policy. There are many reasons for this. First, and most obviously, workers and front-line managers are crucial because they are *there*. They are not occasional visitors, inspectors who must somehow stay on top of thousands of work sites with different problems and needs. When conditions change suddenly – when a machine malfunctions or a chemical leaks – they are on the scene, and few hazards can be hidden from them. Of course, their numbers are not affected by budget cuts, nor their vigilance by political interference. Second, there are as many risks as there are workplaces; even the best-trained professionals cannot be familiar with all of them. Indeed, the facts themselves may be uncertain. For instance, we still lack information concerning the health effects of different levels of exposure to various chemicals, environmental conditions, sources of stress, etc. Individuals frequently differ in their susceptibility to these influences, and under these circumstances public health officials, aware only of laboratory experiments and epidemiological data, may actually be less informed of the health risks undertaken by a particular worker than that worker herself. Third, as we saw in our review of OSHA's performance, a fundamental issue has been the very commitment of the government to follow through on its own mandate. The story of the last two decades since the passage of the OSH Act has been one of failed deadlines, lawsuits to force the agency to set standards, and lax implementation. To a considerable extent, this simply reflects the true balance of power between labor and capital: workers, during their surge of the late 1960s, were strong enough to get the initial legislation passed, but with the erosion of their position during the subsequent years of industrial and union decline, they have had little influence over enforcement. And this explains why policies that empower rank-and-file workers are so important: they not only promote safety today, but also the constituency that can demand safety tomorrow. An approach that organizes millions of workers and gives them tools at their places of work changes its own context, much like a plant that alters the chemistry of the surrounding soil to further its own growth.[11] Finally, it is important not to romanticize the victims of dangerous working conditions. While workers have greater access to information regarding the risks they face than anyone else, we have seen that their perceptions may be colored by factors ranging from cognitive dissonance to machismo. Since workers' care and attention will be crucial whatever the institutional arrangement, an effective policy will be one that encourages workers (and supervisors) to develop a more informed perspective on health and safety. A strategy of empowerment does exactly this; it recognizes that individuals grow in responsibility by *having* responsibility.[12]

The second general principle complements the first: the complex social and technical aspects of production generate demands that only society-wide regulation can satisfy.[13] (1) There are limits to what workers can accomplish on their own. In an age in which toxic exposures are measured in the parts per billion there is an irreducible role for expert standard-setting. Moreover, workers' subordinate position within the firm constrains their ability to safeguard their interests, even in unionized firms. Naturally, this ability is at its nadir in the most dangerous and generally least organized firms where it is needed most. The heightening of global competition, moreover, has eroded worker power in every country, from business-dominated US to social democratic Norway and Sweden. Under these circumstances a complete devolution of responsibility for safety and health to the workplace level would be a disaster. (2) In a competitive economy workers are always torn between their separate interests *vis-à-vis* management and their shared interest in the success of the firm. As discussed in the previous chapter, this can be viewed as a Prisoner's Dilemma: workers in all firms benefit if stringent safety standards are upheld for all, but if workers at one company take the lead and the others do not follow, their own employer suffers and their very jobs are at risk. As with any Prisoner's Dilemma, all parties benefit if they can discourage destructive individualism; government regulation can potentially do this by creating a single standard to which everyone must conform. (3) A recurrent theme in this book, particularly in chapters 4 and 5, has been the central role of social norms in conflicts over risk. Individual judgment is often guided by common benchmarks (recall the discussions of bounded rationality and prospect theory), and these normative tendencies are intensified in the heat of struggle. In this context government regulations play a dual role: they are legal mandates that alter behavior, and they are symbolic communications that can endorse existing norms or promote new ones. Policy analysts tend to dismiss this second aspect of regulation as extraneous or even unworthy, but if the bulk of risk reduction takes place at the local level measures that influence how people think and respond to one another are not to be taken lightly. A well-constructed system of government regulation will take its symbolic role explicitly into account.

With these principles in mind, imagine an approach to occupational safety and health based on these elements:

1   The right to know

The closed, secretive nature of the modern corporation has become so familiar to us we hardly recognize it. Yet it was not always this way, and there has long been a counter-tradition of writers and thinkers to remind us that it could be different. In *Communitas* (1947), Paul and Perceval Goodman envision a community whose public life does not stop at the factory gates, where places of work are public spaces, allowing outsiders to look in and insiders to remain full participants in community life during their working hours. In particular, they deplore what they call the "quarantining" of work – its separation from neighborhood and family. They recognize, of course, that work must be made more benign, technically and socially, to make its reintegration possible. A more recent statement of the same theme can be found in *The Dispossessed* (1974), a fascinating work of social-science fiction by Ursula K. LeGuin which depicts a utopian society one and a half centuries after its founding. Although it is beset by problems endemic to its communitarian ethos, her anarchistic world has much to teach us. Follow Shevek, the novel's rebellious hero, as he makes his way through LeGuin's imaginary city:

The squares, the austere streets, the low buildings, the unwalled workyards, were charged with vitality and activity. As Shevek walked he was constantly aware of other people walking, working, talking, faces passing, voices calling, gossiping, singing, people alive, people doing things, people afoot. Workshops and factories fronted on squares or on their open yards, and their doors were open. He passed a glassworks, the workman dipping up a great molten blob as casually as a cook serves soup. Next to it was a busy yard where foamstone was cast for construction. The gang foreman, a big woman in a smock white with dust, was supervising the pouring of a cast with a loud and splendid flow of language. After that came a small wire factory, a district laundry, a luthier's where musical instruments were made and repaired, the district small-goods distributory, a theater, a tile works. The activity going on in each place was fascinating, and mostly out in full view. Children were around, some involved in the work with the adults, some underfoot making mudpies, some busy with games in the street, one sitting perched up on the roof of the learning center with her nose deep in a book. The wiremaker had decorated the shopfront with patterns of vines worked in painted wire, cheerful and ornate. The blast of steam and conversation from the wide-open doors of the laundry was overwhelming. No doors were locked, few shut. There were no disguises and no advertisements. It was all there, all the work, all the life of the city, open to the eye and to the hand. (pp. 80–1)

Work in such a world would be radically different from what we know today. A truly transparent, accessible workplace *has* to be safe, both because safety is a precondition for community access, and because a knowledgeable public that can see what goes on in production would have it no other way. But safety and transparency are part of a larger vision, of work as truly human activity. While extreme forms of this vision are stuff of utopian novels, we can see its beginnings in such institutions as the Israeli kibbutz and the intentional communities of the United States and other countries. Consider the example of Twin Oaks. I once visited this community in central Virginia, whose luxurious and well-constructed hammocks are sold around the world. All residents take turns working in the hammock shop, which is open to anyone else who might want to pass through. Moreover, meetings of the community's planning committee are held right beside the machines that string rope to the wooden frames, so that the hammock workers can participate. If they are not interested they can slip on a pair of headphones and listen to music instead.

What a contrast to most contemporary work! In most firms workers are subject to increasing scrutiny, as computerized monitoring permits managers to track their subordinates' every word and act. The accumulation of this information in privately held databases constitutes a serious threat to privacy and personal autonomy. At the same time, the firm itself is shielded from view; information concerning its personnel policies, technology, and future plans is proprietary, the exclusive property of its owners. In fact, it should be the other way around: the rights of individuals, whether on the job, at home, or in the community, to privacy and autonomy should be safeguarded, while organizations should be required to open themselves up to public observation. Firms protest, of course, claiming that the pressures of competition make the transparent corporation an impossibility, but the case for openness is fundamentally the same as for any other social obligation. Environmental protection, adherence to labor standards governing wages and hours, the disclosure of accurate financial information – all of these are costly for business. We try to reduce their effect on competition by requiring them of *all* firms: a level playing field in which social obligations are met. There is no reason why more general standards of openness should not be imposed as well.[14]

An excellent place to begin is the right of workers and the general public to know what risks inhere in the workplace. Workers need to know this in order to press for safe working conditions and to determine their own best-work practices. Front line supervisors need to know in order to be able to organize safety as well as production. Health professionals need to know so they can properly diagnose and treat occupational injury and disease. And the wider community needs to know because the risks of modern technology, particularly those stemming from toxic or combustible materials, do not respect the boundaries of company property. Hazards to workers, in fact, often provide the first indication that the general public is also at risk.

Several states and municipalities have instituted worker and worker-community right-to-know laws, but action is needed at the national level, both because of the need for a level playing field and because there are information economies to be tapped when employers and technologies cross state lines. The mechanics of such a policy need not be a mystery, since, as we have seen, many other countries have imposed a similar requirement. One point that ought to be stressed, however, is that a right to safety information cannot be secured simply by writing a statute: it takes organization and funding. Without the presence of either a union or a safety committee, workers will find it impossible to monitor any but the simplest production process. And gaining access to the skills needed to know what questions to ask and how to interpret the answers requires training and research support. An effective right-to-know policy, then, is not just a one-time-only decision; it demands an ongoing commitment.

2   The right to participate

Like the right to know, the right to participate ought to be a cornerstone of economic life. The virtues of taking an active role in issues of common importance are well-known and apply with particular force to occupational safety and health. Recall that perceptions of risk are profoundly affected by judgments about personal autonomy and obligation: workers are more willing to accept risk if they believe that it stems from their own freely made decisions and does not reflect an attempt by employers to profit at their expense. While this attitude can be justified on both ethical (Kantian) and strategic (game-theoretic) grounds – see the previous chapter – it may well interfere with a strictly objective evaluation of relative risks and compensations. For example, worker interest may be deflected from a much greater potential hazard, such as motor vehicle accidents, to a less likely threat like trace chemical exposures, based on imputations of autonomy and violation. Participation has the potential to defuse at least some of this preoccupation with assigning blame, since sharing the decision-making means sharing responsibility as well. With different risks placed on an equal ethical footing, purely safety and health concerns can be given more attention.

But participation is a vague term that can take on a wide variety of meanings, from genuine involvement in decision-making to cosmetic measures whose main purpose is to disguise workers' subordination. The issue is further clouded by the many forms participation can take, the levels at which it can operate, and the importance of its political and economic contexts. The key to achieving effective participation lies in viewing it systematically, rather than as a particular institutional wrinkle. In this spirit, I will take up the various components of worker participation in turn.

1 In virtually every country that has undergone industrialization, unionism has played a central role in defining and pursuing workers' interests. As we saw in chapter 4, there is a broad correlation between the extent of union representation and a country's achievements in occupational safety and health. This is due to both the creation of a favorable political climate for regulation and the greater ability of workers, protected by a union, to invoke statutory safeguards and defend working conditions on the shop floor. But, as we have also seen, union representation in the United States has fallen to levels not seen since the Great Depression. It is naive to think that fundamental reform of this country's workplace safety and health system can be achieved without a reversal of this trend. While this book is not the place for a full discussion of the causes of and responses to union decline, a few general points are in order: (1) Existing procedures governing union election and certification are inadequate, permitting employers to defeat representation through delay and retaliation, even where a majority of workers would want to unionize. At the very least, workers should be able to install a union simply by signing representation cards, bypassing the need for an additional ballot, and complaints of unfair labor practice should be processed quickly. (2) Without an effective right to strike, unionism is toothless. This right is more than a legal formality; it requires that strikes must be at least as costly to employers as to the workers that undertake them. If firms can break strikes with impunity, legal guarantees are

pointless – hence the need for legislation preventing firms from hiring permanent (or indeed even temporary) replacements. Moreover, as interfirm networks, such as joint ventures, outsourcing, and other cooperative arrangements, become more common, strikes restricted to a single employer lose bite. It is imperative to restore to workers the rights, removed in the Taft–Hartley Act of 1947, to engage in solidarity strikes and secondary boycotts. (3) The National Labor Relations Board's customary distinction between "mandatory" and "permissive" bargaining issues, with only actions in response to the first protected under labor law, is obsolete and obstructive. This dichotomy, unmentioned in the text of the law itself, inhibits unions from disputing company policies of broad strategic importance: whether to change ownership, to load or unload debt, to enter new product lines or technologies. To speak of worker participation but then cordon off the most important issues from union response is hypocritical. (4) The denial of labor law protection to managerial workers seeking representation may have made sense in an era when most workers had no managerial responsibilities and the greatest threat to union integrity was company moles. This is no longer the case. Managerial workers outnumber their production and clerical colleagues at an increasing number of firms; existing law makes it nearly impossible for them to organize and virtually inevitable that they will be used to replace organized workers who strike. US labor law should be revised to eliminate all restrictions on who can form a bargaining unit.

No set of legislative changes, of course, can substitute for the energy and good sense of the labor movement itself, but the reforms outlined above could at least give union activists a fighting chance.[15] As the experience of occupational safety and health regulation demonstrates, only those workers with solid union support will take full advantage of whatever standards and procedures are adopted at the national level.

2 Unions are most effective where they are most centralized, but many concerns of the workforce are local and would tend to be ignored by a national or international body negotiating broad standards of wages and employment. The need for independent shop-level representation is universal and has been addressed by a variety of mechanisms, union-based (like the British "combine," a local coalition of separate union locals), company-based (like quality circles), and independent. My main interest here is in the last option, in particular the "works council" now being considered for general adoption in the United States.

Works councils are elected by the workforce, much as union officers are elected, but they are not part of a larger organization and their duties are ultimately consultative, since they lack the ability to call a strike. It would be a mistake, however, to conclude from this that they have no power to strengthen workers' interests. By helping individual workers see that their problems are not all individual, and by speaking to the owners with a common voice, councils alter the balance of power within the firm. Moreover, if management tries to stonewall them they may even provide a basis for eventual unionization. These effects are well-known in business circles, which is why most nonunion firms try to prevent councils from forming or being imposed by legislation. As this is being written, the members of the European Community are debating whether to make mandatory works councils an EC-wide component of its social dimension. (If approved, this stipulation would not apply to the UK, which has been given permission to go its own way on social matters.) Unions and socialist parties have lined up behind the council proposal; businesses and conservative parties are more reluctant. Similar divisions – minus the socialist presence, of course – can be expected when the topic is introduced in the US.

Works councils can function as weak unions in a nonunion environment, but they can also complement existing unions, giving greater voice to local concerns and enabling workers to pursue collaborative and adversarial strategies simultaneously. For these reasons, it is wrong to see unions and councils as competing forms of organization; each (and particularly the works council) functions better in the presence of the other.

As an element of an occupational safety and health strategy, the works council is important for two reasons. First, it offers some protection to individual workers in the absence of a union, and thereby increases the effectiveness of any other aspect of the program. In addition, the works council approach is implicit in worker-led safety and health committees, an essential component of any decentralized system of reform. We have already seen that such committees play a central role in many OECD countries. As similar institutions are introduced in the United States, it is important to recognize that they can serve not only to collect and disseminate information, voice complaints, and discuss solutions. At heart they are also works councils, and to do their job properly – addressing the connections between the work environment and the broader policies of the firm, encouraging individuals to exercise their rights to know and to refuse – they should be embedded in councils with enterprise-wide rights and responsibilities. In practical terms, this means that safety policy and worker representation policy must be devised together, using mandated safety committees to promote councils and mandated councils to empower safety committees.

3 In the previous chapter it was noted that under US law firms are viewed as simple commodities, the sole property of their owners, despite the fact that they do not, and in principle could not, function entirely on that basis. Indeed, other capitalist countries have begun to recognize the insufficiency of property and contract law as vehicles for regulating the behavior of corporations. Germany, for example, requires 50 percent worker representation on the boards of its large enterprises ("codetermination"), while it is widely assumed in Japan that equity owners must share corporate control rights with several other parties, including, in various combinations, labor, government, suppliers, and creditors (Aoki, 1988). Since incorporation is a publicly defined process, there is no intrinsic barrier to similar departures in this country. Firms enjoying corporate status (including limited liability) could be required to include on their boards of directors not only elected worker representatives but designated environmental or public health advocates as well. This particular combination would be especially appropriate for ensuring a safe and healthy workplace: despite common assumptions to the contrary, workers' concerns for a safe environment inside the company fence and environmentalists' concerns for a safe environment outside it are often complementary. Labor and environmental codetermination could advance these objectives both through direct policy intervention and by using their position to support whistleblowers in the ranks.

4 The rules governing the employment relationship are not negotiated from scratch each time a new employee is hired; they are determined socially through a combination of statute, judicial precedent, and custom. Nevertheless, due to the prominence of free-market thinking in the United States every movement away from untrammeled employer discretion, however modest, has had to be conquered through bitter struggle. After a century of limitations on the freedom of employers to pay what they choose, set hours as they choose, or discriminate as they choose, the time has come to tackle their freedom to dismiss as they choose – to challenge *employment at will*. In reality, there is nothing "anti-market" about requiring employers to provide due process for workers they would fire, since the labor market would continue to allocate employment in any event, albeit for a slightly different bundle of rights. It does strengthen labor relative to capital, of course, and that is why it will be strongly resisted. The demand for due process in dismissal has many ramifications, but its significance for occupational safety and health is straightforward: it would greatly increase the ability of individual workers to bring dangerous conditions to light, not to mention refuse dangerous work, by reducing the fear of retaliation.

Indeed, it would be irresponsible to introduce a plan that called on workers to be front-line inspectors of safety conditions *without* providing for their protection.

5 No set of workplace and labor law reforms, however ingeniously constructed, can fully shield workers who challenge dangerous work from all forms of retaliation – harassment, transfer, false write-ups, etc. The ultimate recourse is to go elsewhere. In the textbook world of perfectly competitive labor markets, where all labor is employed (or spells of unemployment are brief and for the purpose of gathering information) and the next best option is just as good as the one you are in, this would not be a problem. Of course, in the textbook world we would have no need for health and safety regulation either, and workers would never have cause for complaint. In the real world widespread and prolonged unemployment, combined with great inequalities between good and bad jobs, make leaving an abusive employer costly or even unthinkable. In the efficiency wage approach developed in the previous chapter, this effect is captured by the cost of job loss, a function of, among other things, the unemployment rate and the extent of social wage benefits. The public policy implication of this type of analysis is unsurprising: government efforts to reduce labor market insecurity through employment programs and social insurance increase the ability of workers to pursue all of their objectives, including safer working conditions.

6 All too often the chief barrier to expanding worker participation, whether in safety and health or in some other domain, is not employer obstruction but failure of the imagination. Recall the central message of prospect theory, that individuals do not evaluate their circumstances on an absolute, unchanging scale, but against the backdrop of their own experiences and expectations. With so few opportunities for significant worker participation – participation on terms that permit workers to advance their interests where they differ from management – available in this society, it is not surprising that workers often take their exclusion from decision-making as natural. Fortunately, public policy can encourage a sprinkling of highly visible examples of egalitarian workplaces more readily than it can transform labor relations as a whole. One approach, for instance, would be to encourage worker cooperatives through preferential credit and support, although, in the absence of a vigorous public health component, there may be a tendency for cooperators to discount their own safety, as we saw in chapter 4. Another measure, oddly underutilized considering its

immediate feasibility, would use existing public enterprises as models of worker participation. Given that the weight of existing evidence supports the connection between productivity and greater worker participation and control (Levine and Tyson, 1990), there is no reason not to introduce democratic practices to the public sector. As workers in conventional, privately owned firms become more aware of the potential for new forms of organization, hierarchy and exclusion will come to be viewed as less inevitable.

Participation, as envisioned in this book, is not a euphemism for labor's willing submission to capital, an achievement of dubious value for occupational safety and health or any other humane goal. On the contrary, taken together, the effect of the above measures would be to bring about a *mutual* participation in which capital would as often be enlisted in labor's cause as labor would in capital's. This egalitarian vision of cooperation is inconceivable without a radical redistribution of power, and, in the end, that is what these initiatives envisage. At a time such as the present, when the prevailing view is that there is no alternative to an economy organized around the single-minded pursuit of profit, it is important to remember that alternatives to promote democracy and participation are as feasible now as they have ever been, that they can be advanced step-by-step starting from the current system of institutions, and that they can be open-ended in scope and depth.

3   *The right to refuse*

Perhaps the central ingredient in a decentralized approach to occupational safety is the right to refuse dangerous work. There are two reasons for this: (1) Even the best standard-setting and monitoring at a company-wide or plant-wide level will omit something – temporary hazards or problems confined to particular aspects of production. When an unforeseen risk arises, workers need immediate instruments to ensure safety; the simplest and most effective is simply the ability to say no. (2) If worker participation is industrial democracy, the right to refuse dangerous work is a civil liberty: it defines a space within which each individual is inviolable, regardless of the views of those in authority. Surely personal safety belongs in this space, and even if the right to refuse is never invoked, simply having it contributes to the worker's sense that he or she is a respected, valued member of the larger community.

As we have already seen, the right to refuse dangerous work appears in the occupational safety and health systems of most industrialized countries to some extent, yet nowhere has it emerged as a major line of defense against avoidable risk. There is a simple reason for this. If workers could refuse *any* risk they viewed as unreasonable, whole branches of production would come to a standstill. Hence there must be a constraint: either workers must be reluctant to invoke their right, or they must fear retaliation, or the government must designate whole classes of risk as beyond refusal. In any case, the result is that the right to refuse is nearly always invoked only in the most extreme circumstances and plays little if any role in day-to-day safety management. But the vision of a workplace safety and health system grounded in the autonomous judgment and experience of the workers at risk is too valuable to discard. It can be saved by introducing a familiar element from economics: workers should be free not merely to reject risks altogether but to set a price on them. In other words, the right to refuse dangerous work can be made the basis for real, not illusory, compensation for risk.

It would be wrong to view this book as an uncompromising rejection of compensating differentials – far from it. Although I have tried to make clear the limitations of compensation as the only response to risk, emphasizing patterns of individual judgment and social interaction that confound monetary mechanisms, my primary claim has been that market-generated wage compensation is simply inadequate. Mohandas Gandhi is said to have been asked by a journalist, "What do you think of western civilization?" "It would be a good idea," he replied, and so would be compensating wage differentials. Compensation for risk not only serves to promote fairness by rewarding those whose working conditions are the most onerous; it also creates incentives for firms to make jobs safer. For generations employers have tinkered with the production process to economize on costly materials and even human skills; let them show the same concern for risk to life and health by being made to pay for it. The problem, of course, is that the present system does not do this – but there is nothing wrong with the objective.

In chapter 2 we saw that, according to conventional economic theory, it is the worker's threat to take a different job that forces employers to provide compensating differentials. Later we found that the theory is wrong: unemployment, labor market segmentation, and the dynamics of labor–management relations on the job are confounding factors, and, in any event, the overwhelming weight of the evidence is against meaningful compensation. This suggests that reliance on labor markets alone does not give workers sufficient leverage to extract wage premia. Logically, new institutions are required to achieve compensation, and this is where the right to refuse can make an important contribution. By offering (if they *choose*) to waive their refusal right for greater pay, workers in more dangerous jobs can negotiate compensation agreements that could, in principle, generate the same equity and incentive effects that economists (wrongly) attribute to the unfettered market. Of course, matters are not quite this simple; additional elements would have to be in place for the system to be workable:

1 A ceiling would have to be placed on the range of risk for which the right of refusal could be waived. Society has a stake in occupational safety and health and may legitimately curb particularly egregious hazards even if there are workers willing to accept them. (The same argument applies to public regulation of product and transportation safety, among other instances.)

2 A minimum level of risk would have to be established below which workers could not exercise refusal rights. It is important that the right to refuse be invoked only for significant threats to health and safety; permitting frivolous or malicious actions would bring the process to a standstill.

3 Workers must be protected against retaliation. As we have seen, this is an indispensable requirement of any safety program that deputizes workers to regulate their own workplaces. As discussed above, measures to promote truly egalitarian labor relations should not be viewed as auxiliary; advances in occupational safety and health are inseparable from worker empowerment in general.

4 Employers must be protected against unreasonable demands. Even if the risks workers refuse to accept are legitimately compensable, they may try to use their right to refuse to shut down the enterprise unless they are paid an exorbitant premium. (In economic terms, they might attempt to appropriate the firm's entire rent, or more.) In most cases public pressure would probably be sufficient to trim excessive demands. As a last resort, however, intransigent workers can be viewed as poor matches, and the firm can justifiably move to replace them – subject, of course, to the due process stipulations discussed above. Clearly there is room for abuse of the system on both sides, but no proposal can avoid this altogether.

5 Negotiation must take place at the appropriate level. From a practical standpoint, a central problem will be to determine just *who* should have the right to bargain over accepting risk – the individual worker, the immediate work group, or a larger, representative organization of workers? This is a difficult matter to resolve. On the one hand, giving each individual the right to determine which risks she is willing to accept, and for what compensation, brings about a closer correspondence between the prices established through bargaining and the real preferences of individual workers. It also gives each worker the greatest possible autonomy, the opportunity to be the subject rather

than the object of the production process. On the other hand, many occupational hazards are shared: if they exist for one they exist for all. It is simply not feasible to parcel them out through negotiations with small groups of workers. Moreover, even where it is possible to make many localized adjustments, there may be great economies to plant- or industry-wide coordination. It is often the case, for instance, that the joint cost of reducing two risks is less than the combined cost of reducing them separately, due to possibilities for reorganizing the overall process.[16] If so, separate negotiations with each group over each risk is inefficient.

There is no universally correct answer to the problem of centralized versus decentralized risk bargaining: the costs and benefits will differ greatly from one situation to another. An effective system would therefore have to be flexible, permitting individuals, work teams, safety committees, and collective bargaining entities to negotiate risk and reward as circumstances indicate.

6 Not all risks can or should be subject to a process that bargains away the right to refuse. At least four additional factors should be taken into consideration: (1) In some situations risks are "public" in the sense that if a few workers face them, all (or at least many more) do. Clearly this suggests the need for bargaining at a level that encompasses this publicness, but that may not always be possible. For instance, workers may have no genuine representation at this wider level, or the risk in question, even though it is common to all, may affect different individuals quite differently. In such cases it is the greater part of wisdom simply to eschew the bargaining mechanism and rely on a combination of regulation and participation, enforced by a residual right to refuse. (2) Agreements to exchange waivers for compensation can logically be written only for *classes* of risks, but many risks do not fit neatly into general categories. For example, workers are exposed to many toxic chemicals, but the classification "toxic chemical exposure" hardly does justice to the differences between exposure to trace amounts of a mild irritant and potentially catastrophic, irreversible exposure to a potent carcinogen. In practice, then, the bargaining mechanism will tend to be used for certain characteristic production hazards, widely recognized and more-or-less intrinsic to the type of work being performed. (3) Hazards can be negotiated only if they are anticipated, but many of the most dangerous working conditions are unpredictable and transient. Even more important, many risks that are normally within a range of potential acceptability can be magnified by sudden, unexpected events. Risk negotiation is clearly better suited to chronic, "stable" risks than

to dangerous episodes. (4) In any society, even one as fragmented and callous as our own, the hardships borne by individuals are not theirs alone. The wider community can legitimately set limits to the type, as well as the amount, of risk in the workplace, just as it does for medical, environmental and other risks. Granted, this can lead to the perception that public authorities have a license for paternalistic meddling, and vigilance is required to make sure that a balance is struck between the competing interests of community standards and personal freedom. The point here, however, is simply that individuals should not be given an unlimited right to exchange life and limb for money.

Subject to these restrictions, we can imagine a system in which workers have a genuine, enforceable right to safe working conditions. This means either that working conditions are fully safe, or that any remaining risks have been freely accepted in return for adequate compensation. A bargaining mechanism such as the one outlined above, whatever its other merits or difficulties, is an indispensable aspect of the right to safety, since without it there would remain unavoidable gaps:

1 A system based solely on maximum allowable standards for risk exposure does not address the less drastic but still important "normal" hazards of production. Jobs are not completely safe or completely dangerous, of course; they contain many gradations of risk from moderate to extreme. To regulate only the most egregious risks is to leave in place a host of lesser ones, each perhaps less objectionable, but collectively still a threat to workers' health and well-being. In addition, with the advance of scientific knowledge and social responsibility many risks that had been thought too slight to regulate have become objects of public concern. An approach that considers *all* risk, and not merely "excessive" risk, anticipates this process and provides workers, and society as a whole, with a margin of security.

2 Unless all jobs are to be made perfectly safe – a perfect impossibility – some workers will face greater risks than others. It is only fair that they be compensated for this. After all, it is just as inequitable to pay workers equally for bearing unequal burdens as it is to pay them unequally for doing exactly the same job. Since fully compensating differentials do not appear spontaneously as a result of the Invisible Hand, public policies are necessary to bring them about.

3 A system of regulation based on maximum standards, if enforced, gives firms an incentive to improve their working conditions until those standards are met. It does not, however, change their cost calculations for risks that pass regulatory muster. A bargaining system, on the other hand, makes *every* hazard costly, and these costs enter into each

decision the firm makes, whether it be how to organize production or design or price a product. In the long run this can only increase the tendency for production to evolve in a more humane direction.

4   Apart from its social and symbolic dimensions, which we have already considered, the optimal provision of risk depends on its costs to workers and benefits in the form of reduced production costs. A bargaining mechanism has the potential to reflect these considerations with much greater precision than any regulatory process could, since it permits both workers and firms to determine benefits and costs for themselves. If the hazard in question is continuous – that is, if, like the ambient concentration of a chemical, it can be set at any given level – the situation can be depicted as in figure 6.3.

Here it is assumed that, as the risk is increased, its marginal (incremental) cost to the worker rises and the marginal cost to the firm of controlling it falls. The most likely outcome of bargaining would be an agreement to set the risk at R^* in return for compensation C^*; at any higher risk employers would choose to reduce the risk level rather than accede to workers' compensation demands; at any lower level employers would gain by producing, and paying for, more risk. Note that this is the same result as that depicted in figure 6.1, which illustrated the concept of efficient risk.

In many cases, of course, risk will be discrete rather than continuous – for instance, whether or not to install a piece of safety equipment. Here we have the two possibilities depicted in figure 6.4. In 6.4a workers are willing to reduce their compensation demands by as much as C_1 if the improvement is made, but it costs employers C_2 to make the improvement. There is a range of potential agreement between these two amounts, since both parties would be made better off. In 6.4b the situation is reversed: the cost of improvement exceeds the maximum amount by which workers would be willing to reduce their compensation demands. Here no agreement would be in the interest of both parties. The upshot is that, while our analysis cannot predict exactly what financial arrangements will be made in 6.4a, it indicates that only improvements whose benefits exceed their costs will be adopted. This is equivalent to saying that the bargaining mechanism, at least in this ideal setting, is economically efficient. Regulatory and even participatory approaches are unlikely to meet this criterion, since the first will seldom make use of the first-hand information of workers and firms, and the second gives each side a strategic incentive to exaggerate its interests. What we have, of course, is a typical case of markets doing better – except that these markets do not appear by themselves in nature: they have to be *created*.[17]

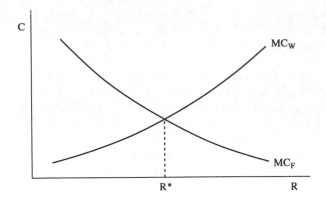

Figure 6.3

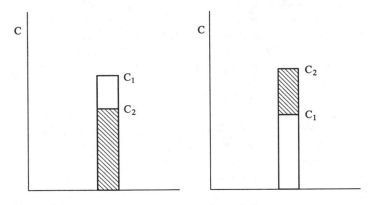

Figure 6.4a   Figure 6.4b

4 Public regulation and coordination

I have already made one case for regulation: it is needed because the other mechanisms are insufficient, even taken together. Above all, there is a need for maximum permissible risk standards, whether to set limits to the range of outcomes from bargaining and participation or to provide a last line of defense for workers beyond the reach of other policies. This is the familiar function of regulation, and little needs to be added here about how it should be carried out. But a second role for regulation can also be found in the foregoing discussion: regulation serves a symbolic function by communicating to workers and managers information about risks that public authorities have determined to be of concern. This shows up in the formation of safety norms, as we saw in the previous chapter, and it is potentially important for the participation and bargaining reforms outlined above. In fact, regulation always performs these dual roles, setting limits and drawing attention, but the problem is that those who make policy usually assume that a single standard can do double duty. It cannot. The maximum permissible level of risk is almost always much higher than the level at which those involved should take notice.

I would argue that confusions over the dual role of regulation are at the heart of much of the controversy surrounding risk assessments not only in the field of occupational safety and health, but product safety and environmental risk as well. Policy-makers, and the scientists upon whom they rely for information, believe that it is their job to determine a level of risk serious enough to force compliance. They look for evidence of likely harm and consequences serious enough to eclipse compliance costs. Workers, consumers, and others on the receiving end of risk, however, view regulation as setting limits to *protection*. From this perspective, the maximum permissible standard effectively sets the *floor* for risk, since the public authority is essentially saying that lesser hazards are fair game. So outraged citizens demand, logically enough, that regulation begin where their concerns begin, at the level of "possible" rather than "excessive" harm.

The solution is to recognize that two *different* criteria are involved, and no one standard can ever do the job. What is needed are *two* regulatory standards, one for maximum allowable risk, the other for minimum actionable (or compensable) risk. The first sets boundaries on permissible outcomes, the second guides public risk norms and suggests to the principals where and how they should take further action on their own. We already have a precedent for two-tiered standard-setting of this sort, although in a very different context: nutrition guidelines. Public health officials publish two guides to healthy eating, minimum daily requirements (MDRs) and recommended daily allowances (RDAs) for vital nutrients. The first indicates an outer limit: if you do not meet this standard you are likely to suffer serious health consequences. The second points to areas of potential concern: if you consume less than your RDA you may have a problem and should consider altering your diet. In a sense, two-tiered regulation would work the same way, by issuing two standards for every hazard, one mandatory, the other advisory. This would free regulators to play both the coercive role customary in our society and the indicative role characteristic of Japan and other corporatist societies without compromising either. If it carries with it a somewhat larger burden of information-gathering (with a concomitantly larger budget appetite), we should not protest, since in any event we need information about both ends of the risk spectrum.

Another advantage to this bifurcated approach to regulation is that it gives regulators at least some activities that will not be subject to constant review and litigation. There can be little doubt that intense business scrutiny of standard-setting in countries like the United States and Canada has created a climate of caution and delay among regulators. From the vantage point of an individual within the public bureaucracy, there is much more to be lost from regulating too much than too little. In an ideal world these pressures would not exist, but in an ideal world we would not need the regulations either. One useful adjustment to a business-dominated environment is to create a class of regulatory standards that have no direct cost to business. This will at least permit research and education over a broader range of hazards than would occur otherwise. Later, when pressures for mandatory standards have reached the critical point, regulators would not have to start from scratch. Again, Japan provides a useful example of a country in which business hegemony is nearly complete, yet the government still takes an active advisory role in identifying and assessing safety and health risks.

Of course, two-tiered regulation also recognizes that the government's role should not *only* be advisory. Mandatory limits on risk ought to be taken very seriously. Experience has shown that laws are obeyed not simply because violators risk getting caught and punished, but far more because most people have an ethical core, and if a climate is created in which laws are viewed as legitimate people will follow them. Indeed, if the only deterrent to theft, tax avoidance, and other infractions were the fear of prison, social order would be an impossible dream. To be effective, upper limits on occupational hazards must be seen as ethical imperatives. But, by definition, organizations are not ethical – *people* are. Those who make decisions that result in unacceptable risks to others must be made *personally* responsible for their actions. Once again Japan excels in this dimension: a manager found to have exposed his workers to excessive risk would be expected to suffer the consequences – demotion or even dismissal, which in Japan's lifetime employment system is tantamount to the end of one's career. Here in the United States we have begun to experiment with criminal sanctions for violation of health and safety regulations. Consider the case against managers of Pymm Thermometer and Pak Glass Machinery, two companies cited for recycling mercury in old thermometers without informing their workers or protecting them from this toxic substance. At least one worker inhaled enough mercury vapor to suffer irreversible brain damage, and the officials were convicted on criminal charges. This action was ultimately upheld by the US Supreme Court (Wermiel, 1991). We should expand on this promising direction, so that it will be generally understood that egregious safety and health violations are acts of *violence*. By appealing to personal responsibility rather than the corporate balance sheet we can end the practice of deciding whether or not to violate the law based only on the risk of getting caught. For the vast majority of managers compliance will instead become second-nature, as it should be.

As envisioned in this model, regulation ceases to be the primary vehicle for safety policy and instead serves to supplement workers' right to refuse dangerous work. It is possible that this change in emphasis may lead to economies in the more conventional functions of inspection and enforcement. For example, with workers, in conjunction with safety and health committees, playing a greater day-to-day role in monitoring risk, fewer outside inspectors may be needed, and more disputes may be resolved within the firm than in the courtroom. At the same time, it would be naive to expect that OSHA, or its successor, could flourish in its new role on a reduced budget. As we saw earlier in this chapter, the current level of funding is completely inadequate, and OSHA is unable to accomplish more than a small fraction of its stated mission. Under these circumstances, any savings from switching to a more decentralized approach are likely to be more than offset by the need to overcome decades of extreme underfunding. Perhaps the best light to put on this issue is that the budgetary increases required to bring about a respectable level of workplace safety are less under the approach advocated here than they would be under a reinvigorated commitment to the old strategy.

5   A supportive role for public health professionals

No system can work unless those who make the decisions have access to the best possible information, and a decentralized system that draws on the talents and energy of thousands of workers and front-line managers needs a much more elaborate structure of research and support than we now have. The organization responsible for studying hazards and suggesting standards in the US is NIOSH, but its resources were never sufficient for the task, even before the drastic budget cuts of the 1980s (see above). The first requirement for researchers and other work environment specialists, as for inspectors and prosecutors, is more money – a *lot* more money. Simply to put workplace safety on the same level as, say, wildlife management will require at least an order of magnitude increase in funding.

In addition to more money, however, public health needs a different orientation. Under a more participatory system, for instance, NIOSH would need to be able to respond to requests for information emanating directly from the country's workplaces; without this capacity, safety committees and other local bodies would simply be unable to do their work. A better model is provided by the Work Environment Institute in Sweden, which is accessible to rank-and-file workers and which also pursues interests of its own. Not surprisingly, it is a world leader in research on not only avoiding risk, but actually making work a healthy and fulfilling activity. In this country the germ of such an approach can be found in local Councils on Occupational Safety and Health (COSHs), city- and state-wide research and training organizations funded by the labor movement. Operating on a shoestring and relying on volunteers for many of their functions, they pursue an agenda set by local needs. Unfortunately, their scope usually does not extend to nonunion workplaces, and many parts of the country have no COSHs at all. An excellent first step would be to provide public support for the COSHs, developing them into a building block of a future public health system.

In addition to research and training, public health activists are needed in the field, as advisors and participants alongside workers and managers. This type of hands-on approach would be facilitated, in turn, by the guarantee of community and worker rights to know – the transparent corporation. Health experts would travel freely and have access to information regarding the work process; with nothing to hide, firms might even view these visitors as a valuable resource. Often improvements in working conditions require not more money, but a fresh, well-informed perspective. Our current system, however, with its secrecy and excessive legalism, does not begin to take advantage of the skills of the public health community.

Here then is an alternative approach to achieving safety and health in the workplace. It is broadly sketched, and I have not attempted to distil its overlapping components into a single, perfectly meshed structure. It does, however, adhere to the two principles I presented at the beginning of this section: it draws on, and in turn reinforces, local knowledge, participation, and control, and it marshalls society-wide authority for effective regulation and the promulgation of reasonable safety norms. It is based on a set of rights whose cumulative effect is to empower individual workers, their organizations, and their communities. Politically, it minimizes coercive government intervention, refuting the facile claim that the only alternative to free-market capitalism is statism. On the contrary, it suggests by its example that there exists a vast and still largely unexplored territory of progressive, libertarian social reform.

No job is an island: making the world safe for safety

A bear is a remarkable piece of work. It has phenomenal strength, enough to rip apart practically any opponent (including us) in a one-on-one encounter, yet it possesses surprising speed and stamina. It can swim and climb trees; it can smell food miles away. Its claws are knives, yet it has the reflexes to catch fish right from the river. It can digest practically anything and then go months without eating at all. It would seem to be nature's perfect survival machine, but its minutes would be numbered on the streets of any large American city.

Everything depends on context. However well-crafted, an occupational safety and health policy would fail miserably unless it is embedded in a larger strategy that makes worker empowerment possible. At a minimum, three larger issues must be addressed:

1   The crisis in industrial relations

By every indicator, workers have less influence over company policy today than at any time since the Great Depression. Private sector unionization declines year after year; it is now below 14 percent and headed for single digits. Meanwhile, strikes are becoming an instrument of management against labor, as employers freely hire replacement workers and terminate collective bargaining. An increasing percentage of the workforce is "casual": part-time, temporary, or without a formal relationship with their direct employer. New computerized technology makes it possible for millions of workers such as assemblers, telephone operators, and clericals to be monitored down to their most minute actions, giving management more control on the shopfloor than ever before. And jobs themselves are increasingly mobile; in an instant an employer with generations-old roots in the community will take flight in search of lower wages or more docile workers. For all these reasons and more, industrial relations for the majority of the workforce is coming to mean "love it or leave it."

As discussed earlier in this chapter this state of affairs is clearly inhospitable to safety and health activism. It is one thing to create documents proclaiming worker rights to know, participate, and refuse, and quite another to enforce them. Without a greater foothold in the workplace, workers who try to exercise their rights against employer opposition will be cut down: it simply is not possible for public authorities to foresee and counteract all possible acts of employer retaliation. Moreover, as Karasek and Theorell (1990) have shown, authoritarian work organization is itself a health hazard, since psychological stress due to the inability to control one's own work has physical consequences. If a vigorous, rights-based policy is to succeed, then, it needs to be accompanied by broader strategies directed at altering the balance of power between labor and capital. I have already considered initiatives that can be taken at the level of government; here I would like to point out that some can be taken by workers themselves – new alliances with environmentalists and other community groups and a new, substantially broader bargaining agenda.[18] In its expansive phases the labor movement was arguably always a social movement, and to revive in these difficult times it must locate new social horizons. For example, by placing the firm's environmental policies in its list of demands a union can win crucial support from environmental groups – many of whose members, incidentally, may be unionists themselves. In return, environmentalists can help organize community support for labor's side in confrontations with management. Similar coalitions are possible, even necessary, with women's groups, minorities, and others whose economic demands are compatible with labor's. These alliances thrive on trust, which can be established only over time, through regular consultations and a record of honesty and reliability. Incidentally, the ability of unions to use their collective bargaining resources for social ends depends on the elimination of the NLRB's mandatory/permissive framework for bargaining issues, as discussed in the section on labor law reform.

2   *The challenge of new technology*

A plant-by-plant approach to safety, undertaken after fundamental technological choices have already been made, is likely to be too little, too late. Many differences between humane and inhumane working conditions are intrinsic to the technologies being used. For example, nuclear power plants will always pose a risk of low-level and episodic exposure to radiation, despite the best efforts of engineers to shield workers. By the same token, using computer-assisted automation to reduce a job to a single motion repeated over and over will place unnatural physical stress on workers however ergonomically that motion may be designed. The deep questions about new technology – whether it will be conducive to a healthy working environment, whether it will encourage or frustrate the development of workers' mental and physical capacities – are largely beyond the scope of the policies advocated in the previous section, since those policies are concerned with conditions that already exist, not those being prepared for the future.

How can society cope with the demands of emerging technology? There is no simple answer to this question. Greater movement toward corporate pluralism – the representation of worker and community interests, supplementing shareholders', on firms' boards of directors – is one possibility, whether mandated by government, as in Germany's codetermination law, or achieved through bargaining, as has occasionally happened in the USA.[19] (We considered this reform under the rubric of worker participation earlier in this chapter.) Another promising approach would have the government play a larger role in subsidizing commercially oriented research and development in return for a public say in the criteria by which research directions are evaluated and chosen. Similarly, public enterprises can be seeded into dynamic sectors of the economy, leveraging their influence through alliances and joint ventures with privately owned firms to influence the course and pace of innovation. The government could also use its massive presence as America's number one consumer to influence new technology, by making occupational and environmental health goals an important determinant of its purchasing decisions.

However we choose to do it, however, it is essential that we establish a public presence at all stages of the innovation process: the social stake in computerization, biotechnology, and other areas of technological change is too important to be left solely to the dictates of private profit.

3   Globalization and the new laissez-faire

One way to stand out from the crowd in the 1990s is to promote *any* new program of social regulation of production; most countries, whether industrialized or (euphemistically) "developing," capitalist or trying to be, seem to be moving in the other direction: they are trimming regulations and generally reducing the public role in their economies, all in the name of competitiveness. This has been equally true for post-Thatcherite England, Clintonite America, and social democratic Sweden. Although there is certainly a large dollop of traditional conservative ideology and class interest involved, the timing and universal character of this development indicate that something more is at work. This additional element is the gathering integration of the world economy.

Many forces are driving the liberalization of global trade and finance: reduced costs of transportation and communication, a greater ability to transfer technology to new locations, the increasingly international character of technical innovation, and the greater sophistication employed by financial wealth-holders to evade national restrictions on the form and movement of their assets. The upshot is a growing integration of what used to be largely autonomous national economies. And when markets are world-wide, so is competition. Public policies that increase production costs, even for a virtuous purpose like safeguarding working conditions or the environment, appear simply impossible, likely to destroy the economy in order to save it. What good does it do to mandate a higher level of social responsibility on the part of firms if the result is to drive production, and jobs, abroad?

This problem is particularly severe in the field of occupational safety and health. Newly industrializing countries, virtually without exception, are exposing their workers to extraordinary risks. The combination of heedless practices, cavalier attitudes toward lethal chemicals, long hours, a ferocious pace of work, and casual employment relations has resulted in a global crisis in working conditions. Indeed, many of the disasters being reported in the new export zones bear a disturbing resemblance to episodes in the grim history of industrialization in the West. In 1993, for example, two disasters took place at doll factories in the high-pressure industrial districts of the new East-Asian "tigers." In May more than 200 workers, mostly women, were killed in a fire outside of Bangkok, Thailand; then in November 81 more perished in another fire in Kuiyong, China. Both factories, in the now-familiar pattern of Triangle Shirtwaist and Imperial Chicken, had locked most doors and windows to keep workers at their stations and prevent theft. In fact, witnesses reported that supervisors in the Thai plant continued to stop workers at the only remaining exits, searching them for stolen toys as the flames and smoke grew more intense (Sivaraman, 1993). Such tragedies are not accidental: they could hardly have been avoided in societies that have come to place production above every other human purpose, and which have chosen as their means the unregulated pursuit of profit. Moreover, by forcing the money (but not the human) costs of production to a minimum, this new breed of exporters forces all producers to meet their challenge. It is not surprising, then, that an ambitious program to protect workers' safety and health, such as the one I have presented in this chapter, would be rejected as destructive of "competitiveness."

There can be no return to the insular political economy of even two decades ago. Just as most forms of aggressive state and local regulation are anachronistic in the age of the national economy, so are most new national initiatives in an age of globalization. And just as social and economic policy made the leap from local to national during the Progressive and New Deal eras, so must we tackle the challenge of transnational regulation today.

Unfortunately, recent trade agreements, such as the new North American Free Trade Agreement (NAFTA) and the Uruguay Round of the General Agreement on Tariffs and Trade (GATT), in the process of approval at the time this is being written, not only fail to take up this challenge; they actually try to codify laissez-faire in international trade law. In part this reflects business dominance of the secretive trade negotiating process, unaccountable to normal democratic mechanisms;

in part it reflects the mistaken belief that unregulated "free trade" is the only alternative to backward-looking protectionism. What is being lost is the opportunity to harness global trade for the common good, by devising forms of regulation appropriate to the twenty-first century. In some instances it may be possible to harmonize national standards across borders, although the lowest-common-denominator approach implicit in the GATT provisions is surely the wrong way to go about this. In most cases, however, national differences in worker and environmental protection, public subsidy and taxation of industry, and other aspects of economic regulation will have to be accommodated without according the most permissive countries a competitive edge. Elsewhere (Dorman, 1988b; Dorman, 1991a; Dorman, 1992) I have argued for a social tariff approach, in which goods produced under weaker social or environmental standards are subject to offsetting border taxes, with the dual purpose of protecting higher standards from the ravages of competition and reducing the incentives to cutting standards in exporting countries. Such a policy is incomplete, of course, since it does not address the problem higher-standard countries may have in retaining their export markets, but it is a great improvement over the nonpolicy of dogmatic liberalization.

Ultimately, defensive tariffs and trade rules alone will not solve the problems created by the competitive devaluation of standards. It will require a democratic revolution, particularly in countries being transformed into low-wage export platforms, that gives grassroots labor and community movements real levers over the policies of their corporations and governments. Here we find ourselves once again at a central theme of this book, the inseparability of politics and economics. There is no contradiction between the much-vaunted "liberalization" of these countries and their authoritarian – generally military or one-party – governments. Laissez-faire is not the absence of politics; it is politics of a particular sort. It imposes autocracy in the workplace under the false supposition that individuals have freely exchanged their autonomy, their right to independent judgment and action, for money, and it requires the suppression of democratic politics throughout society to prevent measures of public regulation that majorities normally support. It can and should be replaced by a different politics, one that enlarges the scope for democratic decision-making and rests on the widest possible distribution of individual rights and liberties. This is a recommendation not only for countries just entering the traumatic process of industrial development, but for our own as well.

Epilogue

This book has two messages. Conventional economic analyses of risks in the workplace, and in society as a whole, are misguided, leading to misunderstanding of current dilemmas and insufficient policy response. Second, the shortcomings of mainstream economics in this sphere illuminate the weaknesses in economic theory itself. Each of these deserves a final word.

Risk, as we have seen in this study, is not all of a piece; how we interpret and evaluate it depends on the circumstances, causes, and alternatives. Indeed, through most of human history the greatest part of risk was viewed as either unavoidable or ennobling. The fatalistic world-view common to traditional societies was an accurate reflection of the real conditions of life: injury or disease could intrude at almost any moment, and stoic acceptance was the only conceivable response. Virtuous risk-taking, the stuff of legend and myth, was the role of warriors and other heroes who embraced danger on behalf of the entire community. Even today we venerate those who willingly assume extreme risk – astronauts, the fire-fighters of Chernobyl, human rights activists who stand up to death squads – and when we tell their stories we often resort to the timeless imagery of quest and martyrdom.

The increasing prominence of social movements opposed to risk in such fields as environmental and occupational health and consumer product safety therefore suggests a vast change not so much in the sheer amount of risk faced in the modern world, as in the way this risk is interpreted and valued. Part of this change can be attributed to the development of technology, which has undermined both fatalism and heroism in the face of danger. We now have the technical ability to eliminate (or at least postpone) many of the hazards that past generations took as given, and this progress has spawned a widespread faith in the powers of science that exceeds its accomplishments. Where the technical necessity of risk ends, the moral judgment of those who impose it begins. Moreover, it is characteristic of modern, technologically sophisticated risk that it assumes utterly unheroic forms, such as the exposure to microscopic amounts of hazardous chemicals or the endless, injurious repetition of machine-like tasks. There is no way to engage these risks in combat, to overpower or outmaneuver them; their force is random and imperceptible. This is not risk that challenges the human spirit, but simply negates it.

Yet it would be wrong to attribute the evolution of risk, and the emergence of modern health and safety movements, to technology alone. Danger of the sort considered in this book is socially constructed; it is borne by some for the benefit of others. This is central to its meaning, as we have already seen. In practice, most people, whether responding as workers to a risk on the job or as residents of a community faced with a hazardous installation, are Kantians: they view risk as a potential violation of their autonomy, as a demonstration that they are valued only as instruments for the satisfaction of others. Indeed, where these feelings fail to arise – in cooperatives or in ostensibly autonomous activities like truck-driving – objectively large and avoidable risks may occasion no resistance at all. Opposition to risk can therefore be taken as one possible indicator of adversarial social relations in general, a principle that applies not only to the workplace conflict characteristic of capitalist firms – the topic of this book – but also the conflict between private and public bureaucracies (Max Weber's "iron cage") and the communities regulated and serviced by them.

The conventional economic view is that such conflicts can usually be mediated efficiently by markets, where risk-creators and risk-bearers can trade off cost against benefit. The historical evidence, however, overwhelmingly demonstrates that this has not been true of disputes concerning occupational safety and health: markets have not contained these conflicts, nor have they produced even remotely efficient outcomes. Various reasons for this have been considered, including the particularities of labor markets and the characteristics of risk perception that diverge from the economist's conception of rationality. Above all, risk is largely contested within economic and political institutions, not between them in the anonymous terrain of the marketplace. This has not always represented an improvement. In general, institutional mechanisms are characterized by unequal power, the consequence of such chronic features of our society as unemployment, a general reliance on hierarchy, and the extraordinary concentration of ownership. In extreme cases this inequality can, ironically, take on the appearance of purely market mechanism. Return to the women of the Triangle Shirtwaist Company one last time and consider the plight of these impoverished immigrant workers, employed on a day-to-day basis by contractors, without even the legal status of employees. Their strike of 1909 broken and their union organizers blacklisted, they had no vehicle for protest or even meek suggestion. We know that they were acutely aware of the danger posed by locked doors and exposed piles of material, conditions that later proved their undoing. Yet even as they went quietly about their work, can we say that they "accepted" these conditions in return for a correspondingly higher wage? Was the suppression of resistance the same as voluntary assent, and, had the Triangle workers summoned the courage to challenge the company one more time, would we say that they had violated the terms of their initial agreement to accept employment?

In the absence of public regulation, human and environmental exploitation can rise to unconscionable levels. This is why we regulate. Rather than viewing such measures simply as constraints on the freedom of markets (which, of course, they are), we might also regard them as attempts to modify the *nonmarket* mechanisms by which economies are governed. This understanding was commonplace during earlier times; today it seems we have to reconstruct it from scratch in the face of skeptical economic doctrine. Moreover, the same vision of perfect markets now used to deny the need for regulation reappears as the basis for making regulation efficient. Hence the use of data from the labor market to identify a value of life that can be employed in benefit–cost analysis. Of course, if markets need to be regulated, their outcomes cannot be used mechanically as benchmarks of public rationality, and, in any event, the incoherent intellectual case for quantifying a value of life should render the entire topic moot.

Where does this leave us? Once we have moved from a narrow worldview dominated by markets and commodities to a broader understanding of the social, psychological, and political dimensions of economic life, we can see that safety policy is necessarily social policy. Risk in its publicly meaningful sense is not the bare statistical probability of suffering a loss; it is a violation of the norms of care and reciprocity that ought to govern relations among people – avoidable harm for the benefit of those who impose it. While regulatory mandates can restrict to some extent the amounts and forms this harm can take, truly effective policy will target these relations themselves. In this work I have argued for measures that would give workers more control over their working conditions, both individually and collectively, but which would also promote more cooperation and communication in matters of work organization and safety. In part these reforms are intended to alter outcomes directly by increasing the power of those with the greatest stake in improving safety and health conditions, but they also have the potential to change the way risk is perceived and evaluated. By assuming responsibility for their own safety, workers – and for that matter all of us – may finally disentangle the strictly technical aspects of modern risk from its strategic and even iconic aspects.

This sober, unblinking confrontation with the benefits and hazards of rapidly developing technology is long overdue. We have evolved over the millennia as sight-and-sound directed beings, locating the hazardous elements of our environment by sensory perception. This has worked; our survival is the evidence. But exotic new threats to life and health, from toxic contamination of our living and working environments to the subtle buildup of physical and psychic stress, pass beneath these perceptual gateways. We do not have time for the plodding trial-and-error of natural selection; our technical ingenuity has seen to that. The future evolution of our species must be social and cultural: the development of institutions that can translate our best understanding of the human consequences of technology into economic policy. The scientific and organizational demands of this project alone are daunting, but we will not even begin to address them if we remain mired in social and class warfare over risk. That is, while fairness is a fundamental goal of social life, its achievement is only a precondition of the effort to harness the promise of emerging technologies for the public good. The British socialist Raymond Williams, in *Toward the Year 2000* (1983), his final major work before his death, argued that the defensible goal of socialism was never to impose the will of one segment of society over another, but, by radically democratizing decision-making, to evoke – finally – a "responsibility for the whole system." The era of permanent industrial revolution into which we are now hurtling demands as much responsibility as we can muster.

It has become common to regard economics as an imperialist among the social sciences, claiming ever more territory for the doctrine of exchange between rational individual maximizers. Increasingly, articles in the *American Political Science Review*, the *American Sociological Review*, and other disciplinary flagships appear indistinguishable from their counterparts in the *American Economic Review* and the *Journal of Political Economy*. Economists see this as a validation of their methods and research agenda, but their celebration may be premature. Just as the imperial army is weakest at its moment of greatest expanse – think of Napoleon at the gates of Moscow – economic orthodoxy may be entering a period of heightened vulnerability. Distended from its half-absorbed conquest of such diverse fields as family relations, the formation of political parties, and now the human confrontation with mortality, economics is ripe for challenge. In fact, to carry the analogy one step further, to capture new ground, whether territorial or intellectual, is also to be captured by it – to acquire through the inevitable practical details of occupation the problems and perspectives of the occupied.

In this book we have surveyed a set of problems historically addressed by philosophers, theologians, public health experts, industrial sociologists, and political activists. Economists have now had their say, and it is not surprising that their analysis does not eclipse the insights of their predecessors. On all the thorny issues, such as the significance of certain death for the things of this world and the nature of power within social institutions, the core message of conventional economics is embarrassingly shallow. If the eventual outcome, on the other hand, is an ongoing conversation between economics and other intellectual traditions, we have much to be optimistic about. I hope I have made it clear that I expect progress to take the form, not of the replacement of one whole approach by another, but of a hybridization in which the partial insights of conventional economics can be combined with those of the other social sciences. Where would we expect this transmutation of knowledge to be most productive?

The division between labor markets and labor relations, as methodologies and objects of study, is artificial. In its modern form it is the result of the rigid application of static optimization methodology to one field and a more inductive, narrative-and-case-study approach to the other. In the study that occupies this book the dichotomy appears in the guise of two different approaches to the explanation of occupational risk, one that sees it as the negotiated outcome of conflict and cooperation within the firm, the other that regards it as simply one more commodity to be transacted in the marketplace. Modern efficiency wage theory, however, represents a first step toward the dissolution of this divide, and more flexible and creative uses of game theory can be expected to take us even further down this road.

But the parallel realities of labor markets and labor relations typify a larger problem, central to the future of economics. Economists nearly always treat market transactions as one-time-only affairs conducted by anonymous buyers and sellers. The static, ahistorical character of most economic theory rests on this foundation. In the real economy, however, a great many interactions are not anonymous; the same individuals do business with one another and expect to do business again. This is true of workers and employers, but also of borrowers and lenders, suppliers of unfinished goods and the firms who assemble them, and even ordinary consumers and the brand-name products they buy off the shelf. As we have seen, this is the world of repeated game theory, and its characteristic features – strategic behavior, multiple equilibria, the potential for both cooperation and conflict, the difficulty in arriving at mutually optimal results – are light-years away from the predictable equimarginal condi- tions of today's economic texts. Moreover, a strategic approach to economic decision-making casts a clearer light on the role of institutions. Unlike the anonymous, come-and-go transactions in the textbook market, the repeated and thickly strategic interactions of real-world markets can hardly be imagined apart from institutions that regulate them and impart a measure of predictability. These institutions, both explicit and implicit, are the product of human beings acting strategically, but they also condition the choices individuals can make and the goals they can pursue. This back-and-forth between individuals remaking institutions and institutions remaking individuals takes place over time and is the stuff of history. This study cannot claim to have done more than sketch the bare outlines of one possible approach to a historically and institutionally sophisticated account of occupational safety and health. I hope, however, that I have conveyed the enormous opportu- nities open to those who are willing to experiment with hybrid methodologies.

As for the economist's favored model of human cognition, expected utility theory, its shortcomings were starkly revealed in the context of workplace risk. In chapter 3 we discovered its inability to grasp the qualitative difference between accumulating goods and extending life – between having and being. In chapter 5 we encountered alternative approaches to the understanding of human behavior, drawn from the work of psychology and decision theory. As I tried to show, in many instances it is possible to graft their insights on conventional economic stock and employ the results to explain real-world behavior. It is difficult to understate the importance of reforming utility theory: its goal is not merely better prediction but the return of genuine human agency – the mirror of recognition – to the study of society.

The purpose of economics is, above all, better economic policy, but current economic doctrine surrounding the definition and measurement of well-being is seriously misguided. We have seen that the treatment of all outcomes as commodities is untenable in matters of life and health; it is equally inappropriate where policies can affect other constitutive goods – in particular, personal freedom. But it is not only the special attributes of human life that undermine the usefulness of willingness to pay (and benefit–cost analysis generally) as the sole criterion for public policy. A major contention of this book has been that private preferences are just that: private. Public policy must be based on public preferences, views arrived at through a social process of fact-finding and debate and for which we are willing to accept social responsibility. The ideal to which democracy bends is not Nielsen ratings or push-button plebiscites for every policy proposal, but the deeply engaged and publicly accountable decision-making of a jury or town meeting. There can be little doubt that our political needs have outstripped our political resources, and the result has often been unfair action, irrational action, or, most often, simply no action. The solution to this dilemma, however, lies not in perfecting new devices to measure our private impulses of Benthamite pleasure and pain, but in revitalizing the instruments of democracy and broadening the scope for collective action. Public participation, discussion, and decision-making are the only basis on which a general climate of responsibility can be cultivated.

Notes

1 The economics of risk and the risk of economics

1 The sample was self-selected: workers were told the nature of the survey and those who agreed were asked to complete a written questionnaire.

2 The low perception of injury risks among financial records and other clerical workers are exceptions. In a private communication, Elaine McCrate has raised the possibility that women in these jobs may not yet be informed of the risks of repetitive motion disorders and the possible hazards of VDT use.

3 The National Institute for Occupational Safety and Health (NIOSH) has conducted exploratory studies of this sort, but has not generated an ongoing data base.

4 It also means that the qualitative data, such as the type and cause of safety and health problems, are not collected, reducing the value of the information for occupational hygiene professionals.

5 In creating this series, Robinson (1988) adjusted the raw data to maintain consistency despite the record-keeping changes mandated by the passage of the Occupational Safety and Health Act in 1971.

6 A technical note: the Bureau of Labor Statistics employs two different surveys to determine, on a month-to-month basis, employment by industry – one of business establishments, the other of households. The establishment survey is generally regarded as the more accurate of the two, but it does not include farm employment. The farm sector is recorded under the household survey, however. Although the two surveys yield somewhat different estimates, I combined the establishment data for nonfarm employment with household data on farm employment. For the purposes of the index, the advantage of more accurate estimates for the seven nonfarm industries outweighs the distortion introduced by using a different source for agriculture. I also combined wholesale and retail trade into a single, employment-weighted industry.

7 A possible exception may be women, who are on average less advantaged economically but who may be less exposed to gross physical risk. There is

some evidence, on the other hand, that women may experience greater stress; see Karasek and Theorell (1990).

8 The data are taken from the combined Young Men's and Young Women's National Longitudinal Survey ($N = 5,174$), The Panel Study of Income Dynamics ($N = 4,452$), the Current Population Survey, and the Quality of Employment Survey ($N = 1,380$).

9 Throughout the book I will refer to the opinions of "economists" and "the economic view" to reference the predominant position within the profession. From my own reading of the literature I am convinced this perception of their position is accurate. Not all economists share the majority view, of course. For one, *I* do not.

10 This last term is widely used in economics to refer to the process of decomposing the price of complex goods into the prices of their constituent elements. The intellectual justification for this practice comes from utilitarian preference analysis, in which consumers are said to adhere to a unitary "hedonic" calculus for all positive and negative outcomes that may arise.

2 The theory of compensating wage differentials

1 This can be translated as, "Minimize the combined cost of safety and wages, provided that you meet the market-clearing level of worker utility u_0."

2 More specifically, identify the conditions on w and s for which the partial derivatives of the constrained minimization function Z equals zero; that is, for which there will be no unexploited possibilities for cutting costs. These are

$$1 = \lambda u_w$$
$$k = \lambda u_s$$

(The condition on λ is satisfied by meeting the constraint $u = u_0$.) The first-order conditions hold if there is an interior solution; in other words, if the optimal compensation package includes, as seems reasonable, at least some wages and some safety. The second-order conditions necessary to show that we have a minimum over all possible combinations of w and s meeting u_0 will not be taken up, although the assumptions on the curvature of employer cost and worker indifference curves are sufficient to satisfy them.

3 Each (w, s) pair is a Pareto optimum.

4 The following analysis is adapted from Rosen (1974), but similar arguments have been made by others, including Viscusi (1983, p. 107) and Zeckhauser and Nichols (1978, p. 174).

5 This of course is another application of the "law" of diminishing marginal returns.

6 Technically, this is the problem that a worker's utility is almost certainly nonlinear in risk of sudden death; each increase in probability is dreaded

more than that which preceded it, and full certainty ($p = 1$) would be avoided at all cost.

7 The following point was made independently by Schelling (1968) and Mishan (1971).

8 A full account of these motives would include not only the costs to employers of having their workers fully informed, but also the benefits derived from being the first to introduce new products or processes which may utilize hazardous substances. Ashford (1976, p. 344) points out, "Considerations of market structure pervasive in the American economy today have resulted in a chronic tendency among many firms to introduce new substances and processes for short-term marketing advantage before the longer-term implications of their use are properly understood."

9 It is interesting to note that deficient worker information not only disrupts wage compensation; it also raises the costs of worker illness against which compensation was intended to work. Selikoff (1985) contends that mortality rates from degenerative occupational diseases could be lowered if workers were properly informed of their condition and if careful monitoring and appropriate medical procedures were instituted. An effective medical surveillance program for workers with asbestos-related disorders, for instance, could reduce mortality (from these disorders) by 15–20 percent.

10 This is a reference to Bayes' Theorem, according to which one's estimate of a probability distribution should be altered with each new piece of information.

11 The worker characteristics included in this study were education, marital status, race, gender, age, experience, number of hours worked per week, and likelihood of being a white-collar worker.

12 About half of these coefficients are statistically significant – primarily those for seniority groups with influence.

3 Putting a value on human life

1 Note that this use of the term "human capital" bears no relation to its accepted economic meaning, investments in worker skills or other attributes that are costly but productive.

2 Discounting reduces the value of an event expected in the future to its equivalent value today according to the formula

$$B_0 = B_t (1 + r)^{-t}$$

where B_0 is the value of a benefit (or cost) today, B_t its value when it occurs t years into the future, and r is the rate of discount. Holding B_t constant, as r increases B_0 falls.

3 According to this approach, pioneered by John Von Neumann and Oskar Morgenstern, the value of a choice with uncertain consequences – commonly referred to as a lottery – is the sum of the values of each of the consequences, weighted by their relative likelihood. In other words

$$EU(L) = \sum_i u_i p_i, \quad \sum_i p_i = 1$$

where L is a lottery and u_i, p_i are the utility and probability of the ith outcome, and all possibilities are taken into account.

4 The multi-period version of this is a sum of future utilities, weighted by the likelihood of surviving into each period.

5 The expected utility models considered in this section can also be critiqued from the perspective of the cognitive theories discussed in chapter 5.

6 It embodies fewer implicit assumptions concerning the relationship between risk, wealth, and utility.

7 In some circumstances a respondent might even surmise that the survey results will be used to increase or lower her own risk, and will therefore have an incentive to respond strategically. This is a survey researcher's worst nightmare.

8 For a more detailed treatment of cognitive dissonance, see chapter 5.

9 This account is drawn from the description in Violette and Chestnut (1983).

10 Violette and Chestnut note that Mulligan's interviewers began each valuation question with a suggested initial bid of $5. It is well known that such a procedure greatly biases the results, and this too could explain a portion of the anomalous response.

11 This account is taken from Jones-Lee (1989).

12 Here I take issue with Jones-Lee (1989), who states: "If, on careful reflection and given 'adequate' information, a person genuinely elects to place a value of zero on a particular effect, then any decision criterion that purports to take account of individual preferences (as does the willingness-to-pay approach) should reflect that person's valuation, even though it is zero and even though, as an independent observer, one regards the valuation as eccentric" (p. 83). In such cases it would, I think, make more sense to ask which ought to be discarded, the assumption that human life is generally of high value or the particular assumptions underlying expected utility theory?

13 This means that characteristic sub-populations were identified and individuals chosen randomly within these sub-groups. In the Smith and Desvousges study, sub-samples were randomly drawn from each of 100 census tracts in the Boston area. The purpose of this technique is to increase the likelihood that the full sample is truly representative of the larger population.

14 This is derived from the value that individuals place on their own lives only; it excludes the monetary benefit from not having other passengers killed, innocent bystanders, etc.

15 Almost, anyway: for one of their risk questions they found a relationship between positive WTP and age.

16 For more detailed reviews, see Violette and Chestnut (1983) and Jones-Lee (1989).

17 Note here the very different responses of the workers interviewed in Nelkin and Brown (1984); almost universally they claim to reject the view that health can be traded off against wealth.

18 For an influential account of the havoc wreaked by this problem, see Mishel (1988).

19 For a review of this history, see Griliches (1971).

20 Formally, this is an example of an "envelope curve."

21 H is upward-sloping because an increase in safety, if it is to leave profits unaffected, must be accompanied by a corresponding increase in prices, and vice versa. It is convex (flatter in the low s region, steeper in high s region) because it can be assumed that it is increasingly costly to provide additional safety as more total safety is provided. Incidentally, the location of the cost curves rather than the indifference curves determines H, since firms are constrained to occupy those particular isocost curves by the zero-profit assumption, whereas the existence of consumer surplus means that the level of utility obtained by consumers may vary.

22 For more thorough reviews, see Violette and Chestnut (1983), US Congress, Office of Technology Assessment (1985), Viscusi (1986), and Jones-Lee (1989).

23 She also assumes that consumers discount future costs and benefits at a rate of 5 percent per year.

24 This is not to say that some or even most smokers do not derive satisfaction from smoking, just that this satisfaction is not the sole determinant of whether, when, and how much they smoke. Incidentally, there is a model of "rational addiction" attributable to Becker and Murphy (1988) in which the Ippolitos' approach is justified. In their view, addiction occurs when the consumer experiences increasing rather than diminishing marginal utility from consuming a particular good. The more you use, the more you want. (Recall that increasing marginal utility of consumption could result from an increasing marginal disutility of failing to consume – withdrawal symptoms.) Although somewhat helpful, what this formulation fails to capture is the notion that, at least potentially, the addict may *want* to stop his addiction but be unable to *act* on this wish. This is central to addiction as a *problem*, since if continued addiction were truly utility-maximizing to the addict, as it is for Becker and Murphy, there would be no dilemma; let the addict remain free to choose in the best Chicago tradition. The alternative view, however, would be based on a pluralistic conception of the self, with the associated problem of self-mastery. This second approach, of course, is inconsistent with conventional utility theory, and its application to the smoking decision would vitiate the Ippolitos' results. For two different expositions of the problem of self-control, see Elster (1979, 1985b) and Charlton (1988).

25 If nonsafety attributes were perfectly uncorrelated with safety we could ignore them, *if* the size of our study sample is large relative to the variance of these other attributes.

26 I use the term "human capital" advisedly, since the view of wages and productivity it has spawned has poisoned much economic discourse. Unwilling to give up the assumption that people are generally paid what they are worth, economists are prepared to attribute worthiness to almost

any social or demographic characteristic. Typical is a passing remark from Krueger and Summers (1986). After noting that higher-paying industries tend to have a different occupational mix and employ fewer women than low-paying industries, they comment: "The general conclusion seems to be that observed differences in average wages between industries do result partially from differences in labor quality with higher wage industries tending to attract higher quality workers" (pp. 20–1). Simply by virtue of their lower pay women workers are deemed to be of "low quality"! Of course, it would be hard to credit discrimination with a role in this if it is the case that the best-paying jobs just happen to "attract" more men than women. It should be noted that Summers is, at this writing, the Under-secretary of the Treasury for international affairs and one of the most talented and influential thinkers of his generation. As one moves down the ladder the practice of blaming the victim becomes more egregious.

27 Formally, we are assuming the diminishing marginal utility of money: as an individual's income rises she gets less additional utility out of an equal increment of income. An extra dollar is worth more to the poor than the rich. Unless we made the adjustment of taking the log of wages we would confuse differences in income for differences in preferences over safety. In practice, the semilog form of equation (1) nearly always yields higher R^2s than the linear specification (with w rather than ln w as the dependent variable).

28 Ruling orthodoxy has it that the models used in regression analysis should be derived strictly from theoretical premises: if theory demands the inclusion of a particular variable it must be given its place, while even the most powerful variables must be left out if they cannot be theoretically justified – whatever the consequences for R^2. The reason is that, if each model is tailored to the data it estimates, the results become captive to the specifics of the study, and the generalizability of knowledge is lost. Increasingly, however, economists are drifting away from this rigid position, since existing economic theories do little justice to the richness of the available data. The opposite extreme is represented by exploratory data analysis, which considers the data from various perspectives and looks, without preconceptions, for emerging patterns. Whatever the merits of the two sides in this debate, computer graphics programs are making the atheoretical, data-driven approach a lot more *fun*.

29 At this point readers may want to know exactly how regression results are extrapolated to produce a value of life estimate. Recall that β_R represents the marginal effect that a small change in risk has on ln w, the left-hand-side of the regression equation:

$$\beta_R = \frac{\Delta \ln w}{\Delta R}$$

R is generally measured as a frequency over a large number of workers, hours, or some other variable; its general form is

$$R = \frac{r}{10^x}$$

For example, risk may be measured as the number of deaths per 100,000 workers in a given year; in this case $10^x = 100{,}000$ and $x = 5$. A "small" change in R is therefore $1/10^x$. Multiplying both sides by the change in risk, then, gives us

$$\Delta \ln w = \beta_R \cdot \frac{1}{10^x}$$

A change in the natural logarithm of w, however, is equivalent to the *rate of change* in w; so we could just as well write

$$\frac{\Delta w}{\bar{w}} = \beta_R \cdot \frac{1}{10_x}$$

where $\bar{w}$ is the average wage for the entire sample. Solving for Δw with respect to a single additional death (rather than $1/10^x$ additional deaths) gives us our final formula

$$\Delta w = \beta_R \cdot 10^x \cdot \bar{w}$$

30 The actuarial data exhibit "selection effects."
31 This objection extends to other studies using this data set, such as Brown (1980), Marin and Psacharopoulos (1982), Arnould and Nichols (1983), and, to an extent, Gerking *et al.* (1988).
32 There are three "layers" to the breakdown of the US economy by industry: major industries (one-digit), major groups within major industries (two-digit), and "detailed" industries (three-digit). Ideally, three-digit data could be matched more precisely with each worker (whose employment at the three-digit level is part of the census survey), but there are too few occupational fatalities in most of these detailed industries to be meaningful. Even at the two-digit level it is common to pool several years' worth of fatalities to increase their frequency in the safer industries and provide a more reliable average.
33 Fluctuations of individual occupations around the industry average should affect the variance of the risk measures but not the best estimate of their values.
34 I am confining this survey to studies conducted on US data. Similar work has been undertaken for other countries, for example Canada (Martinello and Meng, 1992), the UK (Marin and Psacharopoulos, 1982), and Austria (Weiss, Maier, and Gerking, 1986). The first and last of these use industry-level risk data and are broadly comparable to similar studies enumerated in table 3.3;

the second uses occupation-specific actuarial data in the manner of Thaler and Rosen and is subject to similar misgivings.

35 The tendency of hedonic methods to ascribe a higher value of life to the rich than the poor is at the center of a recent controversy surrounding the analysis of global warming. As part of its effort to place a monetary value on environmental costs, the Intergovernmental Panel on Climate Change has relied on a report by the Center for the Social and Economic Research of the Global Environment (Fankhauser, 1992) that attaches a value of $1,500,000 on lives lost in the OECD countries, but only $150,000 for those lost in "poor" countries. While some environmentalists have challenged this methodology for its obvious bias, it is clearly consistent with the "willingness-to-pay" criterion: the poor are not willing to pay as much as the rich.

36 An additional problem with the strategy of merging files is reporting error. Special surveys by the Census Bureau on CPS respondents in 1977 and the Labor Department's 1980 Employment Opportunity Pilot Project generated both employee and employer responses to questions concerning wages, hours, and other variables. It is possible to separate observations where worker- and employer-reported SIC classification are the same from those that are different. Mellow and Sider (1983) re-estimated wage–risk coefficients, where risk was indexed by lost workdays due to industrial accidents, using the merged files approach. They produced zero or negative coefficients for the "disagree" portion of the sample, and more strongly positive coefficients on risk for the "agree" segment.

37 In the first group were mentally demanding work and noise; in the second, hectic and smoke; in the third, punch clock, heavy lifting, shake (strong shakes or vibrations), and poison; in the fourth, inflexible hours, difficult to run errands (without telling a supervisor), otherwise physically demanding, and daily sweating.

38 A similar motivation inspired Freeman and Medoff (1981), who, in the course of a more far-ranging investigation into the union wage premium, found weak and generally insignificant compensating wage differentials for both union and nonunion workers.

39 Also, the NTOF series is broken out only to the one-digit SIC level, whereas BLS data are available by two-digit SIC.

40 In the second portion of the article, the authors performed a Monte Carlo simulation on a regression specification resistant to reduced-form analysis. The results were broadly equivalent.

41 It is necessary to divide by β_w to compensate for the appearance of this coefficient on w in the reverse regression but not in the original.

42 In economic parlance these are her equivalent and compensating variations respectively.

43 This example also exposes what may ultimately come to be seen as the most important flaw in the Coase Theorem: if companies are given the right to do harm they will threaten it whenever they can, in order to accumulate more

payoffs. Coase published his analysis at a time when most economists were not familiar with the study of strategic behavior.

44 Note, however, that it does *not* provide evidence for the doctrine of compensating differentials or for the three hypothetical properties of market determined safety. On the contrary: it is a technique for imputing a value for life despite the absence of Smithian compensation.

45 Due to the relatively small size of their sample (1,033), they represented industries at the two-digit, rather than three-digit, level.

46 There is a fascinating underground history to this study which sheds light on the unfortunate ways economists, like all of us, respond to the incentives of their profession. It is common for published surveys of the compensating differential literature to refer to Dillingham, *but they never mention the disappearing act that risk coefficients undergo in his most controlled estimations*, not even to cast doubt on them. For verification, see Viscusi (1992), p. 53, Viscusi (1993), p. 1926, and Miller (1990), p. 26.

47 Leigh also found comparable results in regressions using other samples.

48 Wage compensation is calculated at the sample means for wages and risk irrespective of whether the risk coefficients are significant. We also implemented a two-stage least squares model to test for the endogeneity of our risk variables. The overall pattern of results, including the negative coefficient on fatal risk, remained the same, although positive compensation for nonfatal risk appeared somewhat larger. A Hausman test on the residuals was unable to reject the null hypothesis that the OLS and 2SLS models are identically biased. Complete regression results for both OLS and 2SLS are available from the authors.

49 The same conclusion was reached by Dickens (1990) for somewhat similar reasons. He also points out that the standard statistical techniques used in the compensating differentials literature are inappropriate, because the use of industry averages in place of (unknown) individual risk reduces the number of genuinely independent observations and biases (upward) the significance levels of risk coefficients.

50 An elegant introduction to the analysis of this problem can be found in Elster (1979).

51 The New York State Constitution mandates that the Adirondack forest preserve be maintained as "forever wild," potentially overruling the commercial motivations of buyers, sellers, and even the public at large. This makes sense as a form of precommitment.

52 The AIDS Quilt project can be seen as an attempt to transform statistical into identified lives so that they will be more highly valued.

53 Of course, Dewey, Habermas, and other democratic theorists also point out that the conditions for effective *public* decision-making are not easily attained; so it is not enough simply to oppose overreliance on the market. Sagoff appears to give inadequate attention to this.

54 Defending strict *ex ante*ism, Thaler (1982) writes that simply because *ex post* evaluations of risk draw on more information is not a reason to prefer them

to *ex ante* evaluations, since "the 'information' is purely distributional – who will lose rather than how much will be lost. When choosing in the original position this information is ignored *by intent*. Its knowledge cannot improve the decisions" (p. 175). My claim, however, is that *ex ante* information can bear upon the content and not just the distribution of expected outcomes.

4   The real world of occupation safety and health

1 The following account draws primarily on the monumental work of P. S. Atiyah (1979), especially in its focus on British law. Atiyah's book combines economic, political, intellectual, and legal history in a sweeping account of the rise and demise of radical contractarianism. Since this doctrine remains, to this day, at the heart of conventional economic thinking, it should be required reading for all who want to understand why economics is so often misdirected.

2 It is for this reason that Adam Smith's model of a free-contract economy earns the designation of "ideology." It represented an unconscious generalization of some of the experiences of commercially active individuals into the presumed basis of everyone's experience. This is an example of the local-global conflation that Elster, among others, sees as a characteristic mechanism of ideology-formation. See Elster (1985, pp. 487ff).

3 There are many accounts of the decline and subsequent reappearance of employer liability; see, for instance, Ashford (1976) or Gersuny (1981).

4 This case was publicized by Theodore Roosevelt as part of his campaign for workman's compensation legislation. See Weinstein (1968, p. 42).

5 Prosser is cited in Gersuny (1981).

6 Liberal insistence on banning contracting out led to defeat of initial employer liability legislation in Britain in 1893. Workman's compensation was passed instead by the Tories in 1897. Ironically, as White has pointed out, "Workers' compensation [itself] can be viewed as one giant 'contracting out' scheme." See White (1983, p. 63).

7 To make matters as simple as possible, we are assuming that work, the possibility of an accident, and all ensuing costs and benefits occur in a single period, so that no adjustment need be made for discounting. We are also assuming that workers who may be killed on the job regard the economic costs and benefits to other members of their family equally with their own.

8 Since the accidents are assumed to be the same – only their probabilities differ – and since the workers have identical preferences, p is the same for both. Strictly speaking, if $\pi_1 > \pi_2$ c would be somewhat greater for the first worker than the second, since the lost wages in the event of an accident would incorporate the compensating differential, but ignoring this does not alter any of the results of the analysis.

9 Clearly this analysis does not remove the incentive for firms to resist negligence suits or other one-shot, nonsystematic worker claims. Even if the result of an adverse legal judgment (upholding claims) is that workers will

increase their expectations of future benefits, this would still harm the firm whose existing wage structure is based on the expectations workers had *before* the decision was handed down.

10 The rousing IWW anthem, "We Have Fed You All for 1000 Years" concludes, "If blood be the price of all your wealth, by God we have paid in full."

11 A good general account of the passage of workers compensation can be found in Weinstein (1968). See also Ashford (1976), Gersuny (1981), and US Congress, Office of Technology Assessment (1985).

12 The most general evaluation in recent years was put forward by *The Report of the National Commission on State Workmen's Compensation Laws* (1972).

13 This result applies to the system considered as a whole. They do find, however, that there is less than a perfect tradeoff at the margin.

14 Like the other analysts who have examined the effect of workers compensation coverage on lost workdays, Moore and Viscusi assume that any increase in workers' sick time reflects a ripoff of the system (the problem of "moral hazard"). There is an opposite possibility, however: perhaps some workers who *should* take time off fail to do so when there are insufficient benefits to make this possible. Since this would also lead to a positive correlation between benefits and lost workdays it is impossible to know *a priori* how to interpret the empirical evidence.

15 For accounts of this type of conflict in the United States and other industrialized countries, see Berman (1978), Elling (1986), Gersuny (1981), Rosner and Markowitz (1987), or Wilson (1985).

16 Interestingly, dangerous working conditions play no role in the preference for representation of *unionized* women. It would seem that unorganized women in risky jobs place their hope in unionization, but they lose this faith once they see from the inside the inability or unwillingness of most unions to challenge these conditions.

17 A prominent victim of this type of accident was Merle Watson, the finger-picking son and accompanist of legendary bluegrass guitar-player Doc Watson.

18 This may be an example of a more general problem: the difficulty in eliciting individual self-discipline in cooperatively organized endeavors. For each member the personal cost of adhering to a work ethic and enforcing that ethic on others appears high relative to the personal benefits of playing by the rules, but at the level of the group the cost of widespread noncooperation is crippling. Strategies for overcoming this obstacle occupy whole subdisciplines of economics, sociology, and political science.

19 It should also not pass without notice that Smith's fable was paid for and disseminated by the trolls themselves at the American Enterprise Institute, a Washington think tank financed by conservative business interests. Smith is in excellent company in this respect: many of the country's most distinguished economists have been in the employ of AEI at one time or another.

20 The US also has a history of private, voluntary standards promulgated by the

American National Standards Institute (ANSI) and the National Safety Council (NSC). While labor has been heavily underrepresented on the boards and committees of these organizations, they have served to bring more uniformity to employer practices. In some cases, voluntary standards have been promoted by insurance companies (Noble, 1986; Cheit, 1990).

21 Two others are Zeckhauser and Nichols (1978) and Viscusi (1983).

22 This and the following point are taken from Berman (1978, p. 171).

23 See, for instance, Weisskopf, Bowles, and Gordon (1983).

24 Although not written into the actual text of the National Labor Relations Act, the distinction between mandatory and permissive bargaining issues has become central to US labor relations. Briefly, management is *required* to bargain over mandatory issues, and union responses, including the use of strikes, is protected – to the extent any labor activity is protected – under the law. Management may choose whether or not to bargain over permissive issues, however, and any actions taken by unions are strictly at their own risk.

25 This is especially true because the texts are uniformly written by true believers in cutting accident rates, even if this means spending considerable money. Without exception, their passages on the economics of safety read like briefs on behalf of safety departments everywhere; they *never* give examples in which the costs of making jobs safer exceed the benefits. Given this interest, the authors of these textbooks have a strong incentive to incorporate any plausible argument that would augment the costs of poor working conditions.

5 Alternative theories of risk, wages, and the labor market

1 There is a large and growing literature on risk perception, spanning economics, psychology, sociology, and political science. For convenience, I will not reference the consensus positions of this literature, since the same citations would be listed again and again. Many summaries are available; one of the most useful and accessible is Camerer and Kunreuther (1989).

2 In a more complete model the worker would also face an *ex ante* probability distribution for c; in that case, the means of c could be used to calculate expected disutility.

3 Note that this is not a claim that workers are unduly alarmist; rather that they may overconcentrate their alarm on a few, potentially unrepresentative hazards.

4 This refusal to make tradeoffs is elevated to the level of a Proposition in Kasperson (1986).

5 There is no analogous "efficiency" argument for the asymmetric treatment of gains and losses, but the "emotional" argument will be considered shortly.

6 For a fuller treatment, see Akerlof and Dickens (1982).

7 In this and the discussion that follows I am assuming the simplest version of segmentation, with two segments only – labor market "duality." Some

proponents of segmentation would further divide the primary sector into "independent" (managerial, professional, skilled craft) and "subordinate" (unionized unskilled, and semi-skilled).

8 Why this is so, and what determines the percentage of good jobs within an economy, remains elusive. I have proposed one type of explanation, based on the relative costs of positive and negative rewards for performance in Dorman (1990).

9 Principal component analysis constructs artificial composites whose value is derived from formulas – add 20 percent of this variable, subtract 10 percent of that one, etc. – which do the best job of summarizing the distribution of the original variables; that is, assigning these new artificial "meta-variables" to workers in different amounts will capture as much of the variation in their components as possible. With each additional composite the simulation of the original distribution of variables becomes closer, but since there are diminishing marginal returns (less additional variation captured with each principal component) generally only the first few are employed. Essentially, it is a mechanism for reducing many detailed measurements to a few overall categories, much as we might reduce all the detail from a physical examination by a doctor to a single variable, "health."

10 According to their sorting rules, none of the primary workers earned less than $15,000 in 1977, and none of the secondary workers earned more than $8,000.

11 A similar view of the importance of unemployment emerges in the epidemiological work of Harvey Brenner. See Brenner (1979).

12 In chapter 2 this was expressed as the constraint $u = u_0$. Incidentally, the joint production model of wage compensation developed by Oi (1974), not discussed in this book, also assumes that labor markets clear.

13 There are one collection of readings and two excellent surveys in this field; see Akerlof and Yellen (1986), Katz (1986), and Weiss (1990).

14 "[W]e require the use of a new term. We may find it in *efficiency-wages*, or more broadly *efficiency-earnings*; that is, earnings measured, not as time-earnings are with reference to the time spent in earning them; and not as piece-work earnings are with reference to the amount of output resulting from the work by which they are earned; but with reference to the exertion of ability and *efficiency* required of the worker" (p. 549).

15 Not everyone is happy with the term "efficiency wage" in this context. After all, a system is said to be efficient if it maximizes the output derived from a given set of inputs, but heightened worker effort represents an *increase* in the inputs devoted to production. To claim that production is more efficient when the sole cause is added effort is to adopt the narrow managerial perspective that (unpaid) effort is costless. It is for this reason that Marxist economists tend to avoid the language of efficiency in discussions of worker effort; instead, there are references to "effort extraction," "industrial discipline" or, more recently, the role of "contested exchange" in labor relations (Bowles and Gintis, 1990). While their point is

well taken, I will follow the path of least resistance and use the conventional terminology.

16 This is a much-abbreviated version of the model developed in Dorman (1991b), which also contains formal proofs for the propositions to come.

17 More formally, in equilibrium, holding v constant, the utility of employment varies monotonically with intensity.

18 Elsewhere I have shown that the tradeoff between wages and safety qualifying as "efficient" depends on the structure of the firm and its resulting incentives. A worker cooperative maximizing net revenue per worker, for instance, would, in this model, choose to make work safer than would a conventional firm (Dorman, 1987). As we have already seen, however, this appears to be contradicted by the evidence because of the far greater importance of the role of autonomy in risk perception.

19 They will nonetheless reduce their work intensity, but this has no relationship to utility, since v has not been held constant.

20 See, for instance, the discussion in US Office of Technology Assessment (1985).

21 This is not strictly true. No such incentive exists at the beginning of the first year, since workers lose virtually nothing by leaving (or being fired) at that point (Akerlof and Katz, 1989). It is not clear whether this should be important in real situations.

22 In a paper cited above, I have developed a formal model contrasting these two incentive strategies. See Dorman (1990).

23 The dissident literature on Taylor goes back to the Master's first public writings; two recent statements are Hirschhorn (1984) and Shaiken (1984).

24 The point is stressed by Bowles (1985), who dubs this view "Neo-Hobbesian." Ironically, his own model develops an efficiency wage mechanism that is formally indistinguishable from the one he criticizes.

25 There is a large and generally excellent body of textbooks on game theory, many of them quite recent. I will not reference the definitions or results which follow, since they are basic to the field and can be found in any of the texts now on the market.

26 In chess terminology, on the other hand, a strategy is an abstract conceptual commitment such as "I will castle on the queenside and open files for my rooks on the kingside." Game theory, which knows only concrete analysis, has no equivalent for this type of thinking. Of course, game theory can live more or less happily with the possibility that particular games may have no determinate solutions, but chessplayers must "solve" the positions that come before them whether they can calculate them to a conclusion or not.

27 I will not address the fascinating issue of whether the consequences of near-rationality approach those of rationality as near-rationality approaches perfect rationality. See, for instance, Akerlof and Yellen (1985).

28 Logically, (1) and (2) serve to establish the players and the options for (3).

29 For a recent, highly detailed treatment, see Elster (1991).

30 Of course, we often engage in acts of altruistic cooperation, even when we do

not expect the situation we are in to repeat itself. For instance, most people would still leave a tip for the waiter or waitress in a restaurant even if they had finished their meal and expected never to come back again. This strong form of normative behavior has recently been subjected to considerable scrutiny by game theorists.

31 Strictly speaking, this theorem holds in generality only for infinitely repeated games. If the players know when the last stage is to take place, they would all (by assumption) plan to defect on the final round. Knowing this, they would also defect on the next-to-final round, since there is no possibility of altering anyone else's last-round behavior. By backwards induction it is established that they will never cooperate in any round. At one time it was thought that this constituted a crippling limitation on the Folk Theorem, since no social situation is truly forever. Over the years, however, theorists have found many plausible ways to make finite games resemble the infinite variety. To take just one example, if the players have only probabilistic, rather than certain, knowledge of when the game will end – a perfectly reasonable assumption – and if this uncertainty is sufficiently large, anticipating the end of the game becomes the equivalent of normal time discounting and the Folk Theorem can be sustained.

32 Another way to establish a cooperative outcome is through evolutionary analysis. In this view, players are myopic; they form their strategies one stage at a time and learn from their past experience. Cooperation does not emerge instantaneously but over time, as players adjust their strategies by trial and error. For a fascinating and deservedly influential account of this approach, see Axelrod (1984).

33 One potential option for preventing defection in times of crisis is the use of force against defectors. Coercive practices at the disposal of unions occupy a spectrum from social shunning on one end, through fines and the denial of economic benefits, and finally to physical violence on the other. Unions that fail to draw a reasonable line run the risk that they, rather than the employer, will come to be viewed as the main adversary by ordinary workers. As to the larger question of the role of coercion, there has been lively debate among game theorists over the potential for completely voluntary paths to cooperation. For an important statement of the cooperative/libertarian position, see Taylor (1988).

34 An additional wrinkle is possible: each time the game is played the payoffs may change as new work practices or production materials are introduced.

35 Employers, of course, will be unwilling to pay fully compensating wages for risks that workers have a substantial chance of mitigating over the duration of the contract.

6 New policies to promote safety and equity in the workplace

1 In the American tradition, the name most commonly recognized in this connection is John Dewey; modern variations drawing on critical theory have

been elaborated by Jurgen Habermas and Paolo Freire. I do not wish to imply that the views of these writers are interchangeable, but their similarities outweigh their differences, especially in this context. For two recent discussions of democratic theory in this vein see Bowles and Gintis (1986) and Cohen and Rogers (1983).

2 Since it has been true of every society since the emergence of settled agriculture that its formal knowledge has been concentrated in a few hands, a conviction such as I describe is a necessary part of a positive theory of democracy. (One could support democracy on the grounds that anything else would be worse, but that is a different matter.) This phenomenological optimism, I would argue, has long been central to democratic theory; it can clearly be found in *The Federalist Papers*; and it is unmistakable in Dewey, Habermas, and Freire.

3 McCaffrey (1982, pp. 139–46), for example, recounts at length an episode in which NIOSH chose not to inform thousands of workers of their exposure to carcinogenic substances. This decision not only obstructed these workers in their attempt to improve conditions at work; it also delayed their treatment, condemning many to unnecessary disease and death.

4 Dionne and St-Michel also found that higher-income workers were more likely to extend their WC claims for back problems. This is consistent with the reduced-claim-suppression hypothesis, since greater income partially buffers workers from the costs of filing.

5 For a recent summary of the literature on this question, see Chelius (1991).

6 The following discussion of comparative health and safety institutions draws on many sources. For convenience I am omitting detailed references. Those interested in more detailed treatments can consult Reschenthaler (1979), Clarke (1982), Kasperson (1983), Gevers (1983), Sirianni (1987), Frick (1990), Sass (1989), Sass (1991), and Wokutch (1990, 1992).

7 The system of just-in-time production, in which inventory buffers are kept to a minimum, does, in fact, increase the cost of accidents to the firm. This logic does not apply to chronic health problems, however, and Wokutch documents the reluctance of Japanese firms to address the long-term consequences of its high-paced, high-stress production system – particularly cumulative trauma disorders.

8 These same norms, however, can also lead both workers and managers to misrepresent their safety performance to the outside world, as we saw in chapter 1.

9 For a fascinating discussion of these issues, particularly the connection between work organization, stress, and health, see Karasek and Theorell (1990).

10 It also restores hundreds of exposure limits previously struck down by the US Court of Appeals. Given the glacial progress of standard-setting under OSHA, this measure is strongly needed.

11 This point is argued convincingly by Noble (1986).

12 Recall that this transformative property of self-determination provides one of the classical arguments for democracy.

13 With this paragraph it should be clear that I have retreated from the more extreme decentralized approach advocated in Dorman (1988a).

14 Some readers may object that requirements of corporate openness conflict with the dictates of intellectual property rights. To the extent that information about production techniques and even the identity of suppliers can be used to replicate innovation, this argument is well-founded. I would counter, however, that the case for protecting intellectual property is not nearly as strong as commonly thought. While this is not the place to take up the matter in detail, it may be enough to point out that innovation in economics and other branches of knowledge proceeds quite nicely without the type of incentives most economists claim are necessary.

15 The preceding arguments for labor law reform are considered at greater length in Dorman (1988c).

16 In technical terms, this represents a nonconvexity in the firm's cost function due to interaction between detailed activities. In Dorman (1991c) I argue that such nonconvexities are ubiquitous for technological, social, and ecological reasons.

17 It might be objected that the historical record considered in chapter 4 demonstrates that workers have generally refused to bargain over risks: few health and safety clauses in collective bargaining agreements include hazard pay, and industrial safety conflicts are usually fought over demands to curtail risks, not increase compensation. Indeed, this record played an important role in that chapter's critique of conventional wage compensation theory. On the other hand, no workers in any period of history have possessed a comprehensive, enforceable right to refuse dangerous work. Without any mechanism by which they could assure themselves that one abuse would not simply pave the way for another, bargaining appears strategically naive. (See the discussion of this point in chapter 5.) In the hypothetical model drawn here, however, such a right exists, and it is difficult to see what workers lose by accepting compensation where the right to refuse is worth less to the workforce than its waiver is to the firm. If new, more onerous risks are added to the old, workers can return to a strategy of refusal and resistance.

18 These initiatives are discussed in greater detail in Dorman (1988c). For a similar prescription, see Brecher and Costello (1990).

19 Effective technology bargaining depends on the existence of a vibrant, independent labor movement; otherwise the criterion of simple profitability will remain unchallenged. For a cautionary tale with this sort of moral, see Kraft and Bansler (1993).

References

Abel, Richard. 1985. Risk as an Arena of Struggle. *Michigan Law Review*. February: 772–812.

Acton, Jan Paul. 1973. *Evaluation Public Programs to Save Lives: The Case of Heart Attacks*. Santa Monica (CA): Rand.

Akerlof, George and William Dickens. 1982. The Economic Consequences of Cognitive Dissonance. *American Economic Review*. June, 72(3): 307–19.

Akerlof, George and Lawrence Katz. 1989. Workers' Trust Funds and the Logic of Wage Profiles. *Quarterly Journal of Economics*. 104(3): 525–36.

Akerlof, George and Janet Yellen. 1985. Can Small Deviations from Rationality Make Significant Differences to Economic Equilibria? *American Economic Review*. September, 75(4): 708–20.

1986. Introduction. In Akerlof and Yellen (eds.), *Efficiency Wage Models of the Labor Market*. Cambridge: Cambridge University Press.

Aldrich, Mark. 1993. Development of Work Safety in the Railroad Industry. Unpublished manuscript.

Ansberry, Clare. 1989. Risky Business: Workplace Injuries Proliferate as Concerns Push People to Produce. *The Wall Street Journal*. June 16: A1, A8.

1991. Hazardous Duty: Nucor Steel's Sheen Is Marred by Deaths of Workers at Plants. *The Wall Street Journal*. May 10: A1, A4.

Aoki, Masahiko. 1988. *Information, Incentives, and Bargaining in the Japanese Economy*. Cambridge: Cambridge University Press.

Arnould, Richard J. and Len M. Nichols. 1983. Wage-Risk Premiums and Workers' Compensation: A Refinement of Estimates of Compensating Wage Differentials. *Journal of Political Economy*. March: 332–40.

Ariès, Philippe. 1981. *The Hour of Our Death*. New York: Knopf.

Ashford, Nicholas. 1976. *Crisis in the Workplace: Occupational Disease and Injury*. Cambridge, MA: MIT Press.

Atiyah, P. S. 1979. *The Rise and Fall of Freedom of Contract*. Oxford: Oxford University Press.

Axelrod, Robert. 1984. *The Evolution of Cooperation*. New York: Basic Books.

Barth, Peter S. 1987. *The Tragedy of Black Lung: Federal Compensation for*

Occupational Disease. Kalamazoo: W. E. Upjohn Institute for Employment Research.

Becker, Gary and Kevin Murphy. 1988. A Theory of Rational Addiction. *Journal of Political Economy.* August, 96(4): 675–700.

Becker, Gary S. and George J. Stigler. 1974. Law Enforcement, Malfeasance, and Compensation of Enforcers. *The Journal of Legal Studies.* January, 3(1): 1–18.

Bergstrom, Theodore. 1982. When Is a Man's Life Worth More than his Human Capital? In Jones-Lee (ed.).

Berman, Daniel M. 1978. *Death on the Job: Occupational Health and Safety Struggles in the United States.* New York: Monthly Review Press.

Biancardi, Michael F. 1987. How to Consider Cost–Benefit Analysis in Occupational Safety Practice. In L. Slote (ed.), *Handbook of Occupational Safety and Health.* New York: John Wiley & Sons.

Blake, Roland. 1963. *Industrial Safety.* Third Edition. Englewood Cliffs, NJ: Prentice-Hall.

Blomquist, Glenn. 1979. Value of Life Saving: Implications of Consumption Activity. *Journal of Political Economy.* June: 540–58.

Bowles, Samuel. 1985. The Production Process in a Competitive Economy: Walrasian, Neo-Hobbesian, and Marxian Models. *American Economic Review.* March: 16–36.

Bowles, Samuel and Herbert Gintis. 1986. *Democracy and Capitalism: Property, Community, and the Contradictions of Modern Social Thought.* New York: Basic Books.

1990. Contested Exchange: New Microfoundations for the Political Economy of Capitalism. *Politics and Society.* June, 18(2): 165–222.

Brecher, Jeremy and Tim Costello. 1990. *Building Bridges: The Emerging Grassroots Coalitions of Labor and Community.* New York: Monthly Review Press.

Brenner, Harvey. 1979. Influence of the Social Environment on Psychopathology: The Historical Perspective. In James Barrett (ed.), *Stress and Mental Disorder.* New York: Raven Press.

Brown, Charles. 1980. Equalizing Differences in the Labor Market. *Quarterly Journal of Economics.* February, 94: 113–34.

Bureau of National Affairs. 1992. *Collective Bargaining Negotiations and Contracts.* April 2. Washington, DC.

Cairns, John. Undated. Risk Attitude and the Value of Life. Unpublished manuscript.

Camerer, Colin F. and Howard Kunreuther. 1989. Decision Processes for Low Probability Events: Policy Implications. *Journal of Policy Analysis and Management.* 8(4): 565–92.

Charlton, William. 1988. *Weakness of Will.* Oxford: Basil Blackwell.

Cheit, Ross. 1990. *Setting Safety Standards: Regulation in the Public and Private Sectors.* Berkeley: University of California Press.

Chelius, James R. 1974. The Control of Industrial Accidents: Economic Theory

260   References

and Empirical Evidence. *Law and Contemporary Problems.* Summer–Autumn: 700–29.

1991. Role of Workers' Compensation in Developing Safer Workplaces. *Monthly Labor Review.* September, 114(9): 22–5.

Clarke, R. D. 1982. Worker Participation in Health and Safety in Canada. *International Labour Review.* 121: 199–206.

Coase, Ronald H. 1960. The Problem of Social Cost. *Journal of Law and Economics.* October, 3: 1–44.

Cohen, Joshua and Joel Rogers. 1983. *On Democracy.* New York: Penguin.

Dardis, Rachel. 1980. The Value of Life: New Evidence from the Marketplace. *American Economic Review.* 70(5): 1077–82.

Dehez, Pierre and Jacques Drèze. 1982. State-Dependent Utility, the Demand for Insurance and the Value of Safety. In Jones-Lee (ed.).

DeReamer, Russell. 1958. *Modern Safety Practices.* New York: John Wiley & Sons.

Dickens, William T. 1984. Differences Between Risk Premiums in Union and Nonunion Wages and the Case for Occupational Safety Regulation. *American Economic Review.* May: 320–3.

1990. Assuming the Can Opener: Hedonic Wage Estimates and the Value of Life. *Journal of Forensic Economics.* Fall, 3: 51–9.

Dickens, William T. and Lawrence F. Katz. 1987. Inter-Industry Differences and Industry Characteristics. In Kevin Lang and Jonathan S. Leonard (eds.), *Unemployment and the Structure of Labor Markets.* New York: Basil Blackwell.

Dickens, William T. and Kevin Lang. 1991. Labor Market Segmentation Theory: Reconsidering the Evidence. Unpublished manuscript.

Dillingham, Alan E. 1985. The Influence of Risk Variable Definition on Value-of-Life Estimates. *Economic Inquiry.* April, 24(2): 277–94.

Dionne, Georges and Pierre St-Michel. 1991. Workers' Compensation and Moral Hazard. *The Review of Economics and Statistics.* May, 73(2): 236–44.

Doeringer, Peter and Michael Piore. 1971. *Internal Labor Markets and Manpower Analysis.* Lexington, MA: Lexington Books.

Doll, R. and R. Peto. 1982. *The Causes of Cancer.* Oxford: Oxford University Press.

Dorman, Peter. 1987. Compensating Wage Differentials, Occupational Health and Safety, and the Value of Human Life: An Efficiency Wage Analysis. Unpublished doctoral dissertation, University of Massachusetts, Amherst.

1988a. A Negotiable 'Workers-Rights' Model of Occupational Safety Policy. *International Review of Applied Economics.* June, 2(2): 170–88.

1988b. Worker Rights and the Global Economy: A Case for Intervention. *Review of Radical Political Economics.* Fall, 20(3): 241–6.

1988c. A Postfordist Strategy for Labor. Unpublished manuscript.

1990. Efficiency Wages and Internal Labor Markets. Unpublished manuscript.

1991a. Trade, Competition, and Jobs: An Internationalist Strategy. In

Margaret Hallock and Steve Hecker (eds.), *Labor in a Global Economy*. Eugene: University of Oregon Books.

1991b. Efficiency Wages and Hedonic Analysis. Unpublished manuscript.

1991c. Externalities, Nonconvexities, and Multiple Equilibria: Property Rights and Nonmarket Interaction. Unpublished manuscript.

1992. Worker Rights, Environmental Standards, and Social Tariffs: Theory and Evidence. In Cheryl Lehman and Russell Moore (eds.), *Multinational Culture: Social Impact of a World Economy*. New York: Greenwood Press.

Dorman, Peter and Paul Hagstrom. 1993. Risk, Wages, and Interindustry Differentials. Unpublished manuscript.

Dorsey, Stuart and N. Walzer. 1983. Workers' Compensation, Job Hazards, and Wages. *Industrial and Labor Relations Review*. July: 642–54.

Douglas, Mary. 1985. *Risk Acceptability According to the Social Sciences*. New York: Russell Sage Foundation.

Douglas, Mary and Aaron Wildavsky. 1982. *Risk and Culture*. Berkeley: University of California Press.

Drapkin, Larry C. and Morris E. Davis. 1981. Health and Safety Provisions in Union Contracts: Power or Liability? *Minnesota Law Review*. April: 635–57.

Duncan, Greg J. and Bertil Holmlund. 1983. Was Adam Smith Right after All? Another Test of the Theory of Compensating Wage Differentials. *Journal of Labor Economics*. October, I: 366–79.

Duncan, Greg J. and Frank P. Stafford. 1980. Do Union Members Receive Compensating Wage Differentials? *American Economic Review*. June: 355–71.

Elling, Ray H. 1986. *The Struggle for Workers' Health: A Study of Six Industrialized Countries*. Farmingdale, NY: Baywood Publishing Co.

Elster, Jon. 1979. *Ulysses and the Sirens: Studies in Rationality and Irrationality*. Cambridge: Cambridge University Press.

1985. *Making Sense of Marx*. Cambridge: Cambridge University Press.

1991. *The Cement of Society: A Study of Social Order*. Cambridge: Cambridge University Press

Elster, Jon (ed). 1985. *The Multiple Self*. Cambridge: Cambridge University Press.

Epstein, Samuel S. 1979. *The Politics of Cancer*. New York: Anchor Books.

Erenburg, Mark. 1989. *Characteristics of Major Private Sector Collective Bargaining Agreements as of January 1, 1988*. Cleveland: Industrial Relations Center, Cleveland State University.

Fankhauser, Sam. 1992. Global Warming Damage Costs: Some Monetary Estimates. Working Paper GEC 92–29. London: Centre for the Social and Economic Research of the Global Environment.

Follmann, Joseph F., Jr. 1978. *The Economics of Industrial Health: History, Theory, Practice*. New York: American Management Association.

Foster, James C. 1984. Western Miners and Silicosis: "The Scourge of the Underground Toiler," 1890–1943. *Industrial and Labor Relations Review*. April: 371–85.

Frankel, M. 1979. Hazard Opportunity and the Value of Life. Unpublished manuscript.

Freeman, Richard and James Medoff. 1981. The Impact of the Percent Organized on Union and Nonunion Wages. *Review of Economics and Statistics*. November: 561–72.

    1984. *What Do Unions Do?* New York: Basic Books.

Freudenheim, Milt. 1991. Costs Soar for On-the-Job Injuries. *The New York Times*. April 11: D1, D6.

Frick, Kaj. 1990. Can Management Control Health and Safety at Work? *Economic and Industrial Democracy*. 11: 375–99.

Fuller, H. R. 1906. Representing the Brotherhood of Locomotive Engineers, Brotherhood of Locomotive Firemen, Order of Railway Conductors, and the Brotherhood of Railroad Trainmen. Before the House Judiciary Committee, US Congress, February 28.

Garen, John. 1988. Compensating Wage Differentials and the Endogeneity of Job Riskiness. *The Review of Economics and Statistics*. 70(1): 9–16.

Gerking, Shelby, Menno De Haan, and William Schulze. 1988. The Marginal Value of Job Safety: A Contingent Valuation Study. *Journal of Risk and Uncertainty*. June, 1: 185–99.

Gersuny, Carl. 1981. *Work Hazards and Industrial Conflict*. Hanover (NH): University Press of New England.

Gevers, J. K. M. 1983. Worker Participation in Health and Safety in the EEC: The Role of Representative Institutions. *International Labour Review*. July–August, 122(4): 411–28.

Gilmore, Charles L. 1970. *Accident Prevention and Loss Control*. American Management Association.

Gintis, Herbert. 1976. The Nature of Labor Exchange and the Theory of Capitalist Production. *Review of Radical Political Economics*. Summer: 36–54.

Glyde, Gerald P. 1984. Worker Participation and Occupational Health Hazards: The Economic Connection. *Labor Studies Journal*. Winter: 275–86.

Goldoftas, Barbara. 1991. Hands that Hurt: Repetitive Motion Injuries on the Job. *Technology Review*. January, 94(1): 43–50.

Goodman, Paul and Percival Goodman. 1947. *Communitas: Means of Livelihood and Ways of Life*. Chicago: University of Chicago Press.

Graham, John D. and James W. Vaupel. 1983. The Value of a Life: What Difference Does It Make? In Richard J. Zeckhauser and Derek Leebaert (eds.), *What Role for Government? Lessons from Policy Research*. Durham: Duke University Press.

Graham, Julie and Don M. Shakow. 1990. Labor Market Segmentation and Job-Related Risk: Differences in Risk and Compensation between Primary and Secondary Labor Markets. *American Journal of Economics and Sociology*. 49(3, July): 307–23

Gray, Wayne B. and Carol Adaire Jones. 1991. Are OSHA Health Inspections Effective? A Longitudinal Study in the Manufacturing Sector. *The Review of Economics and Statistics*. 504–8.

Gray, Wayne B. and John T. Scholz. 1991. Do OSHA Inspections Reduce Injuries? A Panel Analysis. July, NBER Working Paper No. 3774.

Griliches, Zvi. 1971. Introduction: Hedonic Price Indexes Revisited. In Griliches (ed.), *Price Indexes and Quality Change: Studies in New Methods of Measurement*. Cambridge, MA: Harvard University Press.

Grimaldi, John V. and Rollin H. Simonds. 1984. *Safety Management*. Fourth Edition, Homewood, IL: Richard D. Irwin.

Grunberg, Leon. 1991. The Plywood Co-operatives: Some Disturbing Findings. In Russell, Raymond and Veljko Rus (eds.), *International Handbook of Participation in Organizations: For the Study of Organizational Democracy, Co-operation, and Self-Management. Volume II: Ownership and Participation*. Oxford: Oxford University Press. pp. 103–22.

Gupta, Udayan. 1991. Small Companies Help Rein In Workers' Compensation. *The Wall Street Journal*. July 25: B2.

Hammermesh, Daniel. 1978. Economic Aspects of Job Satisfaction. In Orley Ashenfelter and Wallace Oates (eds.), *Essays in Labor Market Analysis*. New York: John Wiley and Sons.

Health and Safety Executive. 1988. *The Tolerability of Risk from Nuclear Power Stations*. London: Her Majesty's Stationery Office.

Heinrich, H. W., Dan Petersen and Nestor Roos. 1980. *Industrial Accident Prevention: A Safety Management Approach*. New York: McGraw-Hill.

Herzog, Henry W., Jr. and Alan M. Schlottmann. 1990. Valuing Risk in the Workplace: Market Price, Willingness to Pay, and the Optimal Provision of Safety. *The Review of Economics and Statistics*. August, 72(3): 463–70.

Hirschhorn, Larry. 1984. *Beyond Mechanization: Work and Technology in a Post-Industrial Age*. Cambridge, MA: MIT Press.

Hwang, Hae-shin, W. Robert Reed, and Carlton Hubbard. 1992. Compensating Wage Differentials and Unobserved Productivity. *Journal of Political Economy*. August, 100(4): 835–58.

Ineson, Antonia and Deborah Thom. 1985. T.N.T. Poisoning and the Employment of Women Workers in the First World War. In Paul Weindling (ed.), *The Social History of Occupational Health*. London: Croom Helm.

Ingersoll, Bruce. 1989. Perilous Profession: Farming Is Dangerous, but Fatalistic Farmers Oppose Safety Laws. *The Wall Street Journal*. July 20: A1, A4.

Ippolito, Pauline M. and Richard A. Ippolito. 1984. Measuring the Value of Life Saving from Consumer Reactions to New Information. *Journal of Public Economics*. November: 53–81.

Johnson, William G. and Edward Heller. 1984. Compensation for Death from Asbestos. *Industrial and Labor Relations Review*. July: 529–40.

Jones-Lee, M. W. 1989. *The Economics of Safety and Physical Risk*. Oxford: Basil Blackwell.

Jones-Lee, M. W. (ed.) 1982. *The Value of Life and Safety: Proceedings of a Conference Held by the "Geneva Association."* Amsterdam: North-Holland.

Jones-Lee, M. W. and A.-M. Poncelet. 1982. The Value of Marginal and

Non-Marginal Multiperiod Variations in Physical Risk. In Jones-Lee (ed.), pp. 67–80.

Kafka, Franz. 1946. *The Trial*. New York: A. A. Knopf.

Kahn, Shulamit. 1990. What Occupational Safety Tells Us about Political Power in Union Firms. *Rand Journal of Economics*. Autumn, 21(3): 481–96.

Kahneman, Daniel and Amos Tversky. 1979. Prospect Theory: An Analysis of Decisions Under Risk. *Econometrica*. March, 47(2): 263–91.

Karasek, Robert and Tores Theorell. 1990. *Healthy Work: Stress, Productivity, and the Reconstruction of Working Life*. New York: Basic Books.

Karr, Albert R. 1987. GM Agrees to Pay Fine of $500,000 on OSHA Charges. *The Wall Street Journal*. October 6.

Kasperson, Roger E. 1983. Worker Participation in Protection: The Swedish Alternative. *Environment*. May, 25(4): 13–20, 40–3.

   1986. Six Propositions on Public Participation and Their Relevance to Risk Communication. *Risk Analysis*. 6: 275–82.

Katz, Lawrence F. 1986. Efficiency Wage Theories: A Partial Evaluation. NBER Working Paper No. 1906.

Kelly, Michael. 1989. A Deadly Delivery Problem: Critics Say Domino's Promise Puts Pizza Drivers at Risk. *The Boston Globe*. July 19: 1, 6.

Kelman, Steven. 1981. *What Price Incentives? Economists and the Environment*. Boston: Auburn House Publishing Company.

Kilborn, Peter T. 1991. Labor Chief Says Coal Companies Disregard Law on Miners' Health. *The New York Times*. April 16: A20.

Kochan, Thomas A., Lee Dyer, and David B. Lipsky. 1977. *The Effectiveness of Union–Management Safety and Health Committees*. Kalamazoo (MI): W. E. Upjohn Institute for Employment Research.

Kraft, Philip and J?rgen Bansler. 1993. Mandatory Voluntarism: Negotiating Technology in Denmark. *Industrial Relations*. 32(3): 329–42.

Krueger, Alan B. and Lawrence H. Summers. 1986. Efficiency Wages and the Inter-Industry Wage Structure. Unpublished manuscript.

   1987. Reflections on the Inter-Industry Wage Structure. In Kevin Lang and Jonathan S. Leonard (eds.), *Unemployment and the Structure of Labor Markets*. New York: Basil Blackwell.

Kübler-Ross, Elisabeth. 1969. *On Death and Dying*. New York: Macmillan.

Lancaster, Kelvin J. 1966. A New Approach to Consumer Theory. *Journal of Political Economy*. April: 132–57.

Landrigan, Philip J. 1992. Commentary: Environmental Disease? A Preventable Epidemic. *American Journal of Public Health*. 82(7): 941–3.

LeGuin, Ursula. 1974. *The Dispossessed: An Ambiguous Utopia*. New York: Avon.

Leibenstein, Harvey. 1957. *Economic Backwardness and Economic Growth*. New York: Wiley.

Leigh, J. Paul. 1986. Wage Differentials and Risk of Death: Comment. *Economic Inquiry*. July: 505–8.

   1994. Compensating Wages, Value of a Statistical Life, and Inter-industry

Differentials. *Journal of Environmental Economics and Management*. Forthcoming.

Leigh, J. Paul and Roger N. Folsom. 1984. Estimates of the Value of Accident Avoidance at the Job Depend on the Concavity of the Equalizing Differences Curve. *Quarterly Review of Economics and Business*. Spring: 56–66.

Leonard, Norman. 1969. Future Economic Value in Wrongful Death Litigation. *Ohio State Law Journal*. 502–14.

Levine, David and Laura Tyson. 1990. Participation, Productivity and the Firm's Environment. In Alan Blinder (ed.), *Paying for Productivity*. Washington: The Brookings Institution.

Linnerooth, Joanne. 1979. The Value of Human Life: A Review of the Models. *Economic Inquiry*. January: 52–74.

Lipsey, Robert. 1976. Comments on "The Value of Saving a Life: Evidence from the Labor Market." In Nestor Terleckyj (ed.), *Household Production and Consumption*. New York: NBER/Columbia University Press.

Lofgren, Don J. 1989. *Dangerous Premises: An Insider's View of OSHA Enforcement*. Ithaca: ILR Press.

Low, Stuart and Lee R. McPheters. 1983. Wage Differentials and Risk of Death: An Empirical Analysis. *Economic Inquiry*. April: 271–80.

Lucas, Robert E. B. 1977. Hedonic Wage Equations and Psychic Wages in the Returns to Schooling. *American Economic Review*. September: 549–58.

Marin, Alan and George Psacharopoulos. 1982. The Reward for Risk in the Labor Market: Evidence from the United Kingdom and a Reconciliation with Other Studies. *Journal of Political Economy*. August: 827–53.

Marshall, Alfred. 1948. *Principles of Economics*. Eighth Edition. New York: Macmillan.

Martinello, Felice and Ronald Meng. 1992. Workplace Risks and the Value of Hazard Avoidance. *Canadian Journal of Economics*. May, 25(2): 333–45.

Marx, Karl. 1976. *Capital*. Volume One. New York: Random House.

McCaffrey, David P. 1982. *OSHA and the Politics of Health Regulation*. New York: Plenum Press.

Mellow, Wesley and Hal Sider. 1983. Accuracy of Response in Labor Market Surveys: Evidence and Implications. *Journal of Labor Economics*. October: 331–44.

Mendeloff, John. 1979. *Regulating Safety: An Economic and Political Analysis of Occupational Safety and Health Policy*. Cambridge, MA: MIT Press.

Mill, John Stuart. 1965. *Principles of Political Economy*. New York: Augustus M. Kelley.

Millar, J. Donald. 1985. Testimony before the Subcommittee on Health and Safety, Committee on Education and Labor, US House of Representatives, Ninety-ninth Congress, First session. July 24.

Miller, Ted R. 1990. The Plausible Range for the Value of Life? Red Herrings among the Mackerel. *Journal of Forensic Economics*. Fall, 3(3): 17–39.

Mishan, E. J. 1971. Evaluation of Life and Limb: A Theoretical Approach. *Journal of Political Economy*. July/August: 687–705.

Mishel, Lawrence. 1988. *Manufacturing Numbers: How Inaccurate Statistics Conceal US Industrial Decline.* Washington: Economic Policy Institute.

Moore, Michael and W. Kip Viscusi. 1990. *Compensation Mechanisms for Job Risks: Wages, Workers Compensation, and Product Liability.* Princeton: Princeton University Press.

1988. Doubling the Estimated Value of Life: Results Using New Occupational Fatality Data. *Journal of Policy Analysis and Management.* Spring, 7(3): 476–90.

Morra, Linda G. 1992. Testimony before the House Committee on Education and Labor. February 26. Washington: GAO/T-HRD–92–15.

Moure-Eraso, Rafael and Theodora A. Tsongas. 1990. Benzene and Cancer: The OSHA Standard, Workers' Compensation and Public Health Policy. *New Solutions.* Summer, 1(2): 13–21.

Mulligan, Patricia J. 1977. Willingness-to-Pay for Decreased Risk from Nuclear Plant Accidents. Working Paper No. 3, Energy Extension Programs, Pennsylvania State University.

National Commission on State Workmen's Compensation Laws. 1972. *The Report of the National Commission on State Workmen's Compensation Laws.* Washington: GPO.

The National Safe Workplace Institute. 1990a. What Indiana Blue Collar Workers Have to Say about Employers and the Role of Government. Chicago: The National Safe Workplace Institute.

1990b. NSWI Discussion Paper: US Multinationals and the Occupational Health Crisis of Mexico's Maquiladoras.

Nelkin, Dorothy and Michael S. Brown. 1984. *Workers at Risk: Voices from the Workplace.* Chicago: University of Chicago Press.

Noble, Charles. 1986. *Liberalism at Work: the Rise and Fall of OSHA.* Philadelphia: Temple University Press.

Oi, Walter. 1974. On the Economics of Industrial Safety. *Law and Contemporary Problems.* Summer/Autumn: 669–99.

Olson, Craig. 1981. An Analysis of Wage Differentials Received by Workers on Dangerous Jobs. *Journal of Human Resources.* Spring: 167–85.

Philips, P. R., I. T. Russell and M. W. Jones-Lee. 1989. The Empirical Estimation of Individual Valuation of Safety: Results of a National Sample Survey. In Jones-Lee (ed.).

Portney, Paul. 1981. Housing Prices, Health Effects, and Valuing Reductions in Risk of Death. *Journal of Environmental Economics and Management.* March: 72–8.

Preston, Anne E. 1986. The Use of Canonical Correlation in Estimating Compensating Wage Differentials. Unpublished manuscript.

Prosser, William L. 1955. *Handbook of the Law of Torts.* Second Edition. St. Paul, MN: West.

Reschenthaler, G. B. 1979. *Occupational Health and Safety in Canada: The Economics and Three Case Studies.* Montreal: Institute for Research on Public Policy.

Risen, James. 1987a. Productivity Push: Peril on the Job. *Los Angeles Times*. March 2: Part I, 1, 12.

1987b. At USX, Safety Turns Into a White-Hot Issue. *Los Angeles Times*. March 8.

Robinson, James. 1984. Non-Competing Groups and Compensating Differentials for Hazardous Working Conditions. Unpublished manuscript.

1988. Workplace Hazards and Workers' Desires for Union Representation. *Journal of Labor Research*. Summer, 9(3): 237–49.

1989. Exposure to Occupational Hazards among Hispanics, Blacks, and Non-Hispanic Whites in California. *American Journal of Public Health*. May, 79(5): 629–30.

1991. *Toil and Toxics: Workplace Struggles and Political Strategies for Occupational Safety and Health*. Berkeley: University of California Press.

Rosen, Sherwin. 1974. Hedonic Prices and Implicit Markets: Product Differentiation in Pure Competition. *Journal of Political Economy*. January/February, 82(1): 34–55.

Rosner, David and Gerald Markowitz (eds.) 1987. *Dying for Work: Workers' Safety and Health in Twentieth Century America*. Bloomington: Indiana University Press.

Saddler, Jeanne. 1987. Panel Questions Method US Uses on Job-Injury Data. *The Wall Street Journal*. October 16: 17.

Sagoff, Mark. 1982. On Markets for Risk. *Maryland Law Review*. (4): 755–83.

1988. *The Economics of the Earth: Philosophy, Law, and the Environment*. Cambridge: Cambridge University Press.

Sass, Robert. 1989. The Implications of Work Organization for Occupational Health Policy: The Case of Canada. *International Journal of Health Services*. 19(1): 157–73.

1991. A Critique: Canadian Public Policy in Workplace Health and Safety. *New Solutions*. Fall, 2(2): 39–46.

Schelling, Thomas. 1968. The Life You Save May Be Your Own. In S. B. Chase (ed.), *Problems in Public Expenditure Analysis*. Washington, DC: Brookings.

Schneider, Keith. 1991. Petrochemical Disasters Raise Alarm in Industry. *The New York Times*. June 19: A22.

Selikoff, Irving J. 1985. Testimony before the Subcommittee on Health and Safety, Committee on Education and Labor, US House of Representatives, Ninety-ninth Congress, First session. July 17.

Selikoff, Irving and Douglas Lee. 1978. *Asbestos and Disease*. New York: Academic Press.

Serrin, William. 1991. The Wages of Work: 300 Dead Each Day. *The Nation*. January 28: 80–2.

Shaiken, Harley. 1984. *Work Transformed: Automation and Labor in the Computer Age*. New York: Holt, Rinehart, and Winston.

Shakow, Don and Julie Graham. 1981. Compensating Wage Differentials and Labor Market Segmentation. Unpublished manuscript.

Shepard, Donald S. and Richard Zeckhauser. 1982. Life-Cycle Consumption and Willingness to Pay for Increased Survival. In Jones-Lee (ed.).

Shilling, Sharon and Robert M. Brackbill. 1987. Occupational Health and Safety Risks and Potential Health Consequences Perceived by US Workers, 1985. *Public Health Reports* (US Public Health Service). January/February: 36–46.

Sirianni, Carmen. 1987. *Worker Participation and the Politics of Reform*. Philadelphia: Temple University Press.

Sivaraman, Satyanarayan. 1993. Thailand: Women Workers Pay Price for Nation's Tiger Cub Status. *Inter Press Service*. July 10.

Smith, Adam. 1937. *Wealth of Nations*. New York: Modern Library.

Smith, Barbara Ellen. 1987. *Digging Our Own Graves: Coal Miners and the Struggle over Black Lung Disease*. Philadelphia: Temple University Press.

Smith, Robert S. 1976. *The Occupational Safety and Health Act: Its Goals and Achievements*. Washington: The American Enterprise Institute.

1979. Compensating Wage Differentials and Public Policy: A Review. *Industrial and Labor Relations Review*. April, 32: 339–52.

Smith, V. Kerry and William H. Desvousges. 1987. An Empirical Analysis of the Economic Value of Risk Changes. *Journal of Political Economy*. February, 95(1): 89–114.

Starr, Chauncey. 1969. Social Benefit vs. Technological Risk. *Science*. September 19, 165: 1232–8.

Stein, Leon. 1962. *The Triangle Fire*. Philadelphia: J. B. Lippincott.

Stiglitz, Joseph E. 1976. The Efficiency Wage Hypothesis, Surplus Labour, and the Distribution of Income in L.D.C.s. *Oxford Economic Papers*. July: 185–207.

1987 The Causes and Consequences of the Dependence of Quality on Price. *Journal of Economic Literature*. March: 1–48.

Stout, Nancy and Catherine Bell. 1991. Effectiveness of Source Documents for Identifying Fatal Occupational Injuries: A Synthesis of Studies. *American Journal of Public Health*. June, 81(6): 725–8.

Stout, Nancy, Michael S. Frommer, and James Harrison. 1990. Comparison of Work-Related Fatality Surveillance in the USA and Australia. *Journal of Occupational Accidents*. 13: 195–211.

Strauss, George and Leonard R. Sayles. 1967. *Personnel: The Human Problems of Management*. Second edition. Englewood Cliffs, NJ: Prentice-Hall.

Taylor, Michael. 1988. *The Possibility of Cooperation*. Cambridge: Cambridge University Press.

Thaler, Richard. 1982. Precommitment and the Value of a Life. In Jones-Lee (ed.).

Thaler, Richard and Sherwin Rosen. 1976. The Value of Saving a Life: Evidence from the Labor Market. In Nestor Terleckyj (ed.), *Household Production and Consumption*. New York: NBER/Columbia University Press.

Thurow, Lester C. and Robert E. B. Lucas. 1972. The American Distribution of Income: A Structural Problem. US Congress, Joint Economic Committee. Washington: GPO.

Tolchin, Martin. 1991. In Walkout by 3,200 at G.M. Plant, Pay and Benefits are Beside the Point. *The New York Times*. June 1: A8.

Tye, Larry. 1991. Poultry Plant Blaze Lights Era of Neglect. *The Boston Globe*. September 8: A1, A25

US Congress, Office of Technology Assessment. 1985. *Preventing Illness and Injury in the Workplace*. Washington: GPO.

US Department of Labor, Bureau of Labor Statistics. *Major Collective Bargaining Agreements: Safety and Health Provisions*, Bulletin 1425–16.

US Department of Transportation, National Highway Safety Administration. 1972. Societal Costs of Motor Vehicle Accidents. Preliminary report. Washington: GPO.

US Executive Office of Science and Technology. 1972. *Cumulative Regulatory Effects on the Costs of Automotive Transportation*. Washington: GPO.

US General Accounting Office. 1975. *Improvements Still Needed in Coal Mine Dust-Sampling Program*. GPO: Washington.

1992. *Hired Farmworkers: Health and Well-Being at Risk*. Washington: GAO/ HRD–92–46.

Violette, Daniel M. and Lauraine G. Chestnut. 1983. *Valuing Reductions in Risks: A Review of the Empirical Estimates*. Washington: US Department of Commerce, National Technical Information Service.

Viscusi, W. Kip. 1979. *Employment Hazards: An Investigation of Market Performance*. Cambridge, MA: Harvard University Press.

1983. *Risk by Choice: Regulating Health and Safety in the Workplace*. Cambridge, MA: Harvard University Press.

1986. The Valuation of Risks to Life and Health: Guidelines for Policy Analysis. In Judith D. Bentkover, Vincent T. Covello, and Jeryl Mumpower (eds.), *Benefits Assessment: The State of the Art*. Dordrecht (Ned.): D. Reidel Publishing Company.

1992. *Fatal Tradeoffs: Public and Private Responsibilities for Risk*. Oxford: Oxford University Press.

1993. The Value of Risks to Life and Health. *Journal of Economic Literature*. December, 31(4): 1912–46.

Viscusi, W. Kip and Charles O'Connor. 1984. Adaptive Responses to Chemical Labeling: Are Workers Bayesian Decision Makers? *American Economic Review*. 74: 942–56.

Weil, David. 1991. Enforcing OSHA: The Role of Labor Unions. *Industrial Relations*. Winter, 30(1): 20–36.

Weinstein, James. 1968. *The Corporate Ideal in the Liberal State: 1900–1918*. Boston: Beacon Press.

Weiss, Andrew. 1990. *Efficiency Wages: Models of Unemployment, Layoffs, and Wage Dispersion*. Princeton: Princeton University Press.

Weiss, Peter, Guther Maier, and Shelby Gerking. 1986. The Economic Evaluation of Job Safety: A Methodological Survey and Some Estimates for Austria. *Empirica*. 13: 53–67.

Weisskopf, Thomas E., Samuel Bowles, and David Gordon. 1983. Hearts and

Minds: A Social Model of US Productivity Growth. *Brookings Papers on Economic Activity*. 381–441.

Wermiel, Stephen. 1991. High Court Lets Stand the Conviction of Employers in Workplace Safety Case. *The Wall Street Journal*. February 20: B4.

White, Lawrence. 1983. *Human Debris: The Injured Worker in America*. New York: Seaview/Putnam.

Williams, Raymond. 1983. *The Year 2000*. New York: Pantheon.

Wilson, Graham K. 1985. *The Politics of Safety and Health: Occupational Safety and Health in the United States and Britain*. Oxford: Clarendon Press.

Wokutch, Richard E. 1990. *Cooperation and Conflict in Occupational Safety and Health: A Multinational Study of the Automotive Industry*. New York: Praeger.

1992. *Worker Protection, Japanese Style: Occupational Safety and Health in the Auto Industry*. Ithaca, NY: ILR Press.

Wokutch, Richard E. and Josetta S. McLaughlin. 1992. The US and Japanese Work Injury and Illness Experience. *Monthly Labor Review*. April, 115(4): 3–11.

Zeckhauser, Richard. 1975. Procedure for Valuing Lives. *Public Policy*. Fall: 419–64.

Zeckhauser, Richard and Albert Nichols. 1978. The Occupational Safety and Health Administration: An Overview. *Study on Federal Regulation*. Committee on Gove.

Index